WISCONSIN CARS AND TRUCKS

A CENTENARY

by Wisconsin Society Automotive Historians

Val Quandt, Editor

Val Quandt, editor

First Edition

Library of Congress Catalog Card Number: 98-060930

ISBN: 0-9664804-0-6

Printed in the United States of America by
Palmer Publications, Inc.
Amherst, WI 54406

Table of Contents

Acknowledgements

The idea for this publication arose around 1980 at early meetings of the newly formed Wisconsin Society of Automotive Historians which had its charter the year before. The society was a chapter of the National Society of Automotive Historians, and an affiliate of the State of Wisconsin Historical Society. It was then felt that at least one of its prime activities should be the writing of a history of automotive vehicle manufacture in the state of Wisconsin.

Some of these earlier articles appeared in the "Spark" magazine put out by the society, appearing once or twice a year. Contributors to the book have come mainly from the ranks of WSAH membership, and a few outside this organization. These have included the following: Bill Cameron, now deceased, Chad Elmore, John Everitt, John Gunnell, Phil Hall, Marly Hemp, Gary Hoonsbeen, Matt Joseph, Michael Keller, John Lundstrom, Keith Marvin, Vince Ruffolo for the Marvin Winther written story, Ray Scroggins, and Wally Wray.

Ralph Dunwoodie supplied voluminous amounts of photocopies of original automotive historical materials out of his extensive archives. Roger S. Smith, of the A. O. Smith Company in Milwaukee, furnished a history of his company production of automobile frames through many decades. Glen Ponczak of Johnson Controls was the source of information on his company's past automobile manufacturing very early in the twentieth century, and its continuing role in improved battery research, and interior automobile design and materials.

Brooks Stevens, in two interviews late in his life, furnished the Excalibur history. This was amplified through interviews onsite at the present Excalibur and Cobra auto plants in West Allis, Wisconsin. The Richard Braunds, father and son, and David Hartje, in Elroy, Wisconsin, both contributed to the section on the Duesenberg II automobile. The General Motors Company offered history from their archives and a tour of their plant for pictures.

Krause Publications in Iola, Wisconsin, through editor John Gunnell, and Greg Smith, publisher, supplied useful information for text and picture illustrations from their publication, "Catalog of American Cars, 1805 to 1942." Also, Patricia Klug, from early on, offered encouragement for the continuation of this project. Beverly Kimes, automotive author, and Jonathan Stein of the "Automobile Quarterly" gave valuable copies of the Kimes article on Nash, together with Nash-Kelvinator by Sam Medway, in an issue of "Automobile Quarterly" in 1977.

The Oshkosh Public Museum, through its archivist, Linda Mittlestadt, furnished the arresting picture of the Oshkosh Steam Car at the beginning of the 1878 steam car race.

Kenneth Nimocks, WSAH president, lent continued support for the manuscript. Dale Anderson, director of the Hartford Auto Museum, has offered the space of his museum for the collection of the manuscript materials, and the location facility and secretarial help of Vivian Whelan for the sale of the book.

Charles Spanbauer, president of Palmer Publications, offered his long-time experience in guiding the manuscript to the finished book. Marcia Lorenzen read through the manuscript several times for corrections of form, and suggestions.

My apologies are extended to those who have helped and yet may have been overlooked in these acknowledgments.

Preface

This is a history of automobile manufacturing in the state of Wisconsin from its origins in the last decade of the nineteenth-century to the present time. Actually, there was even earlier activity in the state and elsewhere with steam-driven vehicles decades before that. The present year, 1998, also coincides with the 150th or Sesquicentennial of the Statehood of Wisconsin.

In the early years of the 1890s there were experimental prototypal vehicles using gasoline engines for power, and some steam-driven vehicles. This activity was on such a small scale and so sporadic as not to represent actual manufacture which implies the use of machinery to produce consecutively.

The initial effort for this publication came as a result of interest shown by the Wisconsin Society of Automotive Historians, a chapter of the National Society of Automotive Historians, and also an affiliate of the State Historical Society. This society had its first state meeting on July 8, 1979. An early issue of its newsletter, the "Spark" in January of 1982, mentioned that "a Wisconsin automobile history book is in the works."

The plan then lay somewhat dormant for the next decade. But beginning in 1992 the society again took up the effort. The Hartford Auto Museum in Hartford, Wisconsin, has been the site of its annual spring meetings. This museum was then chosen to be the custodial location for its society records, the collection of the "Spark" newsletters, and materials relating to the formation of a manuscript for a book on "Wisconsin Cars and Trucks, a Centenary," with modifiers such as "built" and "manufactured" deleted for the sake of brevity.

Earlier this society had referred to the manuscript topic as the "Wisconsin Vehicles Project." Realizing the term "vehicle" by strict definition refers to any conveyance that moves people from place to place, including by land, water, and air, the title was narrowed to "Wisconsin Cars and Trucks, a Centenary."

It is commonly accepted, with some dissention, that automobile manufacture in this country began with the Duryea brothers in 1893, with a single car, to be followed in 1896 with the manufacture of 13 cars. Mr. A. J. Pierce, the founder of the Pierce Engine Company of Racine, Wisconsin, also produced an automobile in 1893, and a second to follow in 1899. Shortly thereafter production began with the early Pierce-Racine automobile. Thus, from the end of the 1890s to the present coincides with the 100 years of automobile manufacture in the State of Wisconsin.

Southeastern Wisconsin was the main location for automobile manufacture during the early history. Three cities were prominent. These were Racine, Kenosha, and Hartford, Wisconsin. There was also notable activity in the Fox River Valley and environs, especially in Oshkosh, Wisconsin. Somewhat later Janesville, with its earlier Fisher body plant, began automobile production at its General Motors plant.

Racine had three major manufacturers, namely J. I. Case, Mitchell, and Lewis and combinations of the latter two companies. There were smaller companies such as Pennington, and Pierce-Racine, soon taken over by J. I. Case.

The longest-lived automobile manufacturing company in Wisconsin was the Kenosha-based Jeffery, Nash, and American Motors Corporation. Its 85-year history to be succeeded by Chrysler with a brief period of car manufacture, and now in recent years making its automobile engines.

The Kissel Motor Car Company in nearby Hartford, Wisconsin, had a 25-year history of automobile manufacture spanning the years 1906 to 1930. It was famous for its Kissel Speedster called the "Gold Bug." It also had a brief history in 1929-1930 making touring bodies for the early front-wheel-drive car, the Ruxton.

This history will document other automobile manufacturers in Wisconsin, past and present. Especially in the early decades of this century there were over 100 small independent companies in Wisconsin, many making only one or a handful of cars. These cannot be included in this study, and others more worthy and not reviewed. Many of these can be found in the Krause Publication "Standard Catalog of American Cars, 1805 to 1942", where the early date refers to steam-driven conveyances.

Advances are continuously being made to make the modern automobile safer to drive and less polluting. Anyone who has experienced driving an automobile a generation or two ago will have been aware of the greater amount of highway congestion today, and the greater speeds producing ever-increasing risks of serious accidents and requiring the greater attention and acuity on the part of the driver. But vehicles and highways will be steadily improved to make driving safer and more enjoyable.

Val Quandt
Hartford, Wisconsin
February 1998

Chapter One
EARLY HISTORY AND OVERVIEW

The following are direct excerpts from several articles that Matt Joseph presented for publication in the auto magazine called “Skinned Knuckles” in early 1991. This material had also been part of lectures that Joseph gave at the University of Wisconsin in Rock County in the winter of 1990.

Joseph is the author of the book published by Krause Publications entitled “The Standard Guide to Automotive Restoration.” He is also the host of the weekly radio program called “About Cars.”

AUTOMOTIVE GOOD CITIZENSHIP

The automobile has done more to realize the dreams of the “full lunch bucket” social benefit mentality of things than any other mechanical or intellectual invention in human history. In this regard it competes successfully with many of mankind's inventions in the realms of social, political, economic, and religious thought.

The inevitable “but” is that the automobile is a great consumer of non-replaceable resources and contributor to many forms of global pollution. It has been allowed to devour these resources and to pollute our planet with abandon. We must wonder how future generations will feel about the mobility that we enjoy today when they discover that in the relatively brief space of 100 years our automobile age has been bought at the cost of degrading earth's resources and environment to the point that future generations may be deprived of things like liquid petroleum for their own automotive and nonautomotive needs.

All of this leads responsible automotive enthusiasts to seek a balance of the freedom that the automobile, the ideas embodied in its hardware and use, makes possible and the prerequisites of good and responsible environmental citizenship. This is not an easy balance to achieve. In part it involves engineering considerations above emotional responses and imposing restraint on many forms of greed.

By now it seems hard to believe that 100 years ago the promise and the problems of the automobile were almost unknown to the world. Consider just a few of the social and cultural changes spawned by man's greatest invention as they have shaped the twentieth century.

Social and Economic Impacts on America

Perhaps the most important change wrought by the automobile on our times is that it has irrevocably changed our concepts of time and space. The limits of almost everything that we think and do is enmeshed in that nexus. Take, for example, the matter of where most people live in this country.

The automobile has played the central role on the way to transforming the USA from a rural to an urban society in the last 75 years. The insularity of rural communities has been progressively broken down and then shattered by the automobile.

Early automotive inventor, Hiram Percy Maxim had an interesting theory about the progress of human transportation. He expressed it in his book called "Horseless Carriage Days." He suggested that successive development of a form of mechanical transportation created a demand that it could not satisfy. It also created some of the technology and infrastructure for satisfying that demand with the next form of transportation. In this scheme animal-driven transportation taught people that they could travel further and faster than was possible by their own unassisted locomotion. Later the railroad accustomed people to moving relatively vast distances very quickly and eventually reliably.

The railroad changed people's concepts of time and space, but its use was limited in application. You had to travel according to train schedules and you had to go where the tracks ran. Often this was very inconvenient, because you might have to travel 35 miles down a spur line, and 35 miles back up another spur line to reach your destination. That destination might be only five or ten miles away from where you started. But the available railroad transit involved traveling 45 miles and making two train changes to go the five or ten crow-fly miles desired. You can see how the train whetted people's appetite for comfortable, reliable and fast transit but failed to satisfy those desires in many respects.

Part of the answer to a desire for complete self determination of destination was the bicycle. It became popular in the last part of the nineteenth century. The creation of the infrastructure of the railroads really set the stage for the bicycle age. The bicycle did not need tracks to run on and could be used according to the schedule of the owner. Unfortunately, it also involved considerable effort. We call that exercise today. The bicycle could not be used effectively in bad weather or over long distances.

In Maxim's theory, as the railroad had created the perceived need and some of the infrastructure for the bicycle age, the bicycle, in turn, created the perceived need and some of the infrastructure for the personally controlled mechanical mobility that was realized in the automobile. Maxim's conclusions about infrastructure are also persuasive. Bicycle manufacturing certainly produced much of the infrastructure and technology for early automobile production. The activities of Colonel Albert Pope and his automotive manufacturing empire attest to the validity of Maxim's theory of this sequence.

While the automobile was diminishing and disintegrating the old limitations of time and space on humankind and opening up new frontiers to extend the concepts of human freedom from these traditional restraints, there remained many who were not convinced that all of this was good or desirable. Change is never universally accepted and its social effects are never symmetrical. What are the changes wrought by the automobile on American society that seemed controversial in the early years of this century? Consider just a few of them.

Residential living patterns changed radically. Cities spread into sprawling suburbs, and by the 1930s workers became decentralized from the factories where they worked. Shopping centers rose to serve new communities and traditional crossroads communities often lost their commercial vitality to the larger enterprises in large communities, stores that now could be reached by automobile.

These changes in living patterns were particularly dramatic when viewed at night from the air. Prior to the advent of wide ownership of automobiles, nighttime aerial views of the lights of metropolitan areas revealed "star patterns" of development. These patterns emanated from communities strung out along trolley lines with the tracks acting as invisible spines in the stars' branches. Widespread automobile ownership changed all of that. It dispersed people into residential patterns that more resembled galaxies and Milky Ways.

The changes in rural areas were at least as great. Tin Lizzies ended the terrible isolation of far-flung farms and rural communities. Localism gave way to regionalism, and regionalism melded into nationalism. Mostly a robust metropolitanism emerged. Much that was quaint was destroyed and forgotten, but much that was efficient and humane also emerged. This revolution is still in progress.

President Hoover named the Hoover Commission to report on the enormous social change that occurred in America in the first three decades of this century. What resulted was effectively the first modern sociological inventory of a nation. Among other things, the Hoover Commission's report on Recent Social Trends concluded that the automobile "...had erased the boundaries which formerly separated urban from rural territory and has introduced a type of local community without precedent in history." Quite an accomplishment no matter how favorably or unfavorably you may choose to view it.

In part, the automobile assaulted traditional values and social concepts. Language changed, for example, when an advertising agency working for General Motors set out to purposely replace the contemporary term "secondhand car" with the more appetizing term "used car." This was done to remove the stigma from buying these cars and thus to make room for the new models. In our own time phrases like "executive driven" and pseudo words like "pre-owned" have been coined for the same purpose.

In 1806 the Federal Government had begun to fund the National Road, roughly the eastern half of the present route of U.S. 40, which was to run from the Potomac to the Mississippi River. However, the advent of railroads shortly after that promised to take care of any problems that the post office had delivering the mail over great distances. The Feds abandoned road building in favor of giving land subsidies to railroads to stimulate construction. The unfinished National Road was given to the states to complete which they attempted to do with varying degrees of success. This was it for federal road building until the automobile age.

Finally 100 years later, and in the face of growing awareness of the need for federally coordinated and supported roads, the 1916 Federal Highway Act was passed. It replaced the ineffective Office of Road Inquiry which had been created in 1893. It completely changed the relationship of the federal government to the states in the area of road building for all time to come.

Other changes in state and federal relationships may have been influenced by this example. The Federal Highway Act created the Federal Highway Administration in the Department of Agriculture and the beginning of national funding for interstate road construction. There were conditions. At first they were easy to satisfy. Each state had only to accept federally-developed road standards and establish a highway department to qualify for some level of federal highway funding. By 1919 all the states had accomplished this.

Even before the 1916 Federal Highway Act, as early as 1912, Carl G. Fisher, president of the Prest-O-Lite Corporation and a founder of the Indianapolis Speedway, was agitating for a transcontinental highway that would connect New York to San

Francisco in time for the 1915 San Francisco Exposition. Here 25,000 automobiles were to join in a convoy to commemorate the opening of the first transcontinental road. It was not to bc.

First there was bickering over the highway's name. Republicans controlled Washington, so it was expedient to call the parent group for this cross-country road endeavor the Lincoln Memorial Highway Association. For the Lincoln Highway the amount of politics in roads was extraordinary. Parts of the Lincoln Highway were completed in the teens and a lot of it was in service during the 1920s.

By the 1920s the frenzy to build the major roads that the automobile was beginning to require, made many different approaches possible. Joining existing roads into a route or system offered very attractive advantages. "Get your kicks on Route 66" was immortalized in song and later by a television program. Of course, Route 66 was a paste-up job of existing roads. It connected Chicago with Santa Monica and was formed in 1926 by connecting 2,448 miles of existing highway through eight states. It was variously identified as "Main Street USA" and the "Gateway to the West." Steinbeck called it the "mother road." Route 66 connected Chicago, St. Louis, Tulsa, Oklahoma City, Amarillo, Albuquerque, Flagstaff, and Los Angeles. Where there had been sleepy country roads and lazy small town streets, there was suddenly the noise, dust, bustle, and excitement of a major highway. It carried goods, people, and change. Mostly it carried change. Route 66 was obsoleted and replaced by the Interstate System and was officially decommissioned in 1985.

The impact of the automobile on the American economy has been so great that it is difficult to consider the automobile and the economy in isolation from each other.

In the eighteenth century the American economy had to adjust to the needs of a new scale maritime shipping. That activity eventually drove and shaped the economy of that period. In the nineteenth century laws, business arrangements, and government policies had to adapt to and accommodate the "release of energy" (Willard Hurst's phrase) inherent in the new scale of activities in the railroads and other mega corporations and trusts in that period of superheated industrialization. In the twentieth century it has been the automobile, and the arrangements necessary to provide for its manufacture, distribution, and servicing that have formed and shaped our economy.

I have very ambivalent feelings about the effects of automobiles on human existence, because I think that our cherished invention has serious downsides and drawbacks. Its progress can cut both ways, for human good or human disaster. However, the current demonology of the automobile that is repeated, and believed in, in some circles, is just amazing. Attempts to legislate a short-term future that requires the greatly reduced use of personal transportation, or its elimination, are unrealistic and counterproductive.

The Virtues of Gasoline

There is nothing magical about gasoline as the fuel for motor vehicles. Its virtues are that it is very compact for the amount of energy that it contains and that it is easy to meter into a device that burns it and converts its heat energy into mechanical power. The problem that we face is that we are coming to the end of an era where we can burn things inefficiently to derive mechanical power. The things that we burn are becoming too scarce for that and the dumping of their combustion by-products into the atmosphere is probably reaching irreversible levels of environmental damage. For the present, we will have to learn to burn things more efficiently to create the motive power for our vehicles. Soon after that we will have to find new, less scarce and less dangerous things to combust or we will have to find non-combustive ways to get the power for our vehicles. Or we will have to replace the very idea of motorized vehicles with some other forms of communication.

In a broad sense, gasoline is simply a storage medium for solar energy. Eons ago rays and or particles from the sun fell on hapless, deceased creatures, and possibly plants too, to create carbon-based liquid compounds with a high energy content. Mankind learned to degrade these compounds by combusting them in air and to derive mechanical and reaction energy from these processes.

The Specter of Global Warming

Even if we do find ways to burn things more cleanly and ways to reduce, halt, or reverse these effects on the atmosphere we must soon begin to think about global warming in terms of simple thermal pollution. When you burn something to create energy from it you must reject heat, usually the majority of that combustion.

There must be a "thermal gradient." Something has to be hotter than something else if energy is to be captured. At some point we will find that the earth's atmosphere has a limited ability to absorb the rejected heat that is required by the energy gradient of our combustion processes. In the 100 years that we have systematically measured global temperatures and atmospheric composition, we have discovered alarming increases in some greenhouse gases and a steady increase in global temperatures. Unfortunately, we don't have enough long-term data to know what kinds of variations are normal in these things and what variations result from human activity. We also do not know what nature's "point of no return" is in these situations, so we cannot be sure how dangerous our present activities are. Already we suspect that we may be causing irreversible changes in our environment.

There is a tendency to want to play an elaborate shell game with matters of energy conservation and pollution control. I think that this game can almost be codified into a law that runs like this: Energy is neither conserved nor wasted, its use is simply moved to a less visible place. So, for example, some naive advocates of electric cars argue that they are pollution free because they have no tailpipes. That is true, but the plants that generate the electricity that they run on have smokestacks or create nuclear waste, once you get beyond the very limited potential of contemporary generation of hydroelectric, wind, and photovoltaic sources of energy.

Plasma reactions hold some promise as sources of energy generation without resource depletion problems, conventional pollution, or serious radioactive waste disposal problems. Photovoltaic energy generation is another possibility. The point is, if a clean form of energy generation that does not deplete scarce resources can be found, the transfer to vehicle power plants is possible. Electric energy has been stored in lead acid batteries and used to power vehicles for a century. New, more efficient battery chemistries will certainly be developed. And battery/capacitor and superconductive donut storage systems also hold much promise in this area.

The hydrogen that advanced power generation could separate from water might be the clean burning transfer medium fuel that we can use to drive our vehicles. Handling hydrogen poses a series of problems, but they are probably solvable. To its credit, hydrogen burns in air, with only water and some easy to scrub nitrogen compounds as its products. It also burns in engines that can be constructed from presently used materials and with existing tooling. Automotive change always keeps an eye towards preserving the investment in the present tooling. It must be an evolutionary process due to the vast amounts of capital involved in this kind of production.

Of course plasma generation, if it is commercially possible, and hydrogen fueled vehicles, if they are practically possible, still do not solve the problems of thermal pollution, generated at the reactor and at the vehicle.

Photovoltaic generation of much of the energy that we use may someday be economically feasible at commercial levels. Photovoltaics are galloping ahead right now, and the progress in this field is very promising. Transfer mediums that do not depend on air supported combustion are also possible. Developments in batteries and fuel cells hold some promise in this regard. Recent developments in high temperature superconductivity also suggest possible storage mediums for the motive power for advanced vehicles.

Alternative Fuels

In the short run we should look at alternative fuels like alcohols, and alcohol petrolatum blends, propane, CNG and synthetic fuels. We should examine various forms of electric and hybrid electric cars and we should subject all of these alternatives to scrutiny that considers the cold facts of their environmental and energy conserving merits and not their support by political or economic interest groups. Some highly touted alternative energy sources are known to involve net energy losses, compared to using petrolatum fuels and they should be refined to the point of effectiveness or eliminated from serious consideration before the whole field of alternative fuels gets a bad rap.

I do not know what the technology will be in 100 years that makes the continuation of personal transportation possible, or replaces it. There are several promising alternatives that are being investigated with regard to the materials, construction and motive power design of the cars of the early twenty-first century. I do know that we will have to get from here to there. We will have to create the technology and infrastructure as we go along, to produce, distribute, and service the personal transportation of the future. That process will necessarily be an evolutionary one.

We must not settle for the human isolation that existed 100 years ago. We must never go back to the highly stratified class structure of the pre-automobile age. The benefits of mobility far outweigh its drawbacks, if we address those drawbacks and solve the problems that create them. I believe that we can accomplish this.

In the Future

The future will see even more variation in automobiles than we have resurrected in the last decade. The sizes, power sources, and types of construction of cars will be based on their intended purpose. No one will argue that a half dozen variations on four- and six-passenger cars is enough to serve the market. Specialty builders and converters will fill any product gaps that the large companies and alliances fail to address. In recent years the phenomenal success of the minivan configuration indicates what can happen when a design fits a need. Many automotive stylists predict that the shape of the car of the future will be a cross between a conventional sedan and a minivan.

Great advances in the materials, mechanisms, electronics, and production techniques of automobiles will be made. New features will be introduced that are hardly comprehensible today. Many advances in the automotive future will be directed at solving resource and environmental problems. Many other advances will be in the areas of safety, comfort, and performance.

The Schloemer Motor Wagon

By John B. Lundstrom
Associate Curator,
Milwaukee Public Museum

The Schloemer Motor Wagon is the first gasoline-powered automobile known to be designed and built in Wisconsin. A Milwaukee entrepreneur, Gottfried Schloemer (1842-1921), with the help of skilled locksmith Frank Toepfer (1850-1918), constructed the buggy-like vehicle at Schloemer's home at 439 3rd Avenue (now 8th and Scott on Milwaukee's near south side.)

The exact date of the vehicle has yet to be determined. Unfortunately no original documents relating to its construction survive. In February 1920, Schloemer stated in a affidavit and in an article in the August 1920 "Wisconsin Motorist" that he built the motor wagon in 1890 and first drove it in 1892. This would, if true, antedate the operation of the Duryea automobile by one year and make the Schloemer a candidate for the honor of the first gas-powered automobile in the United States. In 1920, Fay L. Cusick of West Allis, Wisconsin, purchased the vehicle from Schloemer. In extensive efforts to promote the car, Cusick claimed that the Schloemer Motor Wagon was "the oldest gas-driven car in the world." The source of this error appears to be a patent secured on August 27, 1889, by Schloemer and Edward Hausknecht for an improved "velocipede," or tricycle, powered only by an "oscillating seat." However, this is not the same vehicle later known as the Schloemer Motor Wagon.

A photograph exists of the Schloemer running in what can be dated as an 1898 parade in Milwaukee. The earliest actual mention of the Schloemer Motor Wagon found so far in print occurred in the June 28, 1900, *Milwaukee Journal*. The article highlighting Milwaukee's first automobile parade described the Schloemer as "a curious old lumbering affair" and the "first automobile to be made in the state." It is interesting that as early as 1900 people already considered the vehicle to be a sort of automotive fossil. The Schloemer Motor Wagon lay in storage for nearly 20 years before Cusick obtained it. Hopefully further research will determine once and for all whether Schloemer actually operated his car in 1892. Until then such a claim for priority must only remain an assertion and not a fact.

This is the Schloemer Motor Wagon, made in the early part of the 1890s and possibly as early as 1891, in Milwaukee, and seen in this later photo. It shares at least claim as being the first Wisconsin gas-driven motor vehicle. It presently resides in the Milwaukee Museum.
Photo courtesy of the Milwaukee Public Museum.

When acquired in 1930 by the Milwaukee Public Museum, the Schloemer Motor Wagon was powered by a one-cylinder, four-cycle, Wolverine Junior engine, now known to date no earlier than 1897. However, strong evidence, both anecdotal and physical, argues that the car previously featured a two-cycle engine, probably an early Sintz manufactured in Springfield, Ohio. A recent complete restoration of the car by museum volunteer Herbert Smith revealed prior engine mountings and an altered drive system. Evidently in 1920 when Cusick decided to publicize the car by running it, he replaced an inoperable original engine with the oldest one he could find. Hasty reinstallation is evident in the careless way some internal components were shifted around or greatly modified, as opposed to the excellence of the original workmanship.

A wick-type carburetor of Schloemer's own design and cast with his name in raised letters is attached to the fuel tank. However, he never received a patent for it, as wrongly asserted in many sources. The rest of the running gear is equally primitive and consistent with a vehicle from the early 1890s. Steering is accomplished by a tiller, while the leather belt-and-chain drive has no reverse gear. Sparkbrook Manufacturing of Coventry, England, produced the rear axle and differential in the 1880s to be used in a tricycle. The Schloemer's maximum speed was about ten mph, and the rudimentary cooling system of coiled tubes and a water tank often forced the driver to stop when the engine overheated.

Never a practical vehicle in itself, the Schloemer Motor Wagon represents the vision of Wisconsin's pioneer automobile enthusiasts and points the way to the vast automotive industry that has so revolutionized modern life.

This article is derived from the extensive archives of documents, clippings, and interviews held by the History Section of the Milwaukee Public Museum. The author would like to thank in particular Herbert Smith, the late Verone Kalista, and Vern Kamholtz for their efforts in researching the Schloemer Motor Wagon.

Chapter Two

STEAM-DRIVEN VEHICLES

1878 The Worlds First "Automobile" Race
By Gary Allen Hoonsbeen, Minneapolis

Carhart's Vehicle

An interesting chapter of American automobile history dates back to 1872 and took place in Racine, Wisconsin. Dr. J. W. Carhart (1834-1914) had assembled a self-propelled vehicle he called "The Spark." It was equipped with an upright steam boiler fitted with furnace and smokestack in back of the driver's seat. The fuel was coal and it was stored in the front of the vehicle and passed back, between the legs of the driver, into the burner. Two small slide valve engines were located on each side of the boiler. The 48-inch rear wheels were driven independently from the separate engines through a series of gears.

A report at the time states: ..."when it went down the street, it shot smoke and cinders fifteen feet in the air and with the boiler operating under 120 pounds of pressure, it made such a racket as to drive all the teams off the streets and cause the pedestrians to fear it might explode. For that reason, no whistle was required although one was provided. Wherever it went, there was no team traffic and the streets were cleared for its passage without the request of the driver...."

Chapter 134

[Published March 5, 1875]

AN ACT To encourage the invention and successful use of steam or other mechanical agents on highways.

The people of the state of Wisconsin, represented in Senate and Assembly, do enact as follows:

SECTION 1. There is hereby appropriated the sum of ten thousand dollars, out of any money in the treasury not otherwise appropriated, to be used as a bounty, and to be paid to any citizen of Wisconsin, who shall invent, and after five years continued trial and use, shall produce a machine propelled by steam *or* other motive agent, which shall be a cheap and practical substitute for the use of horses, and other animals on the highway and farm; *provided*, that said appropriation shall not be levied or collected until a successful award is made.

SECTION 2. Any machine or locomotive entering the list to compete for the prize or bounty, shall perform a journey of at least two hundred miles, on a common road or roads, in a continuous line north and south in this state, and propelled by its own internal power, at the average rate of at least five miles per hour, working time.

SECTION. 3. The said locomotive must be of such construction and width as to conform with or run in the ordinary track of the common wagon or buggy, now in use, and be able to run backward or turn out of the road to accommodate other vehicles in passing, and to be able to ascend or descend a grade of at least two hundred feet to the mile.

SECTION 4. The Secretary of State is hereby empowered and authorized, when satisfactory proof that the above conditions have been complied with, to draw his warrant on the treasury for the sum of ten thousand dollars, and pay the same to the inventor of the successful machine.

SECTION 5. This act shall take effect and be in force from and after its passage and publication.

Approved March 2, 1875

Introduced by Rep. Marshall, [No. 163,A.]

THE MARCH 2, 1875, ACT

This is how the original act, introduced by Rep. Marshall, appeared. It was the first of four such "acts" dealing with the world's first self-propelled vehicle race.

It has been suggested that reports of Carhart's invention of a Horseless Carriage was an inspiration to a Republican member of the Wisconsin Assembly by the name of George M. Marshall (1834-1915). For it was Marshall who introduced an act into Wisconsin Laws which was "to encourage the invention and successful use of steam or other mechanical agents on the highways." This bill was approved by the Wisconsin Senate and Assembly on March 2, 1875, thus laying the foundation for the world's first trackless, self-propelled land vehicle race.

What prompted this assemblyman, from the small town of Big Springs, Adams County, Wisconsin, to introduce such an act to the Assembly? Why should such an act be approved by this 100-man body? In the *Milwaukee Sun,* March 1, 1879, author George W. Peck offered the following answer. "He (Marshall) was a mechanic of some kind, hardworking man, but he had a hobby. He was a nice man as we ever met, honest, square, friendly, good-natured, and all that, but he had a hobby. His hobby was a steam road wagon. We have rode on the (Rail Road) cars with him a dozen of times, between Madison and Kilbourn, where he got off to go to his home in the country, and he has explained to us how a steam road wagon could be made. He would illustrate on his fingers, on the car seat, on the newsboy's truck and everywhere; and often, after he left the train, our head would be so full of 'eccentricks,' steam chests, driving wheels, and things that we wouldn't see the conductor when he came along to collect the fare.... Well, Marshall had a bill introduced providing that the state should pay $10,000 to the inventor of a steam road wagon that should be a cheap substitute for horses and mules. The legislature was a good-natured body, and Marshall was a good fellow, and they didn't think anybody would ever go deliberately at work to make a steam mule, and as he had a hobby, why they voted for the bill, just out of pure goodfellowship. The state didn't need a steam mule any more than a dog needed two tails, but they passed the bill...to please Marshall, who had a pretty good head under that coonskin cap, and they all liked him...."

The Act Refined

There were a total of four acts of legislation concerning this Wisconsin race. Marshall, the originator of the 1875 act, introduced the first amendment on March 8, 1876. It eliminated the five-year period for "experimentation" and replaced it with the words "...any citizen of Wisconsin, who shall invent, and within one year after the passage of this act shall file with the secretary of state a statement of his intention to compete for said bounty, and that he has made progress in the construction of a machine...."

The following year, March 8, 1877, a second amendment made it a duty of the Governor to appoint three commissioners to "examine and test all machines which shall compete for or claim said bounty...." Guidelines were also established for scheduling the event. And finally, "Upon the conclusion of said trial" the commissioners were charged with determining if anyone was entitled to the prize, a duty they were to perform without pay, except for their actual expenses.

The Prelude

By the following year the stage was set and the newspapers from around the state were getting out the message.

The *State Gazette* of May 18, 1878, made the following announcement:

"...Governor Smith today appointed the following commissioners to test the competing machines and award the proffered bounty, George M. Marshall, of Big Springs, Adams county; O.P. Olin, of Oakland, Jefferson County, and John M. Smith, of Green Bay...."

As early as June 7, 1878, there was a report in the *Jefferson County Union* regarding participation: "The following persons will present steam road-wagons at the Capital, on the 10th....G. Hubbard, of Fond du Lac; Edwin Roberts, of Richland County; E. P. Cowles, of Brown County; J. E. Bantoer, of Madison; B. Garrison, of Wood County, M. Marshall, of Adams County; Sherman M. Booth, late of Wisconsin, of Free-Sell notoriety, has written to the

Secretary of State for information regarding the entrance of a road-wagon propelled by electricity. Mr. Booth has such a thing, and he desires to enter it for competition."

On June 11, 1878, from the *State Gazette*: "The commissioners have received six entries for trial of steam road wagons, and have decided to meet at Green Bay, July fifteenth, and make that the starting point in the coming trial. J. M. Smith was elected Secretary of Board of Commissioners."

On June 21, 1878, from the *Jefferson County Union*: "At the late meeting of the Steam-wagon Commissioners at Madison, it was decided that the inventors, with their wagons, assemble at Green Bay on the 15th of July next, and start them on a trail trip, touching at Fond du Lac, Oshkosh, Jefferson, Milton Junction, Janesville, Beloit, Evansville and Madison, when the award shall be made...."

The Race

The final day of departure arrived, July 16, 1878, but only two "vehicles" were ready, the Green Bay and the Oshkosh, each named for the city of their origination. They were, in reality, large steam tractors.

The Green Bay had three speeds forward and a reverse. Its engine had two 7-inch cylinders with an 11 stroke, developing about 16 horsepower. It was the second such vehicle built by E. P. Cole of Wequiock, Wisconsin. The machine he had planned to enter was either sold or leased to a logging concern desperately needing its service. The Green Bay machine was put together in the three months before the race and was not complete or ready when it left the starting line on July 16th.

The Oshkosh had two 6-inch cylinders with an 8-inch stroke, developing about 10 horsepower. It had only one speed forward and reverse. There were five individuals involved in the Oshkosh. A. M. Farrand was the chief designer; A. Gallagher and F. Shomer supplied some of the financial support and engineering details; J. F. Morse provided the facility for its construction and M. T. Battis made the boiler. All five of these gentlemen were named by the State of Wisconsin in the final award of the prize money.

The *Wisconsin State Journal*, July 24, 1878, gives us a good summary of the event:

"The start was made from Fort Howard at noon of the 16th instant (in the current month). When the Green Bay emerged from the city limits, it broke down and was sent back to the shop for repairs. The Oshkosh kept on its way, reaching Appleton, a distance of 32 miles, at 8 p.m. Leaving Appleton at 9:30 the following morning, Neenah was reached in time for dinner, and the people of this little 'Flower of the Fox,' were treated to an exhibition of speed on the principal streets of the city, much to the delight and wonderment of the populace. From Neenah to Oshkosh is about 14 miles, and the machine made the trip in two hours, from 1 to 3 p.m.

"At Oshkosh, the Green Bay machine was found; it had made good time on a flat car, over the C. & N. W. Railway, and beat the second city invention by several hours. It was cruel on the Green Bay engine, but the Commissioners, who had followed the Oshkosh in buggies, demanded the former, though feeble, be taken from the cars, and not transported to Fort Atkinson by rail, as intended by the drivers. The "boys" were then summoned by the plentiful blowing of whistles, and each machine being hitched to about five tons of green lumber, in a road wagon, the Oshkoshians were amused by seeing them cavort around, through the sawdust streets.

"The machines left Oshkosh at 7 p.m., of Saturday last, en route for Waupun; the Green Bay machine broke down two miles out of town, and returned to Oshkosh for repairs, spending Sunday in a machine shop, by way of a rest. Oshkosh continued the 34 miles to Waupun, making it in 6 hours and 25 minutes. From Waupun to Watertown the 32 miles over the sand hills was made in four hours and thirty seconds. From Watertown to Fort Atkinson is 21 miles, this distance being accomplished in two hours and ten minutes.

"At Fort Atkinson, a plowing trial was had on Snell's farm. A gang of two plows was furnished, and the Oshkosh turned over a goodly portion of a 60-acre field. A crowd of 500 people were present to witness the novel sight.

"The time from Fort Atkinson to Milton Junction—thirteen miles—was 2 hours and 15 minutes; from Milton Junction to Janesville—eight miles—1 hour and 2 minutes; from Janesville to Madison—forty miles—7 hours and 30 minutes."

The Winner

"The Oshkosh in charge of Messrs. Rank Schomer and Ans Farrand, the inventors, accompanied by Commissioner Olin, arrived in Madison last evening, having made the trip from Fort Howard—201 miles—in 33 hours and 27 seconds, official time. The allowance given by law—five miles an hour—was 40 hours. The Oshkosh therefore beat official time by six hours and thirty-three minutes. This machine has, throughout, hauled a wagon weighing 3,500 pounds. At Oshkosh, it made the tour of the lumberyards, among the sawdust, with 9,100 pounds. The weight of the machine alone is 4,800 pounds, and with water and coal for 8 miles, 6,600 pounds. It is a handsome affair, neatly and simply made, and appears calculated to do any amount of work. The engineers reported no breakages on the trip, no runaways from scared teams, and not a bridge-plank disturbed; while most of the roadway has been hard to travel, being heavy sand and gravel."

The Loser

The *Wisconsin State Journal*, July 24, 1878, continued: "The Green Bay took the road from Oshkosh last Monday accompanied most of the way by Commissioners Smith and Marshall. They arrived this morning reporting it in the ditch at Jefferson. It will be given a dose of physic, and again started on its luckless way...."

The *Jefferson Banner* of July 25, 1878, described the status this way: "The Green Bay passed through Jefferson Tuesday at 4:20 p.m., but in crossing the railroad track south of town, the coupling broke and the tender was ditched. Bad luck seems to have attacked this wagon from the start, and if it ever gets to Madison, it will be a wonder. It is a ponderous affair, weighs about 7 tons and would be a regular bridge smasher...."

Finally, from the *Janesville Gazette*, July 27, 1878: "The steam wagon Green Bay broke down near Evansville last night, and was shipped home without finishing the trip...."

The Controversy

Before, during, and after the event, newspapers in Wisconsin took up sides for and against the steam wagon event. Most vocal was the *Milwaukee Sentinel* of July 23, 1878, "There was a rush to see the $10,000 appropriation, but all persons of a practical turn of mind were disappointed in the machine. It is simply a self- propelled engine with a wagon hitched on behind. There is not, we venture to assert, a farmer in Rock County, who will declare that the 'alleged' steam wagon can be put to a practical use on a farm. The man who gets the $10,000 will doubtless get the best end of the bargain."

Joining in the criticism was the Janesville *Daily Record*, from July 25, 1878. "...Last evening Fraud No. 2, i.e. the second of the steam wagons, put in an appearance on our streets at about half past six. It was what is called the Cole, or Green Bay, wagon, and it would have been a fine thing to have kept it there. The Oshkosh wagon was a big fraud, but this is a bigger one, only because it is a larger machine. If the other was an ill-shaped concern, what under heaven could you call this one? The only practicable thing they are either one good for is to use up coal and water. The Oshkosh fraud had the best of it because they had seven men and a boy to run their machine, and the last one only had four, and consequently the first fraud had fully thirty hours the start on leaving this city for Madison. Any amount would be a large price to pay for either wagon, unless a person had a spite against another and wanted to make him a present. The commissioners have gone to Madison to hold a conference as to the relative merits of each of the frauds, and also to decide which one is entitled to the $10,000 offered by the State Legislature. If the Commission should award the money to either one of the two humbugs, that have passed through this city, they should be disfranchised and forced to make their living on the road with one of these machines—no matter which one. The proprietors of both wagons expect the $10,000 and we cannot blame them if they can beguile the committee into giving it to them. The people of the state would be better pleased if the legislature would pass a law inflicting a fine of $10,000 upon any person guilty of bringing such machines on the roads, much less fostering them by offering them a premium, and furthermore the tax-payers don't take much stock in such foolishness."

The Committee's Conclusion

On July 27, 1878, the three-man committee submitted their final report to Governor William E. Smith of Wisconsin. It agreed that the Oshkosh had made the 200-mile run, was able to climb hills, averaged better than five miles per hour (running time), hauled heavy loads and plowed fields, but did not satisfy the language and spirit of the law, "...a cheap and practical substitute for the use of a horse...." The committee "passed the buck" and recommended "the next legislature make them suitable awards."

There has been little discovered as to the events leading up to the final compensation given to the winners of the 1878 race, but it appears there were some threats of lawsuits over the failure of the committee to award the Oshkosh the $10,000 bounty. But even more compelling was a threat of the 'inventors' to build another "lower-cost" machine and make a second attempt to drive from Green Bay to Madison to gain the bounty. This would draw even more attention to what many considered an already bad situation.

The Bounty

On March 4th, 1879, the Wisconsin legislature agreed the owners of the Oshkosh should be paid "...the sum of $5,000: provided, the parties herein named accept the said sum in full payment of claims against the state...but this act shall not be construed as an admission that said wagon was a satisfactory compliance with the requirements of said acts...." The legislature also repealed the 1875 law!

WORLD'S FIRST AUTOMOBILE RACE?

The French have long laid claim to having had the world's first automobile race, be it the 1892 Paris-Rouen-Paris rally or the 1895 Paris-Bordeaux-Paris race. But the correct title of the "World's First" must clearly be given to those 1878 Wisconsin pioneers who made it from Green Bay to Madison. Any arguments against this are meaningless, just consider the facts:

1. There was at least a one-year notice for the participants to prepare for the race.
2. The routing was clearly defined, 200 miles, from Green Bay to Madison.
3. A minimum speed was required of the winner, five miles per hour.
4. There were a minimum of six and maybe eleven applications for entry.
5. A prize of $10,000 was offered to the winner.
6. Everything about the event was well-documented.
7. There was a sponsor of the event, the State of Wisconsin.
8. Publicity was abundant, before, during, and after the event.
9. The vehicles represented the technology of the day.
10. There was a winner.
11. It was called a race: The *Green Bay Advocate*, August 1, 1878, said "...The people have an immediate interest in it. They don't care whether Mr. Cowles' machine was in the **race** or out of it...."
12. The fact that the Oshkosh and Green Bay were large steam-driven machines is only indicative of fact that this was 1878, 18 years before the official beginning of the American automobile industry. These steam machines were self-propelled, trackless land vehicles, no different from the automobiles of today than the Wright Brothers' first airplane is from today's Boeing 757.

As for the committee members, they turned in their "actual" expenses for judging the event, Marshall and Olin, $75 each and Smith, $175.

AMERICA'S FIRST AUTOMOBILE ?

IN 1873 (SOME SOURCES SAY 1871) DR. J. W. CARHART ROLLED A PECULIAR-LOOKING MACHINE OUT OF HIS WORKSHOP IN RACINE. TO HIS NEIGHBORS IT LOOKED LIKE A BUGGY WITH A POTBELLIED STOVE MOUNTED OVER THE REAR AXLE.

WHEN THE VEHICLE BEGAN TO MOVE UNDER ITS OWN POWER IT BECAME THE FIRST LIGHT SELF-PROPELLED CAR EVER TO TRAVEL A PUBLIC ROAD IN AMERICA — AND PERHAPS THE WORLD.

THIS FIRST STEAM-DRIVEN CAR PRE-DATED HENRY FORD'S FIRST CAR BY TWENTY-TWO YEARS, BUT CARHART NEVER ENTERED THE AUTOMOBILE MANUFACTURING BUSINESS, AND IT WASN'T UNTIL 1893 THAT THE DURYEA BROTHERS OF SPRINGFIELD, MASSACHUSETTS INTRODUCED THE FIRST MARKETABLE AUTOMOBILE IN AMERICA, TWO YEARS BEFORE THE FIRST FORD.

'THE SPARK' ENDED ITS DAYS AS A POWER UNIT IN A RACINE PRINT SHOP!

IT CHANGED AMERICA'S LIFESTYLE !

LOU + JOHN RUSSELL '81

SOURCE: "TREASURY of EARLY AMERICAN AUTOMOBILES · 1877 - 1925" by FLOYD CLYMER, BONANZA BOOKS, NEW YORK, N.Y. 1950

This was the car that started it all in Wisconsin. The above picture was taken from the January 14, 1903, issue of "The Horseless Age." It was sent to this magazine by Dr. Carhart with a letter which read: "...I herewith hand you a photo of my steam buggy 'Spark,' built at Racine, Wisconsin, in 1872. Pneumatic tires were then unknown, and such a thing as ball bearings had not been thought of; nor was oil used as a fuel to produce power. I used hard coal and had a boiler made by the Buttons Fire Engine Company, of Waterford, N.Y. After my buggy was built the State of Wisconsin offered a prize of $10,000 for the steam road wagon that would accomplish certain conditions. Ans Farrand, of Oshkosh, Wisconsin, who at that time had charge of my steam buggy, built the steamer Oshkosh and took the prize...."

(Signed) J. D. Carhart, M.D.
LaGrange, Texas
December 21, 1902

Ansen Farrand, referred to in Carhart's letter was one of the engineers who drove the Oshkosh. He is credited for much of the machine's design. Farrand was for several years the chief of the local fire department.

THE MAP

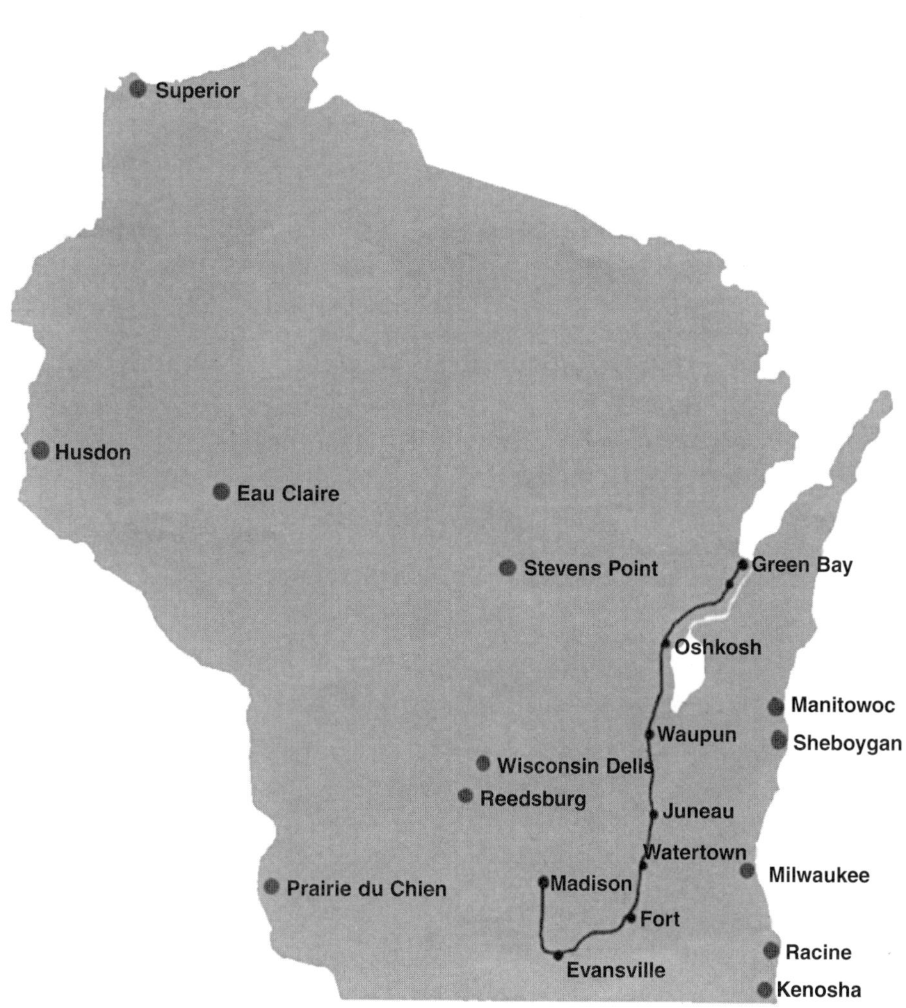

The newspaper articles of 1878 clearly describe the cities touched by the race of 1878. Although the actual path may never be known it is likely the routing was on many of the roads still used in Wisconsin today. This would make a great annual 3- or 4-day tour for the HCCA. It could combine early cars and steam tractors. Anyone interested?

The beginning of the 200 mile steam driven vehicle race Oshkosh to Madison, Wisconsin in 1878. The Oshkosk steam car is witnessed by a crowd of people. Photograph courtesy of the Oshkosh Public Museum.

The picture is the only one known to exist of the 1878 race. The Oshkosh is shown next to the stone building at 201 Ceape Avenue in Oshkosh, Wisconsin, where it was constructed. The building was built in 1853 and was the location where the automobile differential was invented by Alexander Gallinger and John F. Morse. The Oshkosh shown here matches exactly the description given by early magazine writers. Any question about which vehicle first used a steering wheel? Here it is, clearly shown on the Oshkosh in 1878. Notice the wooden spoked wheels both front and back. The two cylinder heads are located above the front axles. According to early records the Oshkosh used a differential to drive the rear wheels. Alex Gallinger is at the steering wheel, in shirt sleeves behind him is Ansen Farrand, the bearded man on the tongue of the water tank is Frank Schomer. There are four wagons hitched to the Oshkosh. Those were the days!

The Spark, The Steam Automobile Invention of Dr. J. W. Carhart
By Val Quandt

The story of Dr. Carhart and his steam car dating back to 1871 is included here because it is a Wisconsin story, and serves as an introduction to the main topic.

In September of 1871, Dr. J. W. Carhart drove his steam-propelled vehicle on the streets of Racine, Wisconsin. He was then 37 years old, and a pastor of a Methodist Episcopal church in Racine. His steam-driven vehicle had a boiler of 20 gallons capacity and with an engine for each of the large four-foot-driving wheels. It had a long steering tiller. This vehicle was made with the assistance of his brother, H. C. Carhart, a physics professor at Michigan State University, who made all the working drawings. Hard coal was used to feed the boilers. The boiler was made by the Button Fire Engine Works of Waterford, New York. Dr. Carhart had moved shortly before from Saratoga County, New York. Much of the machine work on this steam engine was done by the J. I. Case Company in Racine, Wisconsin.

Dr. J. W. Carhart was a Methodist minister who also later trained and practiced as a physician. He is credited with producing the first automobile in the state of Wisconsin, and possibly also in America, in 1871. Assigning a primacy in time, however, is fraught with the possibility that other or less well known figures were doing the same thing at the same time. As Andrew J. Pierce noted in 1909, "The invention of the automobile was not the product of a single mind, or of a single country." As early as 1769, Nicholas Joseph Cugnot in France developed his cumbersome three-wheeled steam vehicle. This was then 102 years before the invention by Dr. Carhart.

Reminiscing later in 1914, Dr. Carhart said, "It was in September of 1871 that my son and myself went out to the barn and fired the machine up for its trial trip. As we turned into the street, I steering and my son wielding the poker, which formed a very necessary part of our touring equipment, the entire town rushed out of doors to see what was happening. The noise of the exhaust, which escaped through the stack, and which shot smoke and cinders fully fifteen feet into the air, was terrific and startling. Of course the steam whistle, with which it was equipped, did not tend to make matters any better. In fact, it was not long before we had the streets entirely to ourselves, for when they had seen it, the citizens were unanimous in predicting that this steam car, the Spark, would blow up."

This was in 1871, as mentioned, and in June of 1878 the state of Wisconsin offered the prize money of $10,000 for the invention and development of "a horseless vehicle that could successfully complete a 200-mile journey as nearly as possible in a north and south direction, within the confines of the state." This then occurred from Green Bay to Madison, Wisconsin.

The Spark inventor did not take out patents on his car nor did he participate in, or drive in, the 200-mile run. Several other of the participants did claim bounties of $5,000 apiece, among which was A. Frand of Oshkosh, Wisconsin. He was the builder of the famous Oshkosh steam carriage, and he was closely associated with the Methodist clergyman in the building of the Spark.

Dr. Carhart was born in 1834 at Coeyman, Albany County, New York, and completed his education in the ministry in schools of New York state and came west around 1870 to Racine, Wisconsin. He was a medical doctor also, with his training in medicine coming shortly after his arrival in Wisconsin. He spent the latter part of his life in Texas, in the practice of medicine combined with ministerial teaching.

Dr. Carhart kept his bias for the steam-driven automobile. In 1905, in an interview, he remarked, "after 35 years of experience and observation, I am of the opinion still that steam will be the power of the future for motor cars."

Just months before his death in 1914, Dr. Carhart was interviewed in his office in San Antonio, Texas, for an article on his steam vehicle, the Spark. The doctor rummaged in his safe among piles of scrapbooks and clippings. At length he produced a suitable picture of his steam car. He remained a firm believer that steam-driven was the car of the future.

In June of 1914 John S. Donald, secretary of the state of Wisconsin, and interested in motor cars by reason of being the administrative officer of the law requiring the registration of motor vehicles, started a movement to honor publicly Dr. Carhart for his first motor-propelled vehicle in America. It was planned to ask the legislature to appropriate funds for a medal and a purse of several thousand dollars in recognition of Dr. Carhart's contribution to humanity. Apparently nothing came of these plans. Several months later in this year of 1914, Dr. Carhart died at age 81.

The end of America's earliest motor car was quite unromantic, for soon it was dismantled and utilized as a power plant for a job-printing establishment run by the inventor's sons.

1900 - 1902
Milwaukee Steamer
Milwaukee Automobile Company
By Walter E. Wray

Most turn of the century steam cars were near carbon copies of the Stanley and the Locomobile. The Milwaukee Steamer, Wisconsin's only native mass-produced steam car, didn't stray from the pattern. Unlike some, however, one of its creators went on to become known in other automotive ventures: W. H. McIntyre who later became the power behind the Kiblinger high-wheeler, the McIntyre auto and the Imp cyclecar.

During the Milwaukee company's short life span, five models were offered, ranging from the typical lightweight Stanhope of Stanley type, also known as the runabout style, to larger versions with increased seating capacity. Prices ranged from $750 for the basic transportation model to $1,300 for the larger units. Larger boilers seem to have been used as vehicle size increased, and all tools and equipment were apparently included in the list price.

The Milwaukee Steamer was located in Milwaukee at 19th and St. Paul Avenue in the old Milwaukee Engineering Company plant. The company was organized in December of 1899. It was a steam car, representing "the oldest artificial power." It had no ball bearings, rather bronze bearings. But the company came to an end in just two years, in 1902. It was thought to have overproduced for a market that was not as favorable as expected.

1900 Milwaukee Steamer, Stanhope

Chapter Three
RACINE-BUILT VEHICLES
Pennington, Pierce-Racine, Case, LPC, Mitchell

E. J. Pennington, Inventive Genius or Rogue
By Val Quandt

When this story begins in 1895, Thomas Kane was in the business of manufacturing school and office furniture, and also with an interest in producing boat launches. In an article in the "Horseless Age" in November of 1895, the writer described the association of Kane and Pennington to form a new business, the Racine Motor Vehicle Company to manufacture a new "hot air engine" developed by the then 37-year-old inventor, Edward Joel Pennington.

Pictures showed the Pennington engine powering both bicycle types of vehicles, and also four-wheel quadricycles. These were basically two bicycles fastened to each other side by side with a platform interposed holding the engine. These were offered in one-, two-, and four-cylinder sizes. Each cylinder was of a two and one-half inch bore, and a six-inch stroke. There was a primary battery, no carburetor, and a copper wire extending from this battery directly into the combustion chamber.

Pennington had his own unique theory of what took place at ignition in the combustion chamber. He claimed it did not need a cooling water jacket in stating, "by utilizing the well-known principle that rapid evaporation produces cold, and both heat and cold are being produced, the cylinder never becomes overheated."

Whatever was the theory behind his engine, it seemed to work in his hands, and was less well accepted by the public. Motor cycles propelled by his engines were exhibited a the Cycle Show in New York in January of 1895, and attracted much attention. At an exhibition given in Milwaukee in 1895, a Pennington powered motor cycle covered a distance of one mile in 58 seconds. Early on these were motor cycles, not motorcycles.

The Pennington Motor Cycle of 1895

Pennington was born in 1858, and it was most likely in Indiana. At least his early years were spent in this state. He worked at various machine shop types of jobs. He matured into a large and tall man of six-feet two-inches. He had an impressive appearance, wearing fashionable clothes and with a tall silk hat.

In 1891, Pennington developed a small model of a flying ship (airplane) that he displayed in Chicago at the old Exposition Building on the lakefront. This was his endeavor to float a big company to manufacture air ships, the site of which was to be in Mt. Carmel, Illinois. The "Scientific American" magazine in its March 7, 1891 issue had an article and a descriptive picture of the Pennington Air Ship. The tone of the article was generally derogatory. It described in quite detail what E. J. Pennington had in mind. The conclusion in the article was that the contraption would not fly, and that it was too bulky to achieve this.

The dimensions are not given, but with 13 passenger windows in view, it must have been about 100 feet long. It in essence was a dirigible with a long cigar-shaped buoyancy chamber, and with a top sail and rudder. It was propelled by a large four-blade propeller driven by a gasoline engine. There were batteries below for lighting the passenger compartment. The writer called it a "stock jobbing" enterprise, and suggested that an actual flying machine was far in the future. Pennington had a better imagination than the writer.

To demonstrate his proposed flying machine Pennington made a small lightweight model that he displayed at the Chicago Exposition Building. This model was tethered to the ground and flew in a 50-foot circle. Current to an electric motor and propeller was fed from a battery on the ground to a wire to the ship. Again the conclusion is rather harsh in saying, "as a demonstration of anything new or promising in the way of aerial navigation it is without value."

Pennington is seen at the controls of his fan-motor bicycle, in Racine, Wisconsin, an ideas-rich genius, c. 1895

He also exhibited his invention of a motor bike at a Chicago bicycle show at the Lakefront Armory in 1894.

What was to develop into his trademark of operation was evident early on in his career. This was an ability to smoothly talk his select audience into parting with their investment money for his enterprises. In all cases he was selling stock in his newly proposed enterprises which would produce great profits for the stock buyers.

The first of this nature was for a company that was to patent a wooden pulley. He convinced citizens to invest $50,000 for a factory and a promotion that never took place. He repeated this sort of experience in several more Indiana towns and cities. This was before migrating to the state of Ohio. With the slow pace of communications, word of his previous nefarious financial dealings was also slow in alerting his new business contacts.

Here in Cleveland, Ohio, he did have a justifiable business with a motor cycle company, producing a four-wheeled vehicle called a quadricycle, with the trade name of Victoria.

The Pennington story now continues with his association with Thomas Kane and his Racine Motor Vehicle Company in 1895.

The "Victoria" a Kane-Pennington product made in Racine, Wisconsin.It was four wheeled and was exhibited at the Cycle Show in New York, in January of 1895.

Ever the showman, this is the Pennington Autocar in 1896, intended for four passengers, and here seen with nine.

The motor bicycle or motor cycles as they were called, and the four-wheeled quadricycles, were now the focus of this new company. Whatever the merits of the product in experiments and in demonstrations to the public, they failed in production and in their ability to be sold.

Then a fire destroyed the factory. To this point the company had made only engines, and stating that they were not interested in making motor vehicles, contrary to the name of the firm as Racine Motor Vehicle Company.

Pennington, in 1896, had a short sojourn in the state of New York where his activities were criticized by the newspaper called *World*, and which he countered with a libel suit. While in Racine, and in the midst of attack by angry stockholders, Pennington shipped off to London, England. Here he remained until 1899, except for some visits back to America.

The "Horseless Age" wrote in June of 1896, 'Realizing that he had outgrown his welcome here, he set out for the green fields of England to repeat his performances there, and from the very moment of his landing the tide of puffery and misrepresentation has been rising in the English press. It is beyond belief that this adventurer has been able to worm himself into the confidence of the promoters of the industry in England.' But Thomas Kane, at least in public utterances, kept up his confidence in Pennington and his motor, at least until he left America.

In England and later in France, Pennington was issuing public challenges for races between his motor cycles and quadricycles and the foreign counterparts. He published one challenge for a prize of 5,000 pounds, and for substantial entry fees, all of which he pocketed.

Pennington saw a market for selling his quadricycles to the English military for war-fighting machines. He described and had pictures taken of his vehicle as fit for military action using armor side plates, and equipped with rapid fire guns. As with all his promotions to date, his ideas were experimental, and the vehicles prototypal, and without a market. This "war automobile" was tested by the English and was capable of traveling a mile in 55 seconds. In spite of their early enthusiasm, there is no record of any production.

In the meantime, Pennington was staying in the finest hotels in London and yet did not have the income to pay his debts. He also was hounded by dealers who had incurred expense setting up facilities to market his promised vehicles, which were never delivered. For all of this Pennington was defending himself in bankruptcy courts. A writer gave his impressions, "Pennington seems to possess a faculty of getting into other people's pockets to his own immediate advantage, and the strange part of his ventures is that he never seems to hold on to any of the money he induces others to lose."

Back in America, and in May of 1901 Pennington was reported in "Horseless Age" to be attempting to organize an automobile company in Carlisle, Pensylvania.

In January of 1902, the Racine Wagon Works was announcing their intention to build a factory for the manufacture of a motor vehicle, and their use of the motor of an inventor from New York, presumably that of Pennington. Nothing developed from these plans.

In December of 1902, Pennington was being sought by the police at the complaint of the Hotel Racine, in Racine, Wisconsin. Pennington had stayed in a luxury suite and failed to pay for his accommodations. The same was true for his experience at a hotel in Cincinatti, Ohio.

What Pennington was doing in these various locations was selling stock in companies that he purported to be developing for the manufacture of his engine and motor vehicles. The companies never developed. He and his wife lived expensively on this money, moving from place to place before his ill repute caught up to him.

At the same time that Pennington's available possessions were being auctioned off by the sheriff in Racine, Wisconsin, he was promoting another deal. This was for purchasing the works of the Racine Boat Manufacturing Company for $300,000. This was a sum of money that he did not possess. Also he was promoting the incorporation of the American Automobile Company with $5 million capital stock for the manufacture of automobiles.

In late December of 1902 Pennington was located in Detroit, Michigan, and Windsor, Ontario, with his wife. She commented at the time that "her husband had spent a fortune in attempting to perfect an automobile and that they were now in sore straits."

In October of 1903 Pennington was in Cleveland, Ohio, with ambitious plans for a Cleveland Motor Company. This was to manufacture gasoline motor delivery wagons and touring cars with 160 hp to cost $20,000 to $30,000 apiece. The delivery wagon with engine was described as a sort of "forecarriage" with motor activating the front wheels to be used for pulling any kind of carriage.

At this time Pennington was being quoted as claiming that he built the first motor cycles and the first automobiles ever constructed in this country. Also Pennington was developing an immense touring car able to hold 20 passengers, even sleeping facilities, and developing 300 hp. This was to be adaptable to railway use by fitting flanged wheels to travel across the rails. He secured the attention of C. D. Schoenberg, president of the May Department Stores, who was interested in purchasing such a vehicle for a sort of traveling land yacht.

By May of 1904 it was known that the latest Pennington endeavor had failed, and stock in the gasoline forecarriage or automobile horse, and the sleeping car enterprise had gone unsold. The Cleveland Motor Company was in bankruptcy.

Various companies were at work to build the forecarriage or automobile horse, and it was reported that at least two examples were made and were seen driving the streets of Cleveland. But the immense 28 foot long passenger and sleeping car vehicle never was completed.

In December of 1905 "Horseless Age" was describing 'Penningtons Wonderful Plugs,' yet another invention of Pennington. This was to be an advanced spark plug produced by the Continental Engineering Company. This spark plug was to have improved flaming properties, and to produce 20 to 50 percent more power from the gasoline. "Horseless Age" commented further, 'Pennington's inventions are always wonderful, but his financing is much more so. Read the back issues of "Horseless Age" before you invest.'

Nearing the end of his career, Pennington was back in Racine, Wisconsin, his old stamping ground promoting a new automobile, of a more conservative size, with 16 hp and selling for just $300, and trying to collect advance orders for these. The motor press was denigrating him.

From 1906 to 1911 not much was published about Pennington, his inventions and promotions. He died in early March of 1911 the result of a fall near his home at Springfield, Massachusetts. When he fell he fractured his nose. This got infected and he died of resulting meningitis.

In his adult years Pennington combined inventive ideas with expansive plans, and not a little bit of financial chicanery. Rather than the descriptive label of "Prince of Fake Promoters" he might have preferred lively "inventive genius" or at least "Airship Pennington."

The Pierce-Racine, 1904-1911

In 1900, the Pierce Engine Company was manufacturing and advertising for sale a 2 hp gasoline engine. This company was operating at 2325 Clark Street, in the Lakeside suburb of Racine, Wisconsin.

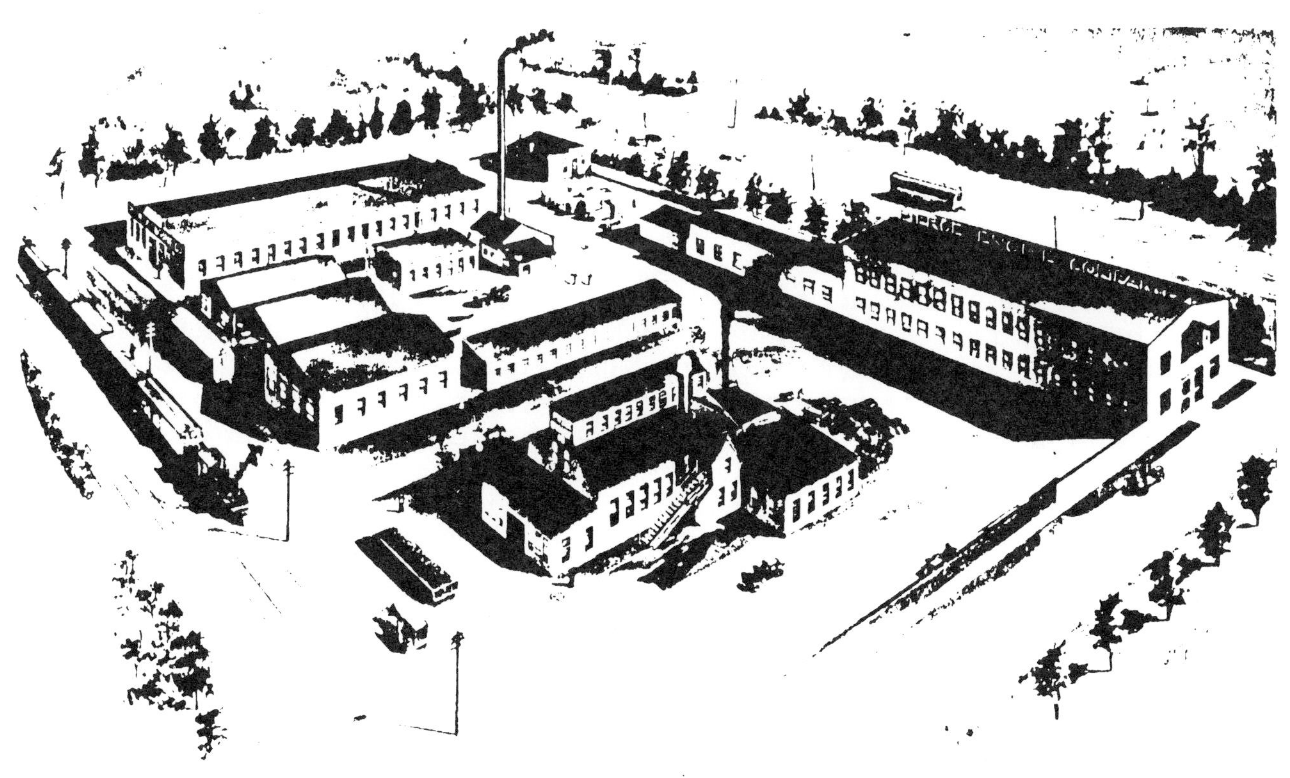

An artist conception of what the Pierce-Racine automobile factory looked like in 1908.

In 1899, the Pierce Engine Company made, and the same held true also in 1901, an experimental car. An earlier effort in 1893 will be described later.

In 1903, the Wisconsin Wheel Works at Racine Junction, Wisconsin, sold all of its bicycle manufacturing business to the Great Western Manufacturing Company of La Porte, Indiana. In the future they would manufacture the Mitchell motor cycles and automobiles, under the name of Mitchell-Pierce Company of Racine. A year later, in 1904, it was stated that the Pierce Company built the Mitchell for the Wisconsin Wheel Works, not mentioning the Indiana firm.

In 1904, at a time that the principal business of the Pierce Company was the manufacture of Pierce marine motors and Pierce launches, it announced that it would build 100 single- and twin-cylinder, water-cooled motor cars, weighing about 1,000 pounds. These were all open cars, in a runabout, and also a tonneau, at prices of $750 and $850 respectively.

In 1905, in referring and commenting on their Pierce-Racine models for that year, this company stated that Mr. A. J. Pierce, president of the company, had already in 1893 experimented with and had running on the streets of Racine, a functioning automobile. So the claim to 100 years of the car in the state of Wisconsin can be made on the basis of the Pierce in 1893, in a factory setting and with multiple vehicles manufactured following in the ensuing decade, much the same as the Duryea experience.

By 1906 Pierce-Racine had enlarged to a four-cylinder-touring car with a 24 hp engine, while maintaining their twin-cylinder cars.

In 1907 Pierce Engine company made a single four-cylinder model D, in three body styles. Mr. Pierce, in that year commented on the progress in automobile manufacture, with "its beginning less than fifteen years ago," and also that "the automobile of today is not the result of a few minds, but of thousands, and not limited to a particular country."

Reorganization of the Pierce Motor Company with its Pierce-Racine cars was realized in 1909 with officers of the Racine located J. I. Case Threshing Machine Company gaining control. The new president of Pierce-Racine was Mr. C. L. McIntosh, who was treasurer and part owner of the J. I. Case concern. He brought with him other officers from the J. I. Case Company. Mr. A. J. Pierce, founder of the Pierce Engine Company stayed on as general manager of the company. His engine company was credited with being one of the very first to manufacture gasoline engines in America, and while making marine engines and launches.

The announcement of August 1910, stated that the J. I. Case Company had taken over the entire automobile output of the Pierce Motor Company, and henceforth the vehicles would be called Case. While gaining financial and production control, it was another year of transition before the output was called the Case automobile. So the Pierce-Racine automobile, so named, essentially ceased with the 1911 model year, becoming the Case. In September of 1912 it was more widely announced that the J. I. Case Threshing Machine Company of Racine, Wisconsin, had purchased the entirety of the Pierce Motor Company and that for the past two years the latter had been the property of the Case company.

Mr. McIntosh died in 1910, and in the same year Mr. Pierce resigned from the business.

Around that time this humorous story was heard at Pierce-Racine: "A traveling demonstrator for a manufacturer of light runabouts recently importuned a Yankee farmer to buy one of the vehicles at a close cash figure. 'I'd rather put the money into cows' was the farmer's answer. 'But think how you'd look riding into town on the back of one of our Jerseys,' said the motorist. 'Perhaps I would look a bit foolish,' replied the agriculturist, 'but think how I'd be sized up if I was caught trying to milk an automobile.'"

Andrew J. Pierce died in January of 1921, at the age of 62 years. He was born in Rochester, New York, trained as a mechanical engineer, and moved to Racine, Wisconsin, at the age of 28 years.

PIERCE-RACINE

General Specifications

H. P., 40.
Cylinders, 4.
Vertical, in front.
Wheel base, 106 inches.
Gauge or tread, 56 inches.
Wheels, wood, artillery.
Spokes, 12, 1⅜ inches.
Tires, 34x4½ inches.
Rims, detachable type.
Body, tulip side opening.
Hood, collapsible.

Speeds, 3 forward and reverse.
Transmission, sliding gear, full ball bearing.
Steering, special screw nut.
Cooling, water.
Ignition, jump spark, storage battery.
Radiator, cellular.
Drive, shaft, bevel gear.
Front axle, tubular.
Rear axle, floating type, full ball bearing.
Brakes, four, two internal and two external, on rear wheels.

Springs, semi-elliptic.
Length springs, front, 42 inches.
Length springs, rear, 50 inches.
Color, body, onyx.
Color, gear, sagamore red.
Trimmings, black.
Fuel capacity, 25 gallons.
Water capacity, 5 gallons.
Speed, 3 to 50 miles per hour.

Equipment

Two side oil lamps.
One tail oil lamp.
One pair acetylene head lamps.
One acetylene generator, piped to lamps.
Body, ironed for top.

Horn, tube and bulb.
Tire repair kit, wrenches, screw driver, plugs and oil can.
Cocoa mat in tonneau; linoleum on floor in front.
Price, ~~$2600~~. $3000

Top, $100.00 extra.
Gas tank, $26.50.
Special color, $15.00 extra.
Crating, $10.00 extra.
Boxing for export, $35.00 extra.
All F.O.B. Racine, Wisconsin.

Dimensions of Body

Height of front seat from floor, 16½ inches.
Height of rear seat from mat, 15 inches.
Width of front seat, 19 inches.
Depth of front seat, 18 inches.

Width of rear seat, 50 inches.
Depth of rear seat, 19 inches.
From front of the rear seat to back of front seat, 26 inches.
Width of door in tonneau, 18 inches. Opens full width.

Height of tonneau back from cushion, 22 inches.
Height of front seat from cushion, 19 inches.
Thickness of cushions, 5 inches.
Diameter from inside of dash to front of front seat, 26½ inches.
Angle of steering column, 35 degrees.

The J. I. Case Company

In an announcement dated August of 1910, the J. I. Case Threshing Machine Company of Racine, Wisconsin, told of their plans to take over the Pierce-Racine Motor Company. Hereafter, and starting with the late 1911 models the Pierce-Racine automobile would be known as the Case car. Case pointed out its confidence in the Pierce-Racine engine as being one of the highest quality. Case had been in business in Racine as the manufacturer of a large line of farm equipment since 1842. In addition to its farm line, Case then went on to produce automobiles for some 17 years.

Case quite rightly felt that its vast farm implement dealership would be an advantage for its automobile sales, especially to farmers.

In 1911, Case offered six body styles for its cars, all with a four-cylinder 30-hp engine. Case concentrated its promotional efforts on state and county fairs, dirt track races, and even had plans to manufacture an aeroplane, as then spelled, to show at these fairs.

What did eventuate was the appearance of three Case race cars for the first Indianapolis 500 race, and that on May 30, 1911. At the pole position was a Case race car. Case entered cars at Indianapolis from 1911 through 1914. In this time only one of their cars finished a 500-mile race.

Already in 1912 Case had 10,000 sales agents and 65 branch houses in the United States and Canada. Many of these were now beginning to handle automobiles.

In January of 1912, the cumbersome name of J. I. Case Threshing Machine Company was dropped for the shorter version of J. I. Case T. M. Company, and in time simply the J. I. Case Company.

In 1912, Case had six body styles, in mostly open cars in the four cylinder offering, with 30 and 40 hp ratings. By 1913 Case had added a six cylinder engine. The 30 hp sold for $1,500 and the 40 for $2,200. The 30 had a 115-inch wheelbase and the 40 had 124 inches. These vehicles had a Westinghouse self starter, and Firestone Universal Quick Detachable Demountable Rims.

In the 1913 Indianapolis 500 mile race, Louis Disbrow drove a Case Jay Eye See II, named after the initials of J. I. Case, whose founder was Jerome Increase Case. There was an earlier racehorse owned by the founder also named Jay Eye See.

While the J. I. Case Company had a solid and successful base for its farm implement business, it apparently was not as successful with the automobile part of its business. Such must have been the case when in 1913 it raised $12 million in an issue to pay off debts and finance into the future.

With its brief foray into the six cylinder field in 1913, Case abandoned this in favor of four cylinder offerings for the next several years. Case continued with its medium-priced four-cylinder cars through World War I. These engines were produced in its own plant, but starting in 1918 it added a 50 hp six with a Continental engine, and it continued to use the Continental engine through the remainder of its existence. Also in 1918, in an effort to establish a separate entity for its automobile manufacture, the company became the Case Motor Car Division of the J. I. Case T. M. Company.

With the European First World War in progress, Case shipped boxcar loads of its vehicles to Russia. In one consignment there were 101 vehicles all meant to serve as war machines.

Case attempted to lure the buyer by offering a range of cars from the small Case 25, selling at $1,350 and with a 5 percent cash discount, to its larger model 40.

In 1914 there were 18,000 cars sold in the state of Wisconsin among 1,202 dealers for an average of 15 cars per dealer.

Some primitive conditions were still in evidence in 1913, as witness this story out of Vermont. In this year a law was passed in this state forbidding an automobile from carrying a red lamp on the rear of their machine. The law was enacted after frequent reports from railroad engineers, who "while running their trains at a high rate of speed have caught sight of one of these red lights on a nearby highway, and have come to a complete stop, only to discover an automobile."

Four cylinder vehicles were offered in

1915, and into 1917, with a price as low as $1,090. The advertising literature also referred to only one color in each of its body styles, mostly in blue, green, and orange-yellow. This was the fact when many of the Case competitors were offering a wide choice of colors, and in some cases pinstriping.

What had been its mainstay for years, their model 40, in 1919 was now renamed their model V, and all were six cylinder. This used the Continental engine with a 3½-inch bore and a 5¼-inch stroke and with a 126-inch wheelbase. There was a rear tire carrier for one or two tires.

Experiencing the market wide difficulty in adjusting to the postwar conditions, Case in 1920 in the magazine "Automotive Industries" announced that 'only a limited number of the four body styles of Model V cars will be produced this year, and the total will be approximately 3,500, of which about one third will be closed cars.'

Case Model X—Five-Passenger Touring

The Case Model X in 1922 to 1924 came in these handsome sedans and touring cars, with other styles.

In 1922, Case renamed its offerings model X and model W. The W was the larger car, and each of the series had both touring and roadsters, together with enclosed cars.

For 1924 the model Y replaced model W, and it became still larger with a 132-inch wheelbase. Also, in this year, Case revived the name Jay Eye See for some of its sport models.

The Case Jay-Eye-See Special

The Case Jay-Eye-See Roadster

The Case Jay-Eye-See Brougham

The Case Jay-Eye-See Sedan for Five Passengers

In the year 1926 Case Motor Car Company was seeing the end of its active production. It was struggling and rearranging the names of its models. This time there was a continuation of the Y and a new JIC on a smaller chassis.

Automobile production ceased at Case in the year 1927, and with little media attention devoted to it, as was the case for dozens of other small independents of this time period.

Mitchell Motor Car Company

Henry Mitchell emigrated out of Scotland to America in 1834. He settled at Fort Dearborn, which later became the city of Chicago, Illinois. In 1845 he moved to Kenosha, Wisconsin, and in 1857 he moved to Racine, Wisconsin.

Here he joined with William T. Lewis in the manufacture of farm wagons and other farm implements. At this point in the last century the Mitchell and Lewis story with their manufacture of farm equipment is similar to that of the J. I. Case Company in the same city and in the same business.

Henry Mitchell had a daughter who married William T. Lewis. The latter had a son who in turn was named William Mitchell Lewis. The middle name was in honor of Henry Mitchell.

When William Mitchell Lewis reached adulthood he went into the business of bicycle manufacture, a business that was in high vogue at the time. His company was called the Wisconsin Wheel Works.

With the interest then in gasoline engines, inventors were motorizing bicycles and calling these motor cycles. Also around 1900 Lewis was experimenting first with three-wheeled vehicles and then four wheel.

William Mitchell Lewis hired John Bates, who had experience in the early days of automobile manufacture, when he had produced an automobile called the Tri Motor. Pierce gasoline engines were then being manufactured in Racine, and these were used for the early Lewis experimental automobiles.

By 1903, Lewis had developed a motor cooled vehicle, single cylinder, called the model 4, and selling at $850. Also there was an air-cooled version model 6, called the Mitchell Junior, and selling at $600.

In October of 1903 the Wisconsin Wheel Works was discontinued and its bicycle plant sold out to the Great Western Manufacturing Company of La Porte, Indiana. Henceforth, Lewis would manufacture motor cycles and automobiles under the name of the Mitchell Pierce Company of Racine, Wisconsin.

In February of 1904 the company had dropped the Pierce name and engine, and incorporated as the Mitchell Motor Car Company. It took over the plant of the Wisconsin Wheel Works for the manufacture of motor cars and motor cycles.

The Mitchell offerings for 1905 were the "Light Cars." There was a two-cylinder air-cooled, 7 hp at $750 and a similar car, water cooled at 9 hp, and the same price. Their slogan was "The car you ought to have at the price you ought to pay." Shortly, Mitchell upped its hp to 18 in a touring car selling for $1,500.

The 1906 car was now selling at $1800. Advertisements were applauding its performance at road races, and in 50-mile endurance races in the midwest, including a mile traveled in one minute and eight seconds.

This is an early model of a Mitchell from 1907.

The Mitchell Motor Car Company in New York at that time was enterprising. He offered to the public a rental department where a Mitchell and driver could be leased for $5 an hour, with daily rates, and up to $500 a month.

In 1909 Mitchell was offering a six-cylinder vehicle, together with the fours, and where the cylinders were cast in pairs, all $4^1/_4$- by 5-inch, and with bodies accommodating three, five, and seven passengers.

In January of 1910, the Mitchell Motor Car Company, and the Mitchell and Lewis Company, manufacturers of farm wagons and buggies, were united in a new company known as the Mitchell Lewis Motor Company. This went under the direction of William Mitchell Lewis, his father William T. Lewis then retiring. This was at a time of officer reorganization and foretold early financial problems in the company.

In the same year there was a convention at the Madison Square Garden in New York City sponsored by the Association of Licensed Automobile Manufacturers (A.L.A.M.). Here licenses were granted under the Selden Patent for the automobile. There were then 62 licenses for the Selden patent including Mitchell, and Kissel in Hartford, Wisconsin, who also buckled under to these pressures. The A.L.A.M. was attempting to bring legal suit against manufacturers who did not agree and pay into this licensing system. The notable holdout to the Selden patent was Henry Ford.

The combined Mitchell and Lewis automobile and farm implement business was now employing 2,800 men. All stock in the company was owned by the Mitchell and Lewis families.

Earlier Mitchell had been manufacturing a few specialty delivery wagon types of trucks. But in 1911 they developed a Commercial Vehicle Department for the output of one-half and two and one-half ton wagons.

Their cars were of the open type, for the S model seven passenger, the T model with five passenger, the R model with three passenger, and limousines. All of their bodies were made in their own plant.

In 1918 Mitchell had the above nomenclature for their models, but in addition, they produced a 6-46, six cylinder and the 46 referring to its A.L.A.M. horsepower rating.

In late 1913 William Mitchell Lewis broke away from his parent company to form the Lewis Motor Company. This was at a time, again, of restructuring of the company, and bringing in banking interests as officers. Then with the confusion with the Lewis Motor Company and its similarity with the Mitchell Lewis Motor Company the name of this new company was changed to the L.P.C. Motor Company.

As it became apparent then and publicized, Chicago and New York banking interests had taken over the Mitchell Lewis Motor Company already in the fall of 1911. The motor company could not fulfill its payments on loans from these banks. Little wonder then that in 1913 the stockholders formed a new management with fresh officers. Thus William Mitchell Lewis was out of control and chose to form his own company.

In an effort to pay off its debts the Mitchell Lewis Company, in February of 1914, sold its entire horse wagon interests to the International Harvester Company.

The Mitchell and Lewis Motor Company, in 1914, was offering to the public a four-cylinder five-passenger model called the "Little Six" touring car, and a "Big Six" touring car, in five and seven passengers respectively.

In spite of all their financial difficulties, Mitchell, in 1916, offered an eight-cylinder model in a V configuration. This was at a time that numerous companies were coming up with eight-cylinder models.

At this time, Packard was offering a twelve-cylinder car, at the same time, in Detroit, an electric car was offered by the Eagle Electric Automobile Company.

In a note in the automotive magazine, "Motor World" in July of 1917, there is reference to the fact that "when the former Mitchell and Lewis Motor Company was purchased by the present owners and renamed the Mitchell Motors Corporation, the wagon department was organized separately as the Mitchell Wagon Company." This wagon company was now sold to Deere and Company of Moline, Illinois. While the wagon works made some of the bodies of the Mitchell cars, the increased space was not used for production. The present owner referred to apparently was the banking interest which had been in control of Mitchell Motors since 1911, and when earlier there was reported sale of the wagon works in 1914 to International Harvester.

In the world war year of 1918, and immediately following, Mitchell offered quite a large array of body styles from the cheapest touring car to the limousine. Mitchell was selling enclosed vehicles using the detachable or demountable top for combined summer and winter driving. This was a novelty that was a first in America in 1914, when it was featured by Kissel Motor Car Company in Hartford, Wisconsin. At this time no further mention was made of their eight-cylinder cars.

Model E-40
5-Passenger Touring Car
120" Wheelbase, 40 Horsepower

The Mitchell E-40 appeared in 1920 at the Racine, Wisconsin plant. From the archives of Wally Rank.

Model E-40 three passenger roadster, in 1920, with 120 inch wheelbase and 40 hp. From the archives of Wally Rank.

Model E-40
3-Passenger Roadster
120" Wheelbase, 40 Horsepower

"Motor Age" in 1921 reported the affiliation of Mitchell Motor Company and Hupp Motor Car Corporation in a new H and M Body Corporation to produce automobile bodies for the two automobile companies.

In 1922 Mitchell devoted about equal production to their open and enclosed vehicles. In a test of stamina and endurance, and for promotional purposes, Mitchell used 109 of their cars to run a total of over one million miles criss-cross over America. Fuel consumption came to 17.9 miles to one gallon of gasoline.

The most handsome of its cars to date was their model F-50. This came in 1923 as a six-cylinder car, in the colors of maroon and blue, with five-passenger seating.

This was at the very troublesome time at Mitchell when they were virtually crumbling as an auto manufacturing entity. A creditors committee that was in charge of Mitchell operations was meeting in Chicago trying to sell the property to the Checker Manufacturing Company of New York.

The Mitchell Motor Car Company lost $2 million dollars in 1922, while selling cars at less than their cost of production.

"Motor World" in 1922 reported 'Development and promotion of an entirely new model was described as the expensive procedure to which the failure of the Mitchell Motor Company of Racine, Wisconsin, is attributed.' This apparently was their model F-50.

At the same time frame in Detroit, 6,700 Fords were made for a record day on May 28, 1923.

Added to these financial problems was the Internal Revenue Service filing for unpaid taxes and penalties going back to 1917, in the amount of $218,248.

Also claims were made by the United States Government, suing for overpayment for work that Mitchell did for the war effort producing trucks.

For sale on September 12, 1923, was the entire plant consisting of 604,800 square feet of space on 35.46 acres of land. The hope to see the plant sold as a single entire unit failed to secure a reasonable bid to purchase. Later the plant was sold in parcels, with partial dismantlement, and purchase made by Charles W. Nash who paid $405,000 for the plant, at quite a come down from the $2 million dollars Mitchell had earlier wanted.

Some general creditors got, at most, 20 cents on the dollar, at least that was the plan.

This was the sorry end of the Mitchell and Lewis enterprises which did well in the last century manufacturing wagons and other farm supplies, and bicycles at the end of the nineteenth century. In their foray into the automobile manufacturing business, they had, at best, some success during their first decade, and declining fortunes during their second and last decade.

The L.P.C.

At a meeting in September of 1913 in Racine, Wisconsin, Captain William Mitchell Lewis, head of the Mitchell Lewis Motor Company, was ousted from leadership. Thereafter, with his removal, the company would become the Mitchell Motor Company.

Already by 1911 the Mitchell-Lewis Motor Company was having financial difficulties. At the meeting mentioned above a new slate of officers was put in place to direct the company. Captain Lewis at that time then went on to start his own company, and with very small capitalization. His new company was called the Lewis Motor Company. By November of 1913 the Mitchell people were complaining about the confusion in names of these two companies and Captain Lewis changed the name to the L.P.C. Company. This letter nomenclature stood for the last names of Lewis, Petard, and Cram. Rene Petard was his French engineer, who used his European ideas of styling on their first car, the Lewis Light Six. James M. Cram was their secretary and sales manager.

This vehicle, the Lewis Six, was six cylinder, with 3½-inch bore, and a long stroke of 6-inches. It had a folding top in a touring style, six passenger, 135 inch wheelbase, a three bearing crankshaft, with cylinders and crankcase cast as a unit, and selling for the competitive price of $1,600. The company advertised, "A rather unusual economy is claimed for the car in getting fifteen miles to the gallon of gasoline." This seems little to boast about, although later it was advertising 18 miles to the gallon.

The factory space was that previously owned by the Racine Sattley Carriage Works at Racine Junction, in Racine, Wisconsin.

By March of 1914, some 200 men were on the job at this new plant working on an initial production of 500 cars. Already there were no plans for a model change into 1915.

In August of 1914 Rene Petard had left the new plant for duty with the French Army during early World War I. As their head engineer and vehicle stylist, he was sorely missed. But the fledgling L.P.C. Company stated that his absence was anticipated and that all refinements of their new automobile were planned up to January 1, 1917. Unfortunately this company never made it that far.

The L.P.C. Motor Company in 1914 in Racine, Wisconsin. The initials stood for Lewis, Petard and Cram.

The Mitchell E-42 was shown in 1920 at the Racine, Wisconsin plant. From the archives of Wally Rank.

In 1915, the L.P.C. Company added an enclosed car to their offerings. This was a sedan, in a bright yellow color, with green hair line striping. It also featured a roof that had a large skylight that could be closed by a silken curtain. In the rear there was a compartment that housed a spare tire. This vehicle had quite rounded lines, especially for its day, and abundant glass areas for visibility.

For 1916, the Lewis Six maintained its price at $1600. It had a Stewart single-cylinder motor-driven tire pump mounted at the right side of the gear box, and with the hose stored in a compartment under the floor board.

A six-passenger touring body and a two-passenger runabout were the 1916 offerings on a single chassis. Gone was the sedan. The Cutler Hammer magnetic gear shift was a $150 optional item. This was mounted on the dash to the right of the steering column. This was a push button mechanism facilitating shifting together with the clutch.

After barely more than a year of production the L.P.C. Company was in serious financial difficulty by September of 1915. At that time a voluntary assignment by a creditors group placed F. Lee Norton in operating charge of the company. Norton had recently retired as vice president and general manager of the J. I. Case T. M. Company of Racine, Wisconsin.

Lewis was still hoping for an improvement at this difficult time, by advertising, "There is a prospect of obtaining a large order which will make it necessary to operate the factory at its utmost capacity for the next twenty-four months. If this order is placed, the company will probably be able to obtain sufficient funds to continue the business at a large profit."

But by February of 1916 there was an auction of the L.C.P. Motor Car Company by order of the assignee, F. Lee Norton, with an estimated inventory of over $100,000.

After the auction it was announced, in early March of 1916, that the American Motor Company of Indianapolis had purchased a parcel at the auction for just $3,400. They were to act as the service house for all owners of L.P.C. cars in the future and would be in exclusive possession of repair parts. Several new 1916 L.P.C. cars were sold at auction for less than one-half of their retail value.

Captain Lewis was true to his word when he promised his creditors that none would lose "even a penny" in the transactions at closing. On August 15, 1916 all creditors were paid 100 percent, with 23.7 percent of claims paid by assignee sale, and the remaining 76.3 percent coming personally from Captain Lewis.

The Lewis family had recently disposed of its holdings in the Mitchell-Lewis Motor Company, which was then to become the Mitchell Motor Company.

The following demonstrates the strength and popularity of the more prominent Wisconsin automobile manufacturers having their cars registered in the state of Michigan, in the year 1915. It also gives a measure of the lack of success that L.P.C. experienced at that time. These were the registrations at a time when there were in excess of 400 automobile manufacturers in the United States, and there were 112,953 cars sold in this state. The Model-T Ford had by far the largest concentration of sales.

Mitchell	662
Jeffery	390
Kissel Kar	158
Case	104
L.P.C.	30
Badger, Clintonville	2

Chapter Four
KENOSHA-BUILT VEHICLES
Jeffery, Nash, American Motors, Jeep, and Winther articles
By Val Quandt

The Thomas B. Jeffery Company

The Thomas B. Jeffery Company had its Wisconsin origins in 1902 at Kenosha. It was the second automobile company that mass-produced its vehicles, the first being the Oldsmobile Curved Dash. By the end of this year and the next, Jeffery had produced 1,500 of its vehicles. Thomas Jeffery, English born, began as a bicycle manufacturer in Chicago, Illinois, in 1879. This was a time that bicycle manufacturing was a flourishing business in America. Their early bicycles had a model called the Rambler,

This rare photograph shows Thomas B. Jeffery at the tiller of his 1897 Rambler, 5 hp. This was at his factory in Chicago called Gormally and Jeffery, and where earlier a bicycle of this name was manufactured. The reader will understand that this predates the Wisconsin history several years later with the 1902 Rambler at Kenosha.
Courtesy of the Phil Hall Collection.

Rambler, 1900 Stanhope, which was exhibited at the nation's first automobile show held in New York's Madison Square Garden, again predating the Kenosha, Wisconsin, manufacture. Courtesy of the Phil Hall Collection.

which later became the name of their first automotive vehicle.

In 1889 Jeffery decided to quit the bicycle business and get into automobile manufacturing, which was just beginning to emerge. Around 1900 he bought the Sterling Bicycle Company in Kenosha, Wisconsin. Both he and his enterprising son, Charles, were experimenting with the early automobile models. So Charles Jeffery, after a few experimental models, began his production of the Rambler. At the same time, in nearby Racine, Wisconsin, George N. Pierce was producing his Pierce gasoline engines and a few prototypal automobiles.

The father, Thomas Jeffery, died in 1910, leaving the business in the hands of son Charles.

Rambler, Model D, the first Rambler offered for sale, out of Kenosha, Wisconsin. It was a 12 hp "run-about" with 1,500 built. It was shown at the Chicago Coliseum on March 1, 1902. Courtesy of the Phil Hall Collection.

Rambler, 1904, listed as "One step from the surrey." Model L, two-cylinders, 25 hp. Courtesy of the Phil Hall Collection.

Jeffery, 1917, handsome custom body. Model right before the Nash takeover.
Courtesy of the Phil Hall Collection.

The very early Ramblers in 1902 were called models C and D. They were single cylinder as was the case into 1904.

By late 1904 there were roadsters and touring vehicles. There were a total of 11 two cylinders in 1906 when the first four-cylinder car was introduced. There were then a total of 60 model numbers until the first six-cylinder vehicle was introduced in 1914. That was also the year when the vehicle was given the company name of Jeffery. The company then produced a mixture of four- and six-cylinder vehicles until 1917 when the company was purchased by Charles Nash.

In 1914 Jeffery was offering trucks in several sizes up to one and one-half ton and their famous truck, the Rambler Quad, which shortly would be called the Jeffery Quad. These were all-terrain vehicles, four-wheel drive, braking and steering. They were used during the years of 1914 and 1918 in the First World War.

The smaller Jeffery trucks were 3/4 ton and were suitable for light hauling such as for grocers, butchers, and retailers generally. The next size up was the one and one half-ton suitable for transfer and express companies. The Jeffery Quad was a two-ton vehicle, with a 25-gallon gas tank, four-speed transmission, 124-inch wheelbase, and a 4,800-pound chassis weight.

In the military adaptation it had a steering wheel front and back and it could travel forward and reverse. The Jeffery Quad was the first in America to feature this reversible drive. The idea was for a vehicle that was able to run in either direction at equal speeds. So if the vehicle was forced to beat a hasty retreat after a charge, it might reverse without backing, and steer with equal facility in either direction.

As early as March of 1925 Jeffery had an order for 750 of its 3/4-ton trucks to be delivered to the French government within 60 days of order.

Charles Jeffery, head of the Jeffery Company, in May of 1915 barely escaped with his life with the sinking of the ocean liner, the Lusitania. He was a passenger on this liner when it was struck by a torpedo from a German submarine off the coast of Ireland. Jeffery had been warned to not set sail on this liner to attempt this hazardous Atlantic crossing. But Jeffery, armed with large contracts for war trucks, insisted on going anyhow.

When the ship was struck Jeffery was in the smoking room. After making a hurried investigation on top deck he returned to his cabin to don his life jacket. Finding no available lifeboat he plunged into the sea. The next four hours were spent swimming, hanging on to the air tank of a lifeboat, and finally getting aboard a collapsible boat that could be inflated. He was rescued finally by a trawler.

Jeffery advertised that their Quad truck could climb a 49-degree incline of wooden planks stacked up. Jeffery was reported to have produced 20,000 of these trucks before the end of the war. After 1917, when Nash took over, these became Nash Quads.

In their passenger car series, the horsepowers never exceeded 40 N.A.C.C. These produced very low numbers compared to later horsepower ratings. This listing is based on a formula, which figures in the number of cylinders, the cylinder bore, and a factor of 2.5 as follows: Number of cylinders, times bore squared, divided by 2.5. Thus for the Rambler touring car with four cylinders, and a bore of 5 inches it produced a rating of 40 N.A.C.C.

Roadsters were two passenger, the touring cars five to seven passenger. Roadsters came in a price as low as $1,200 to $2,800. Touring cars were priced $1,800 to $2,800 but in 1916 and 1917 there were the cheaper models 462 and 472 that were priced as low as $1,095. Limousines went as high as $4,200. By 1910 Jeffery had model year production that reached 3,800 vehicles.

Nash Motors Company

Much has been written about Charles W. Nash, affectionately known as Charlie Nash, and about his very difficult and meager origins. To repeat some of it is to review the fact that Charlie Nash was born on January 28, 1864, on a farm in DeKalb County in Illinois, which is about 60 miles north and west of Chicago. At the age of six years his parents were separated and abandoned him to the mercy of the court system. They sent him out as a very young farmhand to a farmer in Flushing, Michigan, which today is a near-western suburb of Flint, Michigan. Then he was moved to another farm in Mount Morris, Michigan, which is also a suburb of Flint, to the north.

Up through his teen years he did manual labor on farms. But he was enterprising to raise and sell his own sheep at a profit. He married a farmer's daughter, Jessie Halleck, when he was just 20 years old.

Moving into Flint, Michigan, he moved though a succession of jobs beginning with the Flint Road Cart Company. Here he started as a cushion stuffer. By 1895 Nash was vice president and general superintendent of this company. He then moved on to Buick where he became president of the company in time. In 1912 he had become president of the General Motors Company. This he had accomplished by the time he reached 48 years of age. Nowhere in the accounts of his life is there mention of his ever having received any higher education. He was truly a self-made man.

When in 1916 the Jeffery Motor Company was up for sale, Charlie Nash was interested. Nash had had a policy dispute with Billy Durant, and resigned. He brought with him from General Motors, as his assistant, James Storrow. The date of this takeover was July 28, 1916.

During the first year of transition, Jeffery to Nash, the Jeffery badge remained with these first cars. He built his first Nash, model 681, in 1918. This had the Hotchkiss drive, and semi-elliptic suspension. By 1919 the production had increased to 27,000 cars and a 15-month profit of over $2 million.

Charlie Nash was born on a farm in DeKalb County in Illinois in 1864. He was orphaned at an early age. He rose through the ranks, without much formal education, of Buick and General Motors. He took over the Jeffery plant in Kenosha in 1917. It was in 1918 that the first Nash badge vehicles rolled off the assembly line. Such a model is on display here at the Hartford Auto Museum, by the Nash Club.

Charlie Nash and his company succeeded through the depression years of 1929 to 1934. Part of his amazing success was to keep his inventory low, where it stood at less than 8.5 percent of his working capital. At his age of 68 years Charlie Nash turned over the presidency of the company to his close assistant, Earl McCarty, in 1932. At his age of 72 years, in 1936, he brought in George Mason to head his company.

Charlie Nash's wife of 63 years died in August of 1947 and Charlie died ten months later at age 84 years.

In the early years to follow, half of his production was for trucks, and especially the Quad, now the Nash Quad. In 1918 he delivered to the military 11,490 trucks. These four-wheel drive trucks were contracted out to numerous manufacturing companies in America. The Kissel Motor Car Company in nearby Hartford, Wisconsin, manufactured 2,000 of these same trucks, in subcontract with the Four Wheel Drive Company in Clintonville, Wisconsin.

Nash was looking for a new automobile to round out his business in the upscale area. This was the LaFayette Motor Company of Indianapolis, Indiana, which he took over in October of 1919. It was a luxury car. But it did not sell well while the rest of his company was booming.

Around the same time Nash had purchased a one-half interest in the Seaman Body Company in Milwaukee, Wisconsin. Here he also had a four-cylinder automobile plant selling a vehicle for $1,395. By July of 1922 he had moved his LaFayette plant to Milwaukee next to his four-cylinder auto plant where it survived to 1924.

Sales of the LaFayette were slow, amounting to only 2,200 vehicles sold. In 1924 Nash discontinued its four-cylinder models, and went to sixes. Sales were brisk in this year in which Nash made a profit of $9 million.

The machinery for the LaFayette business in Milwaukee was moved to Racine, to the old Mitchell automobile plant. This was for the manufacture of their new Ajax vehicle. This was a low-priced vehicle at $865. Like the experience with the LaFayette, the Ajax also was not a large seller. The badge was abandoned in favor of the Nash Light Six. In Milwaukee the former LaFayette facility was changed to the Nash Special Six. Anything with the Nash appendage seemed to sell.

These cars had the Seaman body made in Milwaukee. The Light Six was a bargain at under $700, as were the Standard Six, Special Six, and the Advanced Six.

In 1928 there was an upscale Ambassador model, and 400 series. In declining order there were the Special and the Standard. Nash was now the leader of the six-cylinder car and a bargain at $885 to $2,190. Nash produced 138,000 cars in 1929

Nash 1918, Model 681, five-passenger touring. Manufactured by the Nash Motor Company of Kenosha, Wisconsin. On loan from James Dworschack to the Hartford Auto Museum.

1921 Model 41 five-passenger Touring. This picture and numerous of the Nash series to follow are courtesy of Beverly Kimes, Sam Medway, and "Automobile Quarterly."

1924 Model 696

1927 Model 266 Special Six Roadster

and netted over $20 million. This was also the year of the Stock Market Crash. It was a year in which many of the other independents were beginning to fail. This would include the Kissel Motor Car Company in nearby Hartford, Wisconsin, which was in serious financial straits in 1929, and out of business in September of 1930.

1928 Model 320 Standard Six four-door Sedan

1928 Model 371 Advanced Six Sport Touring

1929 Model 433 Special Six two-door Sedan

1928 Model 362 Advanced Six Touring

1929 Model 440 Special Six four-door Sedan

1930 Model 457 Single Six four-door Sedan

Charlie Nash had a very close working relationship with Earl McCarty who was his vice president and director of sales. McCarty retired from this position in February of 1929. In spite of the general business decline Nash continued to make profits in 1929 and 1930.

In 1930 Nash for the first time offered for sale an eight-cylinder car. This was one with twin ignition, as did also the six. It had an extended wheelbase of up to 133 inches. This was a lot of car and a bargain for $1,695. In spite of his successes Charlie Nash was expressing some concerns for the financial future. In this atmosphere Earl McCarty was wanting to help his old friend, Charlie Nash. In April of 1930 McCarty rejoined the company as vice president and general manager. In June of 1932 at age 68, Nash turned over the presidency of the company to Earl McCarty.

There was a succession of vehicles in the six- and eight-cylinder classes. There were the series 880, 890, and 900. At the depths of the Depression, Nash also lost money in 1932 and 1933.

1931 Model Eight-80 convertible Victoria

1932 Model 1097 Ambassador Eight Brougham

1934 Model 1297 Ambassador Eight Brougham

Available in 1934 was the attractive model, the 1297, as the Ambassador Brougham, seen here in a photograph.

In January of 1934 Nash reintroduced the name LaFayette. This time it was in a low-priced six, and at the unbelievable low price of $595. Charlie Nash was now 72 years old, in 1936, and admitting to feeling the effects of his age. At this time Earl McCarty retired, and this time for good. Nash was now looking for his successor. His friend Walter Chrysler recommended that he look to George Mason, president of Kelvinator Corporation. So this man who had dealt in refrigerators became Nash president. Mason was a large man physically, and he thought expansively.

George Mason

LaFayette 1936, four-door Sedan. Manufactured by the Nash Motor Company. All steel construction. On loan from Steve Meisner to the Hartford Auto Museum.

1937 Nash Ambassador convertible. Manufactured by Nash Motors in Kenosha, Wisconsin. On loan from Bob and Wendy Walker to the Hartford Auto Museum.

1936 Model 3680 Ambassador Super Eight four-door Sedan

In July of 1936 the Nash Company purchased the Seaman Body Corporation in Milwaukee. It will be recalled that in 1919 Nash had bought a one-half interest in this company.

Business was good in 1937, but poor in 1938. This was in spite of the fact that Nash had new features such as the Weather Eye ventilation system, where interior temperature was controlled through heating, and use of outside air for cooling, all controlled through a thermostat.

The 1937 Nash consisted of the Ambassador Eight, Ambassador Six, and the

LaFayette 400. But barely had the new management taken over when there was a nationwide downturn in business, which lasted essentially until the beginning of World War II.

From here on especially, there was in the Nash and the succeeding American Motors Corporation such a large tangle of yearly new models, that in the brief space allotted here, the reader would be advised to find details such as specifications in a work such as the Krause Publications book, "Standard Catalog of American cars, 1802 to 1942," which includes the Jeffery and early Nash histories.

The LaFayette model bowed out after 1940. It was succeeded by the model Ambassador 600. This was in the lower cost range. It was advertised as being similar to the Ambassador Eight. It had a shorter hood with the six-cylinder engine. With careful driving the vehicle might go for 600 miles on a tank full of gasoline. This model sold well and was the first to be produced again after the war.

1940 Model 4081 Ambassador Eight Cabriolet by de Sakhnoffsky

1941 Model 4160 Ambassador Six four-door Sedan

1944 Nash truck. Prototype pickup truck manufactured by the Nash Kelvinator Company in Kenosha, Wisconsin. Never placed into production. On loan from Thomas Harrington, France, to the Hartford Auto Museum.

1948 Nash Ambassador convertible, manufactured by the Nash Kelvinator Company of Kenosha, Wisconsin. The first American convertible after World War II. Poster vehicle for the Iola Old car Show for 1998. On loan from Vincent Ruffolo to the Hartford Auto Museum.

1951 Model 5168 Ambassador Super four-door Sedan. Owner: Robert Carlen.

1950 Nash Rambler Station Wagon, manufactured by the Nash Kelvinator Company of Kenosha, Wisconsin. Rambler was reintroduced in 1950 to take advantage of the new small-car market. On loan from Willis Moline to the Hartford Auto Museum.

In August of 1947 Charlie Nash's wife of 63 years died. Nash himself died just ten months later.

Perhaps the result, at least in part, of being cognizant of Charlie Nash's declining health, George Mason thought of his own mortality and felt it was time to consider his own successor. In April of 1948 he brought in George Romney. Their first efforts resulted in the production in 1949 of the Air Flyte. This was preceded by aerodynamic studies favoring this new styling. In time this model came to be labeled, in slang, and not as a compliment, the "bath tub." Nash reintroduced the Rambler Badge in 1950, as the first of its new compact cars. The first cars built by the original Jeffery Company in 1902 bore this name until 1914. This car had a 100-inch wheelbase, and the 82 hp six-cylinder engine from the Nash 600.

George Romney

1951 Model 5168 Ambassador, Super four-door Sedan

1951 Nash Statesman, manufactured by the Nash Kelvinator Company of Kenosha, Wisconsin. Front seat back retracts into a bed. On loan from Paul Kipp to the Hartford Auto Museum.

1955 Nash Statesman Super manufactured by the Nash Kelvinator Company of Kenosha, Wisconsin. This vehicle was found in a barn, where it had sat for 20 years. On loan from Wayne Kielisch to the Hartford Auto Museum.

1953 Nash Healey, manufactured by Nash Motor Company in Kenosha, Wisconsin. Hard-top body designed by Pinin Farina of Italy, with input also by Healey of England. Vehicle on loan from Vincent Ruffolo to the Hartford Auto Museum.

George Mason had wished to combine several of the smaller independents into one stronger structure. It was without success, these other companies apparently wishing to keep their own autonomy.

In 1950 Mason and Romney were planning a Nash vehicle with input from Pinin Farina of Italy for styling, and Donald Healey of England. It took one year for this model to appear, and it was on the market from 1951 to 1954. This was the Nash Healey which was featured at many racetracks. There is a handsome model of this car at the Hartford Auto Museum in Hartford, Wisconsin, belonging to Vincent Ruffolo. Not more than 100 of these cars were made in a year.

Packard had earlier been making some V-8 engines for Nash. Mason had tried to get Packard into a merger with Nash to no avail. But Hudson in Detroit was interested and a merger did take place on May 1, 1954, to become the American Motors Corporation.

1953 Nash Healey engine and transmission. Donated by Vincent Ruffolo and Bernard Turco to the Hartford Auto Museum.

American Motors Corporation

George Mason died suddenly and unexpectedly just six months after the merger to become the AMC. George Romney then became the company president. He guided the company the next seven years. He was the impetus in the drive to sell the small car to the American public.

During the early Romney years in the mid- and late-1950s both Nash and Hudson continued to appear in separate showrooms. As time went on this division tended to blur, as Hudson was being phased out. AMC bought out its subcompact, the Metropolitan. This had the tiny Austin engine made in England. The Metropolitan did not sell well and was phased out by 1962. It could not compete well against the Volkswagen.

Nash Metropolitan, 1954 convertible. Manufactured by Austin of England for Nash Kelvinator of Kenosha, Wisconsin. Though not built in Wisconsin it was sold out of Kenosha. On loan from Dan Hill to the Hartford Auto Museum.

1956 Rambler Custom Country Club model 5619-2 manufactured by the American Motors Corporation in Kenosha, Wisconsin. On loan from Ken and Cindy Carmack to the Hartford Auto Museum.

1959 Rambler American 2-dr. This photograph and the following AMC and Jeep photos are courtesy of Krause Publications.

1964 Rambler AMC 2-dr. convertible

The compact Rambler and the larger more luxurious Ambassador were both designed for the small car market. From now on, the vehicle would be the Rambler, the name revived from the modern Rambler Marque in 1950, and its earlier history as the Jeffery Rambler.

Production of the Rambler took off after 1958. For decades automobile bodies had been produced at the Seaman Body Plant in Milwaukee, and where also Nash had purchased a half interest. This was a huge five-story building of 1,700,000 square feet. From 1917 until 1957 this plant produced the bodies for the Nash and Rambler and then they had to be trucked the 42 miles to the Kenosha facility.

By 1958 Rambler had its new body plant in Kenosha, where it could turn out 600 bodies in a day. Then in 1959 AMC took over the former Simmons Mattress plant in Kenosha for a third body plant.

In 1958 AMC offered the small Rambler American, the larger Rebel, and the more upscale Ambassador. The latter had been a Nash label going back to 1932.

But the Big Three, Ford, General Motors, and Chrysler, reacted to the change to smaller and more fuel efficient vehicles by introducing their versions of the small car. AMC was now in acute competition, and their sales and profits were being trimmed.

In 1961 AMC put out the Rambler Classic, a step up in size from the Rambler American. With the competition from the large producers, AMC, now one of the last independents, was in a real struggle to put out a winner.

Roy Abernethy had come to AMC in 1954 from an executive sales job with Packard. In February of 1962 George Romney resigned from AMC to make a bid for the Governorship of Michigan. Roy Abernethy then took over as president of AMC. He guided the company through successful years where it had no debt. By this time AMC had 13 international plants including those in Canada, a few in Europe, many in South America, New Zealand, and Australia.

In an attempt to capture some of the youth market looking for sporty cars, AMC in 1965 came out with its Marlin, a fastback. This was in competition with the Mustang and Barracuda.

1966 AMC-Marlin fastback

In 1967 Roy Chapin Jr., son of a founder of the Hudson Motor Car Company in Detroit, was chairman and chief executive officer while William Luneburg became president and chief operating officer.

In 1967 the Classic Series became the Rebel. Chapin felt that the survival of AMC depended on dropping the price of the Rambler American. He also felt it necessary to develop new models. So in quick succession, first in 1967, AMC introduced its Javelin and shortly thereafter the AMX. These two vehicles seemed to rather duplicate themselves, at least in gross appearance.

1968 AMC-Javelin 2-dr. hardtop

1969 AMC-AMX

In July of 1968 AMC sold its Kelvinator appliance division, allowing the company to concentrate on its automobile manufacturing business. In 1970 AMC bought out the Kaiser Jeep Corporation. These vehicles were made in Toledo, Ohio, and will be included in these descriptions as Wisconsin vehicles, in this case management. The same could be said for its acquisition in 1971 of the AM General Company, which became an AMC subsidiary, making vehicles for the military, and U.S. Postal Service vehicles, again made out of state, in Indiana.

A new name plate arriving on the scene in 1971 was the Matador. In 1974 the Matador was entered in NASCAR racing events. Also in this year the Ambassador models were discontinued.

1969 AMC-AMX model, courtesy of C. L. Zinn II, of Denver, PA.

1976 AMC-Pacer 2-dr.

In 1975 the new entry was the subcompact called the Pacer. It was featured as a hatchback, and much the same styling appeared a year later in the Gremlin.

AMC, as one of the last of the independents, was struggling furiously to compete and maintain its dwindling market share. There was red ink in 1976 and relieved with slight gains in 1977, chiefly due to success of its Jeep.

AMC was negotiating with Renault of France to build a jointly-financed Renault-styled vehicle in Kenosha as early as the 1982 model year. In the meantime AMC was

1971 AMC-Matador 2-dr. hardtop

1978 AMC Concord 4-dr.

distributing the French subcompact car, the Le Car. France was to sell the Jeep. Gas guzzling large V-8s were being phased out in favor of the smaller models. The Pacer and the AMX were out and the four-wheel drive Eagle was in.

In December of 1980 AMC gave 46 percent of its company shares to Renault. Now in 1981 AMC had a selection of just three models, the Spirit, Concord, and the Eagle. Market share at AMC had now dropped to below 2 percent of national sales. It got a brief

1980-AMC Eagle 4-door station wagon

1986 AMC-Eagle station wagon 4 x 4

boost with the sales of its Renault Alliance.

The Eagles were using the Pontiac four-cylinder engine, and the others were six cylindered. But poor sales persisted into 1986 when the company lost $91 million. President Jose Dedeurwaerder was hopeful that the company could turn it around.

Chrysler agreed to build its M-body cars at Kenosha, and this led to its takeover of the AMC business for $1 billion in August of 1987, just months before Chrysler announced the closing of the plant.

Thus the end came to this proud Wisconsin automobile manufacturing plant in Kenosha, Wisconsin. This covered a very lengthy 85-year span, all the way from 1902. The Kissel Motor Car Company in Hartford, Wisconsin, elsewhere described in this book, came in second with a 25-year career. This discounts the record of the General Motors Assembly Plant in Janesville, Wisconsin, which had a long span making Chevrolets, but a business that was Detroit based.

The Jeep, 1970 to 1987

American Motors Corporation purchased the Jeep from Kaiser Industries in February of 1970. Willis Overland had supplied the military with the Jeep during World War II. The Kaiser Company had purchased the Jeep from Willys Overland in 1953. In turn, the American Motors Corporation had bought the Jeep from the Kaiser Company in 1970 as mentioned. While the corporate structure of this company was at Kenosha, Wisconsin, manufacturing operations continued to be located at Toledo, Ohio. John A. Conde was director of public relations. For continuity the Jeep story is included here as a Kenosha, Wisconsin, enterprise.

The World War II Jeep had an 80-inch wheelbase, weighing 2,315 pounds and had an 800-pound payload and could pull a 1,000-pound trailer. By the end of this war 660,000 Jeeps had been manufactured from its onset.

After the war many Jeeps, to be used for various purposes, found their way into the hands of civilians. But being lightly powered, and somewhat top heavy, they were not suitable for general highway use with its higher speeds.

The origin of the name Jeep may be explained, at least according to this one theory. The army description was that it was a general purpose vehicle, or abbreviated to GP. The phonetic extension of the GP sound could be "Jeep."

1970 *Jeep. First year of AMC-Gladiator*

1972 Jeep Commando station wagon

1974 Jeep Cherokee, 2-dr. sport utility

1977 Jeep Cherokee 2-dr.

1981 Jeep Cherokee Chief station wagon

1986 Jeep Wagoneer

1984 AMC Jeep Laredo CJ-7

There was a new Jeep for the Korean War. The later Jeeps included station wagons, such as the Wagoneer, Gladiator, Jeepster, and the Commander. There were Jeeps for the U.S. Postal Service.

Voyage of the Hard Shell Turtle
By Bill Cameron

Written some time in the mid-'50s by a cruising sailboat skipper, who happened to be in love with antique cars as well as sailboats.

This is a routine report on a "land cruise" from the Port of Thompson, Connecticut, to Key West, Florida. For brevity's sake it will be referred to as "The voyage of the cruiser, HARD SHELL TURTLE via the Inland Super-Waterway" or "In the spring, even a hard shell turtle gets hungry for some sun."

A business committment required the skipper to be in Philadelphia for two days prior to the scheduled day of departure. It was, therefore, decided that the first mate would provision the vessel and terminate the varied and rigid ties-to-the-land, without assistance, viz: cat to the vets, horse to a neighbor, house and dog to the loving care of hired man, collect camping equipment, dig out summer clothes, pack car and pilot the vehicle the first 150 miles single handed (very clever of the skipper).

The rendezvous was established as "Camden Exit of the New Jersey Turnpike at 2:00 p.m. Friday, March 12th." The first mate made landfall at 1:40, relinquished helm to the skipper who guided HST (no! NOT Harry S. Truman - Hard Shell Turtle) back into midstream and headed south by 1:45.

First important decision: should we stop in Washington, see some relatives and perhaps spend a night? Good idea - we'd like to, but the timing is bad - Baltimore late afternoon, Washington rush hour, heavy traffic next morning and Florida still 800 miles away! Rand McNally made the decision: "Avoid Baltimore, stick to the eastern shore of Maryland, use the new Chesapeake Bay Bridge, use new bypass around Annapolis, around Washington and on to Richmond." The map won.

Anchor down at 8:30, moored in midstream at a Richmond, Virginia, motel, then dinner, 25¢ worth of TV and in berth at 10 p.m. Some day!!

On every cruise, there are routes and areas, scenery and towns that are quite important at the time, but by comparison with what precedes or follows it, fade into nothingness when it comes time to prepare the log. Virginia, North and South Carolina, parts of Georgia, a kaleidoscope of scrub oak and pine, cross-road towns, cotton gins, an occasional ultra-modern textile mill (sucking away New England's life blood), intermittent showers, humid warmth, sand, tobacco fields, cigarette factories, truck farms and windmill. You notice with a start that you've gone from March to April to May to June - from snow to pussywillows and forsythia, to trees in full leaf, roses and dogwood.

Rand McNally comes to the rescue by placing a small red inverted "v" on the map at sundown. This symbol (and the navigator is quite adept at spotting them) means a campground, a county, state or national park or recreation area. Sometimes Rand McNally or the pertinent political subdivision is delinquent in supplying the magic symbol at the right place at the right time - then you keep turning up side roads and create a red inverted "v" of your own. But we were lucky, in South Carolina Saturday night, it was the Lee County Park (near Sumpter) and we found a fishing cabin with fireplace, bunk beds, outdoor facilities and complete privacy at $1.00 a night.

Warm and humid with howling winds, thunder and lightning; at midnight, rain.

Sunday night it was Georgia's Crooked River State Park just on the wrong side of the Saint Mary's River. Over there was Florida. But you'd never know it for the brisk winds, October chill and three blankets on the bed. Here we had a one-room housekeeping cabin (dirty) with stove and no fireplace. All this was prologue, for the next day was Monday and Florida.

Up 'til now, and for the rest of the trip, we were forever expressing our gratitude for that new innovation in highway construction, the bypass. Except for Richmond, which we visited intentionally, we had successfully bypassed every major city on the east coast from Connecticut to Florida. And today, our Rand McNally showed a new bypass around Jacksonville, the Buccaneer Highway, a succession of sand dunes, bridges and a car ferry across the St. John River. This was really cruising - almost as much water as land.

But fortunately, a HST is a versatile creature, equally at home on land or at sea. Our cruise, up to this point, had been either in, near, or under, water of various densities from Atlantic Ocean salt to rain pellets, fog and 95 percent humidity. But, now we headed overland from the coast to the north central Florida lake country and on to Winter Park and Rollins College, where daughter Sue is a student. Hook down at 4 p.m. in a landsman's version of a snug harbor - a parking lot, in this case across the street from Mayflower Hall, Sue's sorority house. And shortly along came Sue, tan, healthy, with a smile of welcome on her face.

We took our departure at flood tide and set a southwesterly course for our next port of call, Fort Myers Beach. The HST - once she got a good whiff of the Gulf of Mexico - lost no time and "hit the beach" at 7 p.m. The reader may have gained the impression earlier that this was intended to be a rough and ready camp-type cruise. Sorry to disappoint you, but relatives had engaged a lush, fully equipped cottage not far from theirs, so that for the next three nights we dressed, ate, and lived the way city folks spending the winter in Florida do.

Somewhat more in character, we spent one afternoon swimming, beach combing and bird-watching, and the next day piloting of a friend's 28-foot cruiser from the slip at their back door to its summer mooring where we found a fascinating boat yard some ten miles up the Caloosahatchee River, after ten miles of open water cruising on the Gulf.

Determined to unfurl some canvas (tent), fill some air mattresses, build some campfires and go native, we bade our farewells the night before and got an early start Friday morning - destination: the Florida Keys. So over-country - almost, but not quite to Miami (heaven forbid!) then south to the point where you can stand in one spot and spit first in the Atlantic Ocean and then into the Gulf of Mexico.

By this time the temperature had reached 75 to 80 degrees and we really began to thaw out and peel off. The Keys are mostly built of coral with miles of white beaches and multi-colored expanses of jade green, turquoise, emerald and deep-sea blue salt-heavy water, topped, far out, with scoops of whipped cream and tufts of rabbit fur. A swim and lunch beside a "coral-quarry" - a midnight blue hole in the emerald setting, deep and cold.

As we swung on south under full sail, we passed a harbor with an ominous flag flying and later picked up a weather advisory on the radio - "Full S. E. storm warnings." So we reefed down a point or two but we were soon diverted by a mammoth nautical zoo, a typical Florida institution, featuring all the denizens of the deep, plus "the most highly trained porpoises in captivity." It was really worth the time (and admittance fee) especially to watch the two performing porpoises, one of which jumped 18 feet into the air for a piece of fish.

The clouds were beginning to roll in from the ocean side and the water was turning grey where it had previously been so green and blue. We then knew the time had come to seek a safe anchorage. Rand McNally had long since run out of inverted v's so we began exploring side roads and, after two or three misses, found a strip of beach surrounded by pine trees and coconut palms, plus many evidences that others had camped there before. In rapid sequence - an open fire, beef stew, the Skipper's campfire coffee, tent up, car seats down, screens on, cot up, air mattresses blown up, light out - and "the wind she blew like hurricane." The wind bent the trees, whipped up salt spray, swayed the car and filled the tent: like a kite, like a sail, like a balloon! Then it picked up hands full of sand and hurled it at Sue who was sleeping? (occupying) the tent. HST was designed by Mr. Nash to sleep two, but he should know how comfortably it will sleep three in full gale on Long Key, Florida.

Next day the wind, content with the havoc it had wrought, blew itself out. After a swim and breakfast, we again headed south; the scenery improving by the minute, i.e. - more water, less land. By now we had reached the southernmost city in the United States - Key West. It also turned out to be about the most heavily populated city, for its size, in the U.S.A. The storm warnings had brought the entire fishing and shrimp fleets into safe harbor. The navy has fleet operating bases, air stations and communication centers all over the island and, added to this, is a large native population and an even larger tourist influx. Our activities included a seafood dinner at Fisherman's Wharf, a visit to the city's marine museum and a quick tour of the more interesting attractions - Ernest Hemingway's home, old Spanish houses and, best of all, the docks, moorings, wharves and shipyards.

If you think you are tired, (having read this far) so were we! So, out of the hurly-burly and back on the bridges - one is seven miles long. For variety, we spend Saturday night on the Gulf side. This time the state furnished a roadside rustic table and primitive powder room - also bugs, mosquitoes, gnats, nits, and other varieties small enough to fly through screens without bending a wing. Also heat of the mid-summer, mid-August, mid-hell variety. But these inconveniences were offset by a wood fire, dinner, swim and breakfast and, most of all, by clearing skies, soft winds and sensuous scenery.

The rest is anti-climax - return trip successful and uneventful, taking the shortest possible routes in order to get home quickly.

Thus ends the saga of the good ship "Hard Shell Turtle."

Sure wish I still owned it.

The Winther

Winther was mainly a truck building company in Kenosha, Wisconsin, which for a time also made its trucks at Winthrop Harbor, Illinois, just inside the border of that state with Wisconsin. This was the period of 1917 to 1927. For whatever reasons the company felt it could also compete in the market making automobiles. So the Winther car, conceived in 1920, came out in 1921. It featured a staid appearance with a wheelbase of 120 inches, six cylinders, and 60 hp. It was a touring car with a five-passenger seating capacity. It was somewhat overpriced in its first year, at $2,890, and was reduced in price to $2,250 in 1922. But by 1923 it was discontinued. It is estimated that not more than 500 of these cars were ever made.

What was useful remaining of the company in the way of machining capacity was sold to G. D. Harris of Menasha, Wisconsin. This then surfaced as the Harris Six automobile, which also was short-lived and is described elsewhere in this book, amongst cars manufactured in the Fox River Valley of Wisconsin.

The Winther Six, 5-passenger Touring, 1921. Picture courtesy of Vincent Ruffolo.

Chapter Five
SOUTHEASTERN WISCONSIN
Other Cities Activity

MOHS - 1947-Present
Mohs Seaplane Corporation
Madison, Wisconsin

By W. E. Wray

Bruce Baldwin Mohs is an unusual man, and it can be fairly said that everything he touches reflects, more or less, his flair for the abnormal. That he's a success doing what he does is obvious. He owns a restaurant, motel, seaplane flying service, an automobile factory and museum, is a licensed automobile and motorcycle manufacturer, and is the holder of numerous patents.

It is hard to separate the man and his various enterprises. This is especially true with the automobiles he creates, for much of himself is to be found in each of the models he has built since the age of 12. He freely admits that the automobiles are, for the most part, an outward expression of several of his patents, and that in building them he is not afraid to stretch a point to make a point. That customers have not exactly beaten a path to his door is not surprising, nor, apparently, terribly upsetting to him. Indeed, of the handful of cars he has built to date, very few have found homes away from their place of birth.

Actually, Mohs has been building vehicles since the mid-forties, but his factory in the Madison suburb of Riley did not go into production of 'consumer' cars until the debut of his Ostentatiene Opera Sedan in 1967. By any standards, this one of a kind is one of the most unusual vehicles ever built.

Constructed around an International Travelall chassis and drive train, the three-ton, four-passenger luxury car is an eye stopper. Four of Mohs' patented pivoting, safety-bucket seats adorn the interior and for added creature comfort, such niceties as deep pile shag carpets, refrigerator and cooking stove are thoughtfully provided. Also included are the necessities of motoring, CB, 24k gold inlaid walnut dash, and stereo AM/FM radio.

Body design is what really sets it apart, though. The slab-sided body panels run unbroken from nose to tail, windshield panels and side windows sweep nearly uninterrupted, providing nearly unbroken 270°

The Mohs Ostentatienne Opera Sedan, manufactured in Madison, Wisconsin, by the Mohs Seaplane Corporation, around 1967, seen with its inventor Bruce Baldwin Mohs in a 1975 advertisement.

vision. A huge pseudo-Classic grille fronts the whole thing. One would be hard-pressed to name the single-most unusual design concept, but one might well choose the fully cantilevered roof and the wing up single rear door it provides for. When this is opened, steps slide into place, and the effect is totally UFO-like. Of these, only the prototype was built and can be seen in Mohs Museum, although they are still available on special order.

The second Mohs vehicle offered to the public was the SafariKar. A hardtop convertible, this vehicle is scarcely less iconoclastic, though not so asthetically pleasing. Three of these padded Naugahyde-covered vehicles were built and sold, the last bought from Mohs Seaplane Corporation by Bruce B. Mohs himself. Like its forerunner, SafariKar was based on International chassis, and carries out the same general styling theses. Triple safety-bucket front seats and rear seats that fold out into beds compliment the interior of these two-door cars.

Mohs' most recent project is a more practical appearing three-wheel commuter car utilizing aluminum frame, 16 hp Fuji-built Wisconsin engine, and variable speed Salisbury transmission. Speed and gas mileage are both given as being in the 45-50 range. With today's uncertain fuel situation, it may yet be possible for something to come of this design on a fair-sized scale.

One may well question the wisdom of creating such avant-garde vehicles in such a hard-line business as today's automobile industry. Why does Mohs do it? Besides using the vehicles as a showcase for his patents, he admits it's largely for fun. Apparently the combination of business and pleasure have achieved a happy marriage, for Mohs seems a happy and satisfied man. Few other automobile manufacturers today can claim as much!

The Petrel

This vehicle had an early history in 1909 for a brief period in Kenosha, Wisconsin. It was then moved to quarters in Milwaukee. This unusual name for a car derives from a word which means a seabird with long wings and presumably rapid flight, the Petrel. Another meaning has a connotation to the name Peter, as in biblical St. Peter, and his walking on water.

This vehicle, in Milwaukee, received its first bodies in the W. S. Seaman plant which was in this business and which it later did for Nash.

But success was not in the future for this company. It was bankrupt by 1910. It was rescued then by a company which manufactured steam engines. But the company closed in 1910 with a total number of manufactured vehicles of less than 1,000.

1910 Petrel, model F, touring

Commander, Stillborn Scion Of The Ogren

By Keith Marvin

This article by Keith Marvin appeared in the "Upper Hudson Valley Automobilist," Autumn 1978. The portions of this article that pertain to manufacture outside the state of Wisconsin, will be summarized briefly, leading into the production in Milwaukee, Wisconsin.

Hugo W. Ogren was a born designer and engineer who combined his love of racing with precision, quality, and a flair for aesthetic design. Unlike Ford or Olds, he felt that there was ample room in the contemporary automobile roster for a car that would be the best, regardless of price, and for sale to those who recognized such worth and bought accordingly.

The Ogren of 1922

The Commander of 1922

In 1911 Ogren became affiliated with the Colby Motor Company, of Mason City, Iowa, and designed the car bearing that name. A year later he assumed the post of manager of the Chicago branch. In the summer of 1914 he set up the Ogren Manufacturing Company of Chicago. In January of 1916 the company was reorganized as the Ogren Motor Works and its base of operations was moved to Waukegan, Illinois. By 1919 the All-American truck was being built at this plant.

In August of 1919, an announcement with a Milwaukee dateline appeared, heralding the gladsome news that Ogren had been incorporated in that city as the Ogren Motor Car Company with $500,000 capital and would build a factory to "manufacture the Ogren passenger car." At least one source believes that some 50 units were put together before the end of 1919 and that this marked Ogren's largest production in a given year. The company was reorganized in July of 1920, with H. S. Ogren, president; Elmer Freolk, vice president; and Fred G. Smith, secretary and treasurer.

For 1920, specifications at Ogren included a 132-inch wheelbase, Beaver six-cylinder engine, a 3½ by 5-inch bore and stroke, and a displacement of 303 cubic inches. The L-shaped engine developed 65 hp. Carburetor and ignition were by Rayfield and Bosch respectively. Wheels were optional with wooden artilleries generally gracing the closed models, and wire or disc the open ones. Tires were 33 by 5.00 inch and the four-passenger touring car sold for $3,500 and other models included a roadster, coupe, and sedan.

The line was unchanged for 1921 except for a two-inch increase in the wheelbase and a jump in price, due to the recession, which placed the seven-passenger touring at $3,900, and a handsome new catalog was published.

The clouds were gathering though, whether because of insufficient production and sales, the result of the post war recession, or just plain lack of demand, or possibly a combination of all three. In August the creditors met and shortly thereafter the company was in their hands.

In spite of all this the company in 1922 published another lavish and complete catalog. This listed some changes such as a new Continental engine upping the hp.

In June, what was probably the last bit of Ogren promotion, there showed a truly handsome disc-wheeled touring car. What made the car unusual was the presence of the "Whyte Motorcontrol," a unique gadget which placed the instrument cluster in a container within the steering column. The advantage of this, according to the promotion, was that it enabled the driver to gaze at and have access to the spark and throttle levers, horn button, clock, speedometer, motometer, oil gauge, ammeter, ignition switch and starter without turning his head.

Whereas the Whyte Motorcontrol was available on the market as an accessory, it was standard on Ogren, or at least on its Phaeton model.

At this stage of the tale it is time to leave the Ogren and turn to the Commander, and things happened fast.

It became apparent that the time had come to phase Ogren, or the Ogren name at least, out of the picture and strike out for a new image. Consequently, the decision was made to once again reorganize the company and to start anew under a new name. Commander Motors was therefore formed to take over the Ogren, and to build the Commander car. Contemporary promotion played up the fact that the Commander was also designed by H. W. Ogren.

None of the Commander activity, or plans at least, were Wisconsin based. A new manufacturing site in Chicago was planned, with Chicago officers in addition to Hugo W. Ogren. There was a succession of grandiose plans, with promotional catalogs, attempts to raise $2 million capital. All of this resulted in failure without a single Commander having been built. Liquidation of the company was announced in January of 1924, with the further information that neither stockholders nor creditors got anything as a result of the sale of assets, with the tax claims taking the entire amount received at sale.

A Plaintive Cry in the Wilderness: GM's 1919 "Whole Family Car"

By Keith Marvin

This interesting account appeared in the Wisconsin Society of Automotive Historians publication called the "Spark" in 1988.

When an easterner thinks of Janesville, Wisconsin, he is apt to think of the Parker Pen Company and leave it at that. And, alas, Janesville has been noted for very many other things, of which, one of the most forgotten is the former Samson Tractor Company which flourished, sort of, for six or seven years.

Now a tractor company is not generally ever going to become much more than that, but Samson was an exception to the rule, having been spotted by the eagle eye of the late William C. Durant, who at the time was president of the General Motors Corporation, and who, in addition, was buying just about everything he could lay his hands on to add to GM's holdings. This was at the period of what has come to be known as "Durant's Second Empire" as he had previously headed the prestigious GM conglomerate and been fired from the same, only to reestablish himself in control all over again by a brilliant stock maneuver.

Durant's empire was vast, his sales excellent and the profits therefrom just out of this world. Durant and GM were riding high but ignoring the fingers on the wall which were not writing "Mene mene tekel uparson" but rather "Pride goeth before a fall." Durant was a spendthrift and his non-working crystal ball did not clue him in on the upcoming 1921 recession.

The Samson Company had been around since 1916 producing a creditable line of trucks and tractors, but it was the tractor aspect which caught Durant's eye because the way he saw it, it was an upcoming product and the world of the smaller farm tractor was just coming in with names like Fordson, Uncle Sam, and John Deere to do the work that was the former responsibility of such enormous steam juggernauts as the Case of Racine.

So Durant bought Samson and whereas truck and tractor production continued in their easygoing manner, he decided that in addition a special sort of automobile could be added to the production line in Janesville. This idea, as it turned out, would be a large passenger car, which could accommodate nine persons, and be used as a pleasure car on Sunday to take the family to church, and as a farm work vehicle during the week by removing the rear upholstery.

The Samson Whole Family Car was thus introduced in 1919 at Janesville and put on display there, where Durant probably felt, it would revolutionize the entire farm industry. And an attractive piece of machinery it was, too, with a 118-inch wheelbase and a Northway four-cylinder engine, identical to that being used as the power plant for GM's Chevrolet model FB. I have always felt that Mr. Durant's successes in the automotive field, which God knows were frequent and many, were bound to produce a second generation of successes and even surpass the existing records.

The Samson was an attractive novelty of a car with room for three in both the front and rear seats, and three jump seats as well. At the same time, GM was at its zenith with Chevrolet, Scripps Booth, Oakland, Oldsmobile, Buick, and Chevrolet truck with more than a single model on most of these chassis. In that year of 1919 when Samson made its debut to the good folks of the Badger State, Chevrolet alone would produce 149,904 cars in its Detroit plant plus another 17,431 north of the border. Impressive? You better believe it.

But life is full of strange, wondrous, and sometimes downright unpleasant things, and the Samson family turned out to be one of the latter. Exactly why, I am not entirely certain. This was 1919 remember and only a year from the lean days of World War I, where cars were in great demand. The Samson was attractive, and it certainly was a utilitarian vehicle for large families, and it was dual purpose. Seemingly, everything was going for it. And yet production was concluded with the completion of car number one, which was subsequently sold to a farmer in Green County, and despite years of checking its ultimate fate, I have come up tilt. It seems to have disappeared into thin air, and perhaps it did.

I think it would have been killed off in the 1921 recession in any event. But by that time Durant had been fired by General Motors for the second and final time. In 1922 the corporation would discontinue the Scripps Booth from its line of offerings. It also divested itself of the Samson Tractor Company at Janesville which subsequently became another Chevrolet plant, and which exists yet today.

Durant went on to produce the Durant, Star, Flint, and Locomobile, plus the Mason truck. Two other attempts failed, the Eagle and the Princeton. Durant died in 1948.

The Schuler of Milwaukee

By Keith Marvin

There was little doubt about it, as we may readily see from hindsight. The Schuler was simply the wrong car to promote at the wrong time.

Perhaps, but only perhaps, it might have done a bit better, say in the 1921 recession. But even then the auto buyer probably wanted a bit more than a two-cylinder and two-seater. After all, there's always that unexpected couple who calls, or doesn't, and shows up at the door. With a Ford Model T coupe an evenings entertainment may be readily provided.

Certainly $245 may be a bargain for the times. But what is one to do if that couple shows up unexpectedly on your doorstep at the last minute. Four cannot squeeze into a narrow front seat. There is no rumble seat and only room enough on either running board for one. Scratch that if you anticipate a 1924 Christmas card from your good friends on the doorstep!

Still, the Schuler did have a certain charm of its own if we are to believe the picture shown in the ad which appeared in the *Milwaukee Journal* for Sunday, January 20th, 1924.

Mr. Harry Schuler, backer of the enterprise, was also involved with the Mar-Tan, a small engine manufacturing company. He decided that a 78-inch wheelbase in a 800-pound runabout would be just the thing for economy or childless couples, and who had no friends to entertain.

Thus he embarked on his dream and built the thing. How many no one seems to know. But it did appear and was widely advertised, albeit locally and for a very short period.

It is of interest that if one checks back three or four years, the cycle car craze had risen from square zero with the appearance of a rocket, only to come down rapidly, as did the apple that invented gravity for Sir Isaac Newton.

Yet after the War to End All Wars, 1914-1918, anything built on four wheels which ran was a viable commodity in the marketplace. Two-cylinder cars such as the Spacke, and its successor, the Brook, would come and go quickly, like fast ships that pass in the night. The Hanover was another, but this was produced primarily, if not entirely, for the export market. The Peters was waiting in the wings to make its bid, and subsequent pratfall.

Indeed, the only successful two-cylinder car in production, if one could call it production, was the Stanley Steamer, and that was winding down its twilight years.

But apparently with Mr. Schuler hope sprang eternal. He had a vision, a vision of a viable car which could appeal to the lesser affluent and practical motorist of the day.

Had Mr. Schuler had a good crystal ball which could foretell the future, and which most good crystal balls are able to do, he could have seen that there wouldn't be a successful car marketed in these United States until Powell Crosley Jr., would surprise the world in the fall of 1938 with his 1939 line of air-cooled, two-cylinder cars. On this, the writer cut his driving teeth, and still considers it one of the best cars he ever owned.

The Schuler was available in both two seater open and closed models. It was guaranteed to get 50 miles to a gallon of gasoline, and which at 17 cents a gallon, was something to have seriously considered.

Whether the advertising campaign fell short and the potential buyer's imagination wasn't ready for it, or whether the onus of a new make and untried car killed it, I don't know.

But few Schulers found buyers and the death knell of the make came about almost as quickly as its first newspaper advertisements.

It was a lost cause in any case, although Mr. Schuler and his associates couldn't have known it in January of 1924. In less than a year the Ford hit rock-bottom prices with a roadster car available at $290. Thus, in a relatively short period, one could buy a good solid car for about the same price and still have the option of taking the shivering couple on the doorstep out to dinner. Life has loveliness to sell, but there must be the wherewithal to buy.

The Schuler made its mark on the American motoring scene, if briefly. Its idea was sound, but the market wasn't quite ready for it. It would be 14 years before Powell Crosley Jr., was able to prove successfully a theory which had been tried but had failed a generation earlier.

Ray Besasie - A Lifetime Of Discovery

By Ray Scroggins

Ray Besasie had a shop in back of his east side Milwaukee house since the time when cars were more a novelty than a necessity. He started building and rebuilding cars in his youth, yet even into his eighties, he continued to come up with new ideas. Over the years, Besasie has built cars such as the first Excalibur, the futuristic "X-3" and "X-4" dream cars, and the body of the rocket-powered Blue Flame speed record car. His mechanical talents extend to designing and building everything from gas-saving gadgets to airplanes. Continuing the tradition, he has passed these skills along to his sons, who introduced the classic-styled Baci in 1992.

An Early Start

Young Raymond's mechanical interests developed early. Born in 1904, he remembers watching the early automobiles as a child and wondering, "Gee, what makes those things move? There's no horse in front of them." Sitting with his Italian immigrant father on the front porch of their home in Milwaukee, he would look up at the moon and say, "Pa, someday man is going to go to the moon."

At seven years of age, unable to afford a coaster wagon, he built his own with parts scavenged from the city dump. It easily won a race with a neighbor boy when a friend pushed Besasie backwards up the hill to wind up the rubber strips he had cut from a Model T Ford inner tube to power his creation.

By the time he was ten, Besasie had a regular business repairing most of the fruit trucks in the city's 3rd Ward, then the center of the local Italian community with its many fruit and vegetable peddlers. Still, he longed for his own automobile on which he could try out some of his ideas.

The opportunity came when he was 14 and his brother woke him in the middle of the night to tell Ray his 1914 Cadillac was sitting frozen five or six blocks from home and he could have it if he could get it started. Bundling up against the cold, he set out into the night and soon returned with the car humming away. It quickly became his test laboratory. "I performed experiments in high compression, dual carburation with dual manifolds and even built a new body," he recalled.

Gas-Saving Invention

Some years later, after marriage and while raising a family in the home on North Van Buren Street where he lived for most of his adult life, Besasie got an idea for a gas-saving gadget that took off beyond his highest expectations. As he tells it, the inspiration came to him in a restaurant.

"I went quickly to the cashier and asked her for a piece of paper. I scribbled a little drawing of what came to my mind, and the following morning, I couldn't wait to get to the shop. I made two of them and called them the 'Spiral Jet Gas Saver.' I no sooner finished with them when a friend came into the shop and said, 'Say, Besasie, my LaSalle eats an awful lot of gas. What can you do for it?' I lifted the carburetor and dropped these two Spiral Jets down into the port and told him it wouldn't cost him anything."

"Next, I put one in the Chief of Police's Chrysler. Throughout the week, I made a half-dozen installations, all for nothing, with the understanding that they would give me a report on it in a week or so." He installed several dozen others, including one for the foreman of the H. O. Stenzel Tire Company. "He turned out to be my biggest salesman," Besasie remembered.

After two months, his hands blistered from working the tin shears, Besasie turned production over to his sons, who were then students at Lincoln High School. He recalled, "I said I'd pay them a nickel for each one they made. That evening when I came back, both of my kitchen tables were heaped full of them. I advertised in the *Milwaukee Journal* and even had a radio set. I used to come into the rear door with my pockets loaded with money. I'd stand in the center of the kitchen and let the money fall out. Then I'd sit down in the chair and burst out laughing."

In a few months, however, the thrill was gone. "With me, it's building one. Who wants to build a second one, whether it's an automobile or an airplane? The thrill is in completing the first one. After that, I got sick of it. No matter how much money I made, it never interested me." About the same time a buyer appeared, offered $2,000 and a ten percent royalty on every one sold. Besasie said, "I used that $2,000 to take a trip down to Florida, and I forgot about the idea. I never went back to collect any royalty."

Flying High

As a young man, Ray spent a year building an airplane that he called the "Besasie Midget." The mid-wing, 2-cylinder creation was completed in 1926, and extensive publicity brought a large crowd to see its first flight at what later became Mitchell Field. When it failed to get off the ground, the crowd quickly dispersed, and the *Wisconsin News* (which later became the *Milwaukee Sentinel*) carried the headline "Besasie Plan Failure." Although he eventually managed to get the plane aloft for a few feet, he wasn't satisfied and sold it soon after.

Another try a few years later was more successful, when he built an airplane he named "Sonny Boy," which he flew for about two years. One windy day, after a successful flight at the airport now known as Timmerman Field, a friend, Eddie Lamb, asked Ray if he could borrow the plane to take his girlfriend for a ride. Because it was almost out of gas, Eddie promised Ray he would stay over the field but then took off toward the city. In a half-hour, the plane had crashed in a backyard near the airport. "About ten fellows and I got into my Caddy, on the running boards and all, and rushed across a potato field so fast that I lost both spare tires. They both were standing there next to the plane, covered with blood."

Eddie said, "Take this girl to the hospital. I think she's dying."

After a harrowing ride to the emergency hospital and a promise from the head nurse to try to keep the story out of the newspapers, Ray and Eddie went back to destroy the "evidence."

Ray said, "The plane was a total washup. The engine was up in the wing, and its nose was buried in the mud. In the dark, with 10 or 15 other men using chisels and hacksaws, we cut the plane up into a hundred pieces and hid the wreckage in back of the Green Tree Tavern on Highway 41." The next morning, after pooling their resources, they went back to the hospital with all of $7 in hand to see about burying the woman. As it turned out, she was very much alive and "hollering to get out of there," Ray remembered. The plane, of course, was beyond hope.

But it was the government, not the accident, that put an end to Besasie's experiments with aviation. "I immediately started building a vertical takeoff plane...something like the Concord, where the angle of attack changes. I built the entire plane, which was powered by one of the three-cylinder engines I used to build. I have to thank the Department of Commerce, which passed a law in 1935 that you couldn't fly an unlicensed plane unless it had a stress analysis for a fee of $2,000. Who had $2, let alone $2,000? I sold it to a young man across the street from me, and he took all the rigging off, then sold it to a man from Sussex. It flew there for a couple of years, but with a straight wing. I guess the 101 slip joints I put on were enough to scare anybody."

On Solid Ground

Over the years, Besasie concentrated mainly on automobiles, repairing, inventing and building as his fertile imagination led him. Turbocharging was always of great interest to him. "I built my first turbocharger in 1935," he noted. Although World War II soon intervened, he started producing and selling the Besasie Turbo-Supercharger immediately after the war, in 1945.

Of another company's design that became popular later, he said, "The only time it starts supercharging is if you are in excess of 30 mph and tramp on the throttle. The pressure in the intake manifold will rise above atmosphere, and that is the only time you can say the engine is supercharged. At all other times, you're running a normally aspirated engine. You can be going 50-, 60-, 70-mph, and as long as the throttle is partially closed, you're not supercharging the engine. It's there as a standby. The type of charger that I made rotated on ball bearings, and the friction load was so little that I would pull to the curb and people would say, 'You left your engine running.'"

For the first one, he used a turbine blade from a cream separator. Later, he manufactured the turbines from high-nickel stainless steel alloys. Referring to other units on the market, he said, "Their exhaust gas temperatures had to be controlled. You cannot run the exhaust from the port up against the turbine, so you run it to a point where the temperature drops to around 1,300 to 1,400 degrees. I used to run at 1,700 degrees, and the turbine would glow red-hot. I even went to Europe trying to get some metals that would stand 1,800 degrees."

The First Excaliburs

Besasie's reputation for innovation led Brooks Stevens to ask him to build his new American sports car, which would be named the Excalibur J. The three vehicles that were built, in the early 1950s, had little in common with later production Excaliburs, except the name. Based on the 100-inch wheelbase Henry J chassis, the first two models were powered by the compact Kaiser's 6-cylinder, 161 cubic inch F-head six, modified to produce 100 hp. The third used a 1900cc Alfa Romeo engine with factory-approved tuning. In an article in August, 1981 "Car Collector", Brooks Stevens recalled that the idea "was planned more as a control experiment than for possible production, to compare performance." All three vehicles featured an aluminum skin over a lightweight tubular structure. Besasie Engineering Company built these early Excaliburs in 1952, and Stevens won an award from the New York International Motor Sports Show "for having created an outstanding American competition sports car in the low-priced field." On the road race circuit, they occasionally beat vehicles that included cad-Allards, Ferraris and Jaguars XK-120 and C-Types. The original cars continue to reside at the Brooks Stevens Museum in Mequon, Wisconsin.

The X-Cars

Always ready to try out an unusual idea by building it, Besasie built several cars with attention-getting "futuristic" styling in the 1950s, which he designated with names like "X-3" and "X-4." Some included such non-traditional ideas as center tiller steering.

The "X-1," the first of Besasie's "dream cars" was built around 1953 and named the "Barracuda," not related to the Chrysler Corporation car of the same name built several years later. It toured the country, making appearances at various auto shows and was followed by Besasie's "Batman" car, also known as the "X-2," in which he invested 5,000 hours between 1955 and 1957. Powered by a modified Cadillac engine, it featured a sliding roof that let passengers into the doorless body. The engine, supercharged by one of Besasie's designs, was said to produce 400 hp, giving the car a 0-60 time of six seconds and a top speed of 135 mph, according to an article in the September 10, 1957, *Milwaukee Journal*.

Besasie X-3

Besasie X-4

The complicated dash of the Besasie X-4

Unhappy with its road ability, Besasie sold the car and started on his "X-3," based on a 1958 Cadillac, followed three years later by the "X-4," which started life as a 1960 Chevrolet sedan. While little is published on the specifications of these unusual vehicles, the most noticeable mechanical feature was the driver's placement along the vehicles centerline, with a passenger seat on either side. Steering was by a modified tiller arrangement, with a dual handgrip that pivoted in an arc from side to side. In the first two years after he built it, Besasie drove the vehicle over 60,000 miles, including a trip to the Bonneville Salt Flats.

The Blue Flame

Besasie's experience was put to good use when he was called upon to build much of the body of the Blue Flame. The rocket-powered car that set a world land-speed record of 622,407 mph, driven by Gary Gabelich at Utah's Bonneville Salt Flats on October 23, 1970. Besasie formed major portions of the body, including the nose cone and tail section of the vehicle, and was at the Salt Flats during the speed attempts. The car's record stood for over a dozen years, and it was eventually donated to a museum in Duesseldorf, Germany.

His experience with the record-setting vehicle led to another job building the shell for a streamlined Honda motorcycle. Unfortunately, it held the two-wheel land-speed record for just a day before being displaced by a Harley-Davidson.

A Legacy Continues

Production models of the Excalibur designed by Brooks Stevens and his sons had only their name in common with the first Excaliburs that Ray Besasie built. However, his son, Ray Besasie Jr. was the company's vice-president for manufacturing, sales, and marketing. Leaving the firm after 17 years, when it shut down following several sales and bankruptcy proceedings, Ray Jr. and three outside investors founded Besasie Automobile Company, Inc. in August 1991. He was also joined by his brother, Joseph, who had spent ten years as a designer for Brooks Stevens Associates and worked on the original Excalibur design. The new company, on Milwaukee's south side, employs several other Excalibur alumni.

The "new neo-classic" roadster introduced by the firm was named the Baci, which is both an acronym for the company's name the Italian word for "kiss." The car, a two-seat roadster with classic-styled fiberglass body built by Fibertech of Milwaukee, uses Ford Thunderbird mechanicals that include a 5.0 liter V-8 engine, electronics and climate control system. The company builds its own all-welded steel tube space frames of ladder configuration with a 125-inch wheelbase, some 3.5 inches longer than a 1993 Cadillac Fleetwood. The engine is set back about two feet further than in the Thunderbird. Appointments include leather interior and power windows and roof, and the roadster is the only body style available. A planned four-seat Phaeton exists strictly on the back burner.

Ray Besasie Jr. says that the Excaliburs were difficult to build and developed maintenance problems as they aged because their design was more complex than necessary. As a result, the Baci has about half the number of parts, requires fewer hours to build, and weighs about 3,700 pounds compared to some 5,000 pounds for the Excalibur. The price is also about $20,000 less, with a 1993 retail price of $49,900, which Besasie says is comparable to a Chevrolet Corvette.

The Badger, 1909 - 1911 of Columbus, Wisconsin

By Val Quandt

The Badger was one of two automobile manufacturing companies named after the official state animal of Wisconsin, the badger. This story concerns that made in the small town of Columbus, Wisconsin. The other was the Badger of a company in another small town in Wisconsin, Clintonville.

The effort to build an assembled car with this name began in early 1909. In March of that year, Mr. E. W. Arbogast, son-in-law of a wealthy Watertown, Wisconsin, grain merchant, outlined his plans for the

Exterior view of the Badger Motor Car Factory in Columbus, Wisconsin, in 1910.

Photos courtesy Hartford Heritage Auto Museum.

Interior scene at the Badger Motor Car Factory in 1910.

manufacture of a $1,250 four-cylinder and four-passenger vehicle. His proposal did not meet with favor in Watertown, and it was at a meeting in Columbus that he received reception.

The potential shareholders in this $100,000 subscription were cautious and skeptical enough that they sought the opinion of an attorney in Fond du Lac, Wisconsin, a person who had been raised in Columbus. He suggested that they build the first single car, and then evaluate it and the builder. In fact, he recommended that they seek the advice of Fred Werner, successful body engineer for the Kissel Kar built in nearby Hartford, Wisconsin. There is no record that this advice was followed. Mr. Arbogast was quoted as saying he expected to build 1,000 cars the first year, and the attorney denigrated this claim.

Mr. Arbogast was described as being "a skilled mechanic who has sold and studied automobiles for years." Also, "he has made a study of foreign types and the result is he has planned a car different from, and years in advance of the average American construction."

The first car was built in rented quarters of a local warehouse. This and a subsequent rental space tended to be owned by the Columbus Canning Company, in existence the previous seven years. The officers of the new Badger Motor Car Company formed later in 1909 were all mostly, also, officers in the canning business. By trade they were grocer, lumberman, clothier, and banker.

There were expansive plans in early September of 1909, when the new auto company reported that the sales department had been moved to a building on Michigan Avenue, in Chicago, Illinois, and that all of the finished automobiles would be on display there.

By the end of 1909 they still only had this one prototypal car. And they realized that they would need a factory. Within several months they had constructed a small factory building 50 x 150 feet, with several accessory smaller additions attached to it.

Mr. Arbogast was scurrying about the midwest, notably in Iowa, and Illinois, trying to set up agencies to sell his car to interested people. A problem was apparent, that this was difficult and that many of the potential sites had already engaged other vehicle brands.

Early on, the Webb Jay Company in Chicago, Illinois, was quoted as wishing to purchase 250 of the new Badger cars. In the end they took not a single car.

To compound their problems, the Badger Motor Car Company had not planned any storage space for completed vehicles, rather expecting to ship them out as fast as they were manufactured. There was this plan, and the fanciful plan to send them to the Chicago sales agency mentioned above.

The 1910 Badger, toy tonneau, of Columbus, Wisconsin, vehicle named after the official animal of Wisconsin, the Badger.

Some cars were made in 1910 and being sent to such agencies as a small town in Iowa, and at Morrisonville, Illinois, together with Omaha, Nebraska. In Nebraska a trade was made for about ten Badgers for farmland. Similar trades, cars for land, were made in Wisconsin. Even trades were made for Badger cars with corn huskers, the latter useful for the canning interest in Columbus. In January of 1910 the Badger Motor Car Company could advertise that it had shipped cars to New Orleans, Omaha, Kansas City, and Chicago. Most of the selling was done by Arbogast, and his directors. With their fortunes dampening, numerous letters were sent out pleading for buyers to consider the Badger, often at a reduced price.

By February of 1910 a few vehicles had been assembled. They needed storage space. The Columbus Canning Company had recently put up a warehouse where the third floor was vacant. Two ramps built on 60-foot telephone poles were used and the vehicles driven up the ramps and up to the third floor. This maneuver also gained publicity for the company indicating the proficiency of the vehicle in hill climbing.

Mr. F. A. Stare an official both in the Columbus Canning Company and in the auto company wrote in 1956, "Some cars were sold in 1910, but the vaunted sales ability had been overly estimated. Agencies established were few. Apparently the officers of some of them made an effort to sell cars to friends and business acquaintances, but without much success." Rejection letters were received back at the Badger Motor Company from prospective buyers who stated their preferences in buying better known vehicles such as Ford, Stearns, and E.M.F.

A brighter moment in time came in July of 1910, when several Badger cars were entered in an endurance race of 808 miles. This was sponsored by the Wisconsin State Automobile Association. It had a circuitous route between numerous Wisconsin towns and villages. A Badger finished and in a favorable rank.

Blame was being heaped on Mr. Arbogast with statements such as, "While Mr. Arbogast might know cars, he was a novice when it came to business as a whole." It would seem more proper that the blame should have been leveled at all the automobile inexperienced people in this story. At any rate, Arbogast resigned in early 1911 and his place was taken by George Holtz, secretary of the firm.

Mr. F. A. Stare, again reporting in 1956, mentioned that "careful search of local newspapers shows no Badger items from July of 1910 to May of 1911." Also considering the fact that the first Badgers made in their new factory space first were produced in latter December of 1909, most of the activity must have been in the short span of the first six months of 1910.

1911 Badger, touring

A special meeting of the officers was called on April 10, 1911, for the purpose of trading automobiles for lands and selling lands earlier purchased through these trades. It was at this meeting that Holtz was authorized to take over the failing company.

In the fall of 1911 an assessment against the stockholders was needed to pay off debts. The stockholders would not hear of this. Finally a decision was reached to liquidate the company. So the assets were parts unsold, some of which could be used to assemble a few vehicles, and the lands in Nebraska and Wisconsin.

Production figures are not available, but Fred Stare listed the figure at 237 and disposed of in one manner or another. Even this appears to be a gross exaggeration. The company was now out of existence, with total loss to the stockholders.

Charles Abresch Company

This company was quartered in Milwaukee. The automotive connection in this company spanned somewhat over a decade from 1899 to 1912. Charles Abresch was the proprietor of the Abresch Carriage Company since 1871. In 1899 he announced his intention to manufacture motor vehicles. There was at least one. What is more certain is that his company produced the coachwork for early Ramblers and the Kissel Motor Car Company. A copy of a 1908 Kissel Kar with an Abresch custom body is shown on page 86. "The Standard Catalog of American Cars," 1805-1942 lists Abresch as the Milwaukee agent for the newly formed Kissel Motor Car Company and their Kissel Kars in the year 1908.

Earliest Car Assembled In Hartford In 1902

By Val Quandt

Virtually unknown and unrecognized is a bit of Hartford history. This is the fact that several ambitious and enterprising young men, in Hartford, Wisconsin, assembled a car in late 1901 and had it running in February of 1902. These individuals were James Favour and George Snyder. This accomplishment was noted at the time in the *Hartford Times* newspaper. It was also mentioned in the national press in an article in the "Horseless Age" on March 5, 1902, Volume 9, Number 10. This magazine detailed a number of other vehicles being assembled across the nation, many or most of them being of the one "off" or one of a kind development. In the case of this early Hartford gas-driven automobile, no mention was ever made of any attempt to duplicate or to factory produce it. There was an appreciable quantity and availability of engines and other vehicle component parts available even at this early time to excite the enthusiasm of young men to try their hand at putting together an automobile and without the money or capacity to factory reproduce it.

The garage built in Hartford, Wisconsin, in the 1880s, where in 1902 James Favour and George Snyder built an automobile out of assembled parts, an activity that was prevalent in the country at that time.

The following interview took place in the home of Ben Favour, son of James Favour who produced this first car. The date of this meeting was September 2, 1993. Ben Favour was born in 1904, and now at age 89 he fortunately retains a keen memory for past history. And this goes back to virtually the first decade of automobile manufacture in the United States. The very first production of a single vehicle in our country is generally conceded to be that of the Duryea brothers in 1893. Even this history giving credit to the Duryeas is in dispute, as there were others on the trail of single auto production by this time.

This 1902 vehicle by these local men was assembled from then existing parts and components. Four-cycle engines had been in existence for over two decades before this, credited to a Professor Otto of Germany. These men were influenced in their design by the White Steamer. By 1907 they had assembled yet another vehicle. This was while the Kissel Motor Car Company was in its early existence and they used a Kissel body and a Waukesha motor. A picture exists of the James Favour family in this car with the father at the wheel, and with his wife and three children, Ben being in the rear. It was used for a family car until 1926 when it was scrapped, according to Ben Favour, and the aluminum body was worth $500 as scrap metal. Kissel generally used steel in their auto bodies, but occasionally they used aluminum, based on availability.

Ben Favour recalls that in these very early days of the automobile, roads were primitive and generally the domain of the horse and buggy. It was common for the animals to be frightened by the unaccustomed automobile and bolt out of control. The farmer was inclined to consider the car a menace and something he would not wish to own. Of course, this all soon changed.

This is the car assembled by entrepreneurs James Favour and Snyder of Hartford from available parts. It was a one of a kind effort and not repeated by them. 1902.

Around 1904 James Favour together with three of his friends each decided to buy a Stanley Steamer, at a price of $2,500 apiece. These four were in addition to James Favour, Louis Portz, George Snyder, and Bill Kissel of the Kissel Motor Car Company. Ben recalls that his father chose his car in the color of Brewster Green. When the vehicles arrived, Ben recalls that the others envied the striking appearance of the Brewster Green White Steamer. A picture survives of this early car, and the only thing remaining today of this vehicle is its bulb horn. This is shown in an accompanying picture with Ben Favour holding it, taken on the interview date.

A *Hartford Times* newspaper account dated October 7, 1904, featured a two columned article entitled, "James Favour Smashes Auto Record." In this account that appeared earlier in the *Oshkosh Times*, James Favour and John Zurn made an automobile trip to Oshkosh from Hartford, a distance of 65 miles, in one hour and 36 minutes. The trip was made in their White Steamer and was referred to as "one of the fastest trips made in this country during the present year."

Favour recalls that the steam boiler in the White Steamer car was called a quick flash boiler. It was made up of 3/8-inch seamless steel pipe two feet in diameter and 18-inches high, rolled up in a coil and heated from below by gasoline. The boiler was heated without water in it for about one and a half minutes, and then water injected into it to produce instant steam. The boiler had a 750-pound steam gauge. Also the White Steamer car had a folding rubber bucket to scoop up water from rivers and creeks along the road.

Alongside of the above mentioned men, several others were tinkering with the same idea of making a car. These were George Hall, Heston Knickerbocker, Gustav Frederickson, and Sam Toles. The latter two men were pattern makers for the Kissel family with their Plow Works. Sam Toles also was instrumental in developing the first experimental car for the Kissel brothers.

Knickerbocker was a top mechanic who was trained in Detroit, Michigan. He had the first garage in Hartford in the building owned by James Favour on his property just south of his home. The home was built in 1866. Ben Favour recalls that this garage building was put up in 1885. This was the date that an earlier St. Kilian's Church across the road was torn down for a new structure. Left over were two-inch-thick pine boards which were then used for a floor in the garage building. Favour recalls the large sign using 18-inch letters on the front of this building, stating the Hartford Garage.

In addition to the space used for the automobile assembly there was room for a steam engine which drove a sawmill. Also there was a threshing machine used by area farmers for this purpose. Intact in the building today one finds an original heating stove, and steam-driven pulleys and belts. With homespun ingenuity, James Favour had rigged up a contraption of wooden arms from the steam engine in the garage to a hand pump 50 feet away, to pump water from this well and to direct it through wooden troughs under the ground back to the garage to use as water for the steam engine.

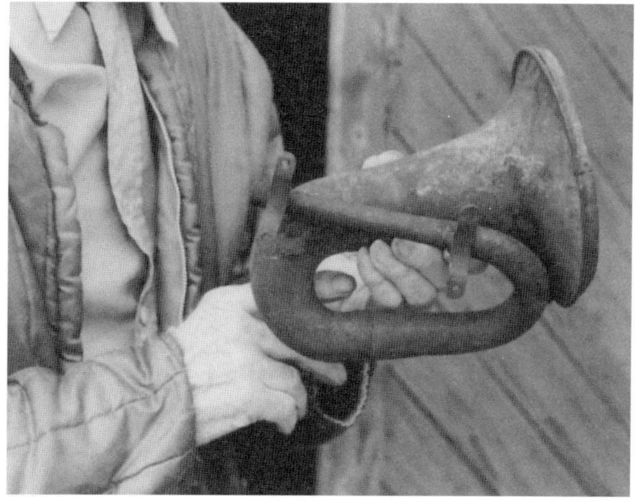

Ben Favour, son of James Favour, in 1993 and age 90 years, holds the bulb horn of this first car.

It is fortunate for us today that we have written records of some of these earlier times and a waning few people living today to verbally testify to it.

The Classic Kissel Automobile
By Val Quandt

The antecedents of the Kissel Motor Company existed way back in 1890. At that time Louis Kissel took into partnership his young sons Adolph P., Otto P., William L., and George A. Kissel. At that time they were living on a farm just north of Hartford in Washington County, called Addison Township. Father Louis had emigrated to America from Germany in 1857.

Shortly thereafter, in 1892, Louis purchased what was to become the Hartford Plow Works, from an existing business in Hartford, Wisconsin. Fourteen years later this location became the focus for the entry of Kissel brothers into the automobile business. Of the four brothers two were engaged in the business of building homes, and mainly for their employees. These were Adolph and Otto. Over a decade and a half they had built 300 homes, and owned another 200.

In 1905 brothers George and William were experimenting at building an automobile from existing vehicle components. By the next year they were putting together their first prototypal car. The first meeting to form the Kissel Motor Car Company took place in Hartford, Wisconsin, on June 25, 1906. The sum of $50,000 was raised. Early officers of this company were H. K. Butterfied, the president, who was a United States district attorney, Otto P. Kissel, the vice president, and George A. Kissel, the secretary and treasurer. Will Kissel was to assist his brother George. Within a few years George Kissel had become company president and William its secretary and treasurer, positions they then kept for the duration of the company.

Louis Kissel, wife and six children, picture taken c. 1895. Future president of the Kissel Motor Car Company George A. Kissel at the far right, and brother William L. Kissel to the far left. Father Louis Kissel killed with pistol shot fired by an angry employee in 1908.

The 1906 experimental model of the new Kissel automobile.

KisselKar, body Roadster with tonneau, early 1906.

This is the first KisselKar produced, for the model year of 1907, of which 100 were produced for McDuffee of Chicago, Illinois.

Their first order was for 100 touring cars for Joseph McDuffee of Chicago, Illinois, an auto dealer for Stoddard Dayton and Royal Intourist. The Kissel automobile was called the KisselKar. This name held into 1918 during the First World War, when anti-German sentiment caused Kissel management to delete the Kar affixed name and to call it simply the Kissel. The radiator badge was then changed from "KisselKar, Every Inch A Car" to an emblem of Mercury, the Roman mythology messenger god.

The KisselKar 1907 tonneau style, note drivers wheel on the right side as was the case for these very early cars.

By 1908 Kissel had established dealerships in most large U.S. cities and was a regular participant in the New York, Chicago, and Milwaukee auto shows. In 1908 father Louis Kissel, was shot and killed by an angry employee. The company was now solidly in the hands of the young Kissel brothers, George and William.

The early Kissel models were four cylinder, and except for the first year, the motor blocks were manufactured in the Kissel plant. These were 30 horsepower and selling for $1,500. In 1909 Kissel produced its first six-cylinder car, and this sold for $3,000. There were already 13 body styles including a five-passenger touring, a baby tonneau, and a coupe all called the LD-9, in 1909. The highest-priced vehicle was a seven-passenger limousine, selling for the top price of $4,200.

The year was 1908, and Abresch of Milwaukee manufactured these elegant custom bodies for a Kissel, at a time when Kissel, in its infancy, needed these bodies.

The KisselKar, coupe, model 4-40 of 1912. The vehicle had acetylene fuel headlamps and side lamps.

The KisselKar, Semi-racer, of 1912. Note the precarious position of the gasoline tank just behind the driver seat.

The most unusual and striking model was its Semi-racer. This had two bucket-shaped seats, a slanted oval gas tank right behind these seats, a tool chest and cylinder for storing acetylene for headlight illumination on the left side running board. By 1910 Kissel was producing its special design motor trucks and continued to do so for the remaining years of their existence.

Kissel automobiles had its driver's wheel on the right side into 1912 when it was placed on the left side. Also in this year the Kissel Motor Car Company purchased the Romadka Trunk Company in Milwaukee on Center Street between 31st and 32nd Streets. This site was to be used for the assembly of Kissel six-cylinder 48 and four-cylinder model 40 vehicles. This company addition, for reasons not clear in the extant company records, never succeeded and records do not show any manufacturing activity there. By 1914 Kissel was out of this plant when it was sold to the Westinghouse Lamp Company of New York.

By 1913 Kissel featured a foot-operated electric starter with a storage battery and dynamo for electric headlights and taillights. Also in the same year Kissel introduced its double kick up frame. This allowed a lower center of gravity with the kicked up or elevated front and back chassis portions over the axles.

Kissel used the Motometer for its radiator temperature gauge. This also served as a radiator emblem as it was situated right over the top of the radiator casing. A window in the gauge showed a colored fluid which when elevated warned against engine overheating, leaky radiator, open drain cock, broken fan belt, and other conditions causing radiator temperature rise.

Kissel motor trucks were now made in sizes all the way from 1,500 pounds, one and one-half ton, two-ton, three-ton, four-ton, and the five-ton behemoth. The smaller trucks were powered by the 30 horsepower, four-cylinder engine, and the larger from the three ton up, by the four-cylinder 50-horsepower engine. Kissel offered to build whatever the customer wanted. The standard was the stake body. They also offered the chemical and hose fire wagons, police and patrol wagons, and the KisselKar ambulance.

In September of 1912 KisselKar trucks of the one and one-half ton size were being sent to Greece in Europe. The European War was being fought. These trucks were being loaded two to a boxcar with numerous spare parts in huge wooden boxes. The shipment was comprised of 50 vehicles. William L. Kissel, long after retiring, recalled that this shipment never made it to Greece, as the ship was sunk by German submarines.

The new KisselKar model 36 came out in late summer of 1914. This model featured the detachable sedan top for winter use. The alternative was the soft top for summer use. This sedan top was a demountable one that could be installed in several minutes, or less than one minute by factory experts, replacing the open car summer soft top.

Six bolts and sockets, three on either side, four top irons, one on each corner, were the only fastenings. The electric wiring connected automatically as the upper and lower halves met. This option remained for about five years. By this time there was a change in buying habits from the open car concept to the firm top. Most buyers opted to just keep the firm top in place, especially in the more northern climates. Some owners also had difficulty in getting the winter top to fit, what with contraction of metal occurring in the colder climates. In their advertising, Kissel showed this as the "All Year Car" serving both warm and colder climate changes.

The engine in its new 1914 model six-cylinder 42 was standard L head type, cast en bloc at the Kissel foundries, with a bore of $3^5/_8$ inches and a long stroke of $5^1/_2$ inches. The valves measured $2^3/_{16}$ inches with nickel steel heads.

Miss Anita King, a Paramount Studio Hollywood star, was the first woman to cross the American continent alone in a car in 1915. She did this in a KisselKar in 49 days. She traveled from San Francisco, where there was a world's fair exposition, to New York City. This was a perilous journey over very poor and primitive roads. The Kissel Motor Car Company was involved in the planning and advertising of this event, and hosted her after the completion of her journey.

In 1916 Kissel employment stood at an all-time high of 1,100 employees. These were mostly men, and women in stenographic positions. By this time Kissel operated out of a space of more than a 500,000 square feet.

Coincident with the high production of cars and trucks in 1916 and 1917 was the growing need for more and improved roads. The average road was still dirt scooped up from the roadside into a roadbed. This turned into an impassable quagmire when it rained hard. With state, county, and city monies Washington County in Wisconsin spent $1 million in bonding for 80 miles of concrete highways.

Kissel 1914 model 6-48 Touring, five-passenger Gibralter. Manufactured by the Kissel Motor Car Company. On loan from Earl Young to the Hartford Auto Museum where it is on display.

The Kissel of 1917, here a 12 cylinder, or double six, made for a very brief period of time.

Kissel ceased making four-cylinder cars after 1916. Its advertising then was featuring the slogan "Hundred Point Six." This featured an assemblage of points that a Kissel buyer could find in its vehicles. The engine bore was three and one-half inches with a stroke of five inches. It had a top speed of 55 to 60 miles an hour. The wheelbase was 117 inches. The cars had a lustrous finish imparted by a 22-step process. The overall base price in 1917 was $1,095, their lowest since their earlier days.

In the early part of 1917 Kissel Motor Car Company was road testing its new "mystery car." This it did in Wisconsin, Illinois, Massachusetts, New York, and California. Kissel had the hood tightly sealed on each of these vehicles, and tried to convey the impression that here was a very special and powerful engine.

But it was no mystery what happened to the effort. It failed after two years. This was a Weidely V-12 engine purchased by the Kissel Motor Car Company. This model did not sell well, and with the slump in its entire passenger car lineup there weren't the ready buyers.

Their new effort now was World War I related. This was for the production of their three-ton trucks for the war effort. President Woodrow Wilson had formally declared war against Germany on April 3, 1917, after German submarines had sunk American shipping. Kissel went on to manufacture 2,000 three-ton trucks, four-wheel drive, in subcontract with the military effort at Clintonville, Wisconsin, for the same vehicle. These trucks were chiefly used as ammunition carriers. Many of the boys from Hartford, Wisconsin, with experience in the Kissel plant then became drivers for these trucks, and other vehicles such as ambulances.

While their war production was going on Kissel was active in developing a new roadster, at first called the Kissel Silver Special, and later the Kissel Speedster. Conover Silver was a New York City distributor for the Kissel automobile. Silver and Fred Werner, Kissel chief body designer, drew up this design. This car, in the color of chrome yellow, became well-known as the "Gold Bug." This was so named because of its bug-like shape and the gold color resemblance of chrome yellow.

Kissel 1918-1920, custom-built five-passenger Tourster.

Kissel 1919-1920 seven-passenger Touring car.

Factory picture of the 1919-1920 Kissel custom-built Speedster, of the very first of this design.

Kissel 1920 custom-built Coupe, six cylinder.

The stimulus of the war effort showed in the attention given to improving the roads of the nation. The Highway Transport Committee of the Council of National Defense sent pathfinder cars over various routes to find the most feasible ones for sending overland the government standardized trucks. The National Highway Association was fathering a system of 50,000 miles of national highways which would serve the nation of its then 84 million people. This at least in part has become the basis of many of the smaller secondary roads in existence in our nation today.

Right after the war the most notable mechanical invention coming out of the Kissel Motor Car Company involved improvements in the oiling system of the vehicle. Kissel mechanical engineers, Herman D. Palmer, and Joseph A. Tarkington devised a new Automatic Oil Control, and with it a new oil basin which had a patent date of May 14, 1919. This oil control worked with the throttle so that the correct amount of oil was provided according to the amount of throttle or power used.

Kissel was now using the advertising slogan of the "Custom Built Car." This was an exaggeration. But it was warranted, in part, by the fact that it was a 90 percent manufactured car rather a mostly-assembled car.

Nationwide there was a reduction in motor car sales, and this drop was also felt by Kissel in 1921, when its total output for the year was 506 passenger cars and 323 trucks. Their six engine was now called the 6-45 with a cylinder bore of 3 5/16 inches and a 5 1/2-inch stroke.

Kissel 1921, model 6-45 Speedster, manufactured by the Kissel Motor Car Company. This vehicle is seen on the book cover as the "Gold Bug" in the color of chrome yellow. It features a slide out "suicide seat." Donated by Beatrice Kissel Schauer and her husband Frederick Schauer to the Hartford Auto Museum.

Kissel 1921 Touring car, owned by Chester Krause of Krause Publications, Iola, Wisconsin.

Kissel 1922 the famous Gold Bug, this vehicle owned by the aviatrix, Amelia Earhart.

The 1922 De Luxe Sedan custom-built by Kissel Motor Car Company.

Kissel 1922, custom-built Bus, 17-passenger, four seating rows with separate door entrances.

Kissel in 1922, showed its innovation, by manufacturing a 17-passenger bus called the "Deluxe Coach Limited." It was built much like a regular passenger car sedan by lengthening the regular 124-inch wheelbase to 202 inches. There was room for 17 passengers besides the driver. Passenger entry was made comfortable by a series of four doors on the right side to rows of seats.

Automobile sales improved in 1923 and 1924. Further road building activity took place and with federal input. Of the 57,178 improved roads in Wisconsin, 1,105 were concrete, the remainder of the roads being gravel, and early forms of macadam.

Kissel 1923 model 6-55, five-passenger Phaeton, six cylinder and 61 hp, manufactured by the Kissel Motor Car Company, on loan from Delyle Beyer to the Hartford Auto Museum.

Kissel 1923, model 6-55, body 4-door Brougham. Manufactured by the Kissel Motor Car Company. Donated by Lyn Schuette and L. Wolbrink to the Hartford Auto Museum.

Kissel 1923 Fire Truck, Model 5159. Manufactured by the Kissel Motor Car Company, fire fighting equipment outfitted by the Pirsch Company, four-cylinder Wisconsin Motors engine, on loan from the Hartford, Wisconsin, Fire Department to the Hartford Auto Museum.

Kissel Speedster, of 1924, 6-55, "Gold Bug" style and such, if chrome yellow color. Drum head lamps and solid bumper.

To gain somewhat of a sales perspective the following figures existed in a week in May of 1923. The Ford Motor Company produced 39,053 cars and trucks while in the same week the Lincoln division of Ford produced 176 cars and the Kissel plant averaged 42 cars and trucks a week. So it can be seen that the average buyer could better afford the Ford than the more expensive vehicle. Kissel was aware of this, and down priced its cheaper models into the $1,000 range.

Billed as an innovation in a sport car was the introduction in January of 1924 of its enclosed Speedster. This model was a departure from its open Speedster as being an All-Year car. It was powered by the Kissel Custom-Built 6-55 engine that came out in 1922. This was not a steel top now, nor was any Kissel through the remainder of its manufacturing years. Rather it was a weather resisting material, generally the patented Pantasote, reinforced beneath with wooden ribs, and a cloth interior lining.

Kissel produced its first eight-cylinder vehicle in 1925. This was the straight 8-75. This engine was imported from the Lycoming Manufacturing Company in Williamsport, Pennsylvania. This was offered in four body styles including a four-door Brougham Sedan, seven-passenger Berline Sedan, and Victoria, all on a 126-inch wheelbase, and the Speedster both open and enclosed.

Kissel 1925 model 6-55 body Enclosed Speedster. Manufactured by the Kissel Motor Car Company. Six-cylinder, 61-hp engine. Donated by Robert Troller to the Hartford Auto Museum.

Kissel 1925 model 8-75 body enclosed Speedster. Manufactured by the Kissel Motor Car Company. Eight-cylinder, 75-hp engine. Donated by Delyle Beyer to the Hartford Auto Museum.

Kissel 1925 model 8-75, four door Brougham, manufactured by the Kissel Motor Car Company. Original unrestored condition. Donated by Robert Troller to the Hartford Auto Museum.

The Kissel Motor Car Company, by 1926, had grown to its maximum manufacturing space of 1,000,000 square feet. Remaining as its two chief officers were George Kissel as president, and brother William as secretary treasurer. Also 97 percent of the stock in the company was owned by the four Kissel brothers.

In the same year Kissel produced its combination hearse and ambulance, its numbers soon to be increased with its contracts to build these for the National Casket Company.

The 1926 Kissel model year expected to get a big boost with the introduction of their All-Year Coupe Roadster. This came in both a two- and four-passenger configuration, the latter the result of having a rumble seat for two in the rear deck.

Both the two- and four-passenger creations allowed the top to be folded down in less than a minute by the owner. These models came in both the six- and eight-cylinder engine sizes. Within a year Kissel claimed that the All-Year Coupe Roadster was copied by 20 other manufacturers as convertible coupes, an idea that had become popular.

Kissel 1926 Model 6-55 body is the All-Year Coupe. Manufactured by the Kissel Motor Car Company. Features are the rumble seat and convertible top. Donated by Aaron W. Johnson to the Hartford Auto Museum.

Kissel Fire Truck 1926 model 52376, manufactured by the Kissel Motor Car Company in Hartford, Wisconsin. Body outfitted for fire fighting by the Pirsch Company, six-cylinder Waukesha Motors engine, price when new was $6,064. On loan from the Juneau, Wisconsin, Fire Department to the Hartford Auto Museum.

In 1925 Kissel produced 2,125 vehicles, cars and trucks, and slightly less in 1926. It is estimated that in its 25 years of existence between 32,000 and 35,000 cars and trucks were produced by the Kissel Motor Car Company. A pinpoint exact figure cannot be reached. The demise of the company was in September of 1930, and a few vehicles, mostly taxicabs were assembled in 1931. It is now apparent that not a lot of concern was shown to preserve production records. In some year periods these are available, and in others not. Here less accurate estimates need to be made on sales incomes, and over a broad range of body styles. As most of the Kissel manufacturing space in the decades to follow was used for outboard and other marine manufacturing, the Kissel Motor Car Company records were mostly discarded and carted away.

Now in the succeeding years after 1926 Kissel offered both smaller and larger six- and eight-cylinder models. The large eight, now model 8-90 had a long wheelbase of 139 inches. The smaller eight was the 8-80. In 1928 Kissel called its new production of vehicles the Kissel White Eagle, and within a year simply the White Eagle.

1926 Kissel Eight, four-passenger Speedster.

William L. Kissel, secretary and treasurer of the Kissel Motor Car Company, picture taken c. 1926 at his age of 45 years.

George A. Kissel, picture taken in late 1930s. He was president of the Kissel Motor Car Company through almost all except the first few years of it's existence. He lived 1881-1942.

Kissel 1926 seven-passenger Sedan, 3-bar bumper.

Kissel 1927, close-up view of the dash instrument display.

Kissel 1927 Sedan plush interior mohair seating.

The 1927 Kissel Speedster, with William L. Kissel at the wheel. Will Kissel helped direct the Kissel Motor Car Company from its beginning in 1906 to its demise in 1930. His brother George Kissel was the president of the company all the years starting in 1910. Standing alongside the Speedster was Richard (Dick) Braund who restored many Kissels in Elroy, Wisconsin, and where for many years his company built the Duesenberg II, his son Richard remains an officer today building the famous Duesenberg II.

It limited this name to its deluxe eight-cylinder series. Its hearse ambulances were selling well. These were elongated vehicles on a 162-inch wheelbase.

1927-1928 Kissel National Funeral Car, as custom made for the National Casket Company.

Kissel 1928 All-Year Coupe Roadster, with a folding top.

Kissel Speedster 1928 8-80, a later model of the Speedster series.

Kissel 1928 model 8-90 White Eagle Brougham sedan. Manufactured by the Kissel Motor Car Company. Vehicle rested unrestored for 30 years in Harrah's Reno, Nevada, warehouse, and then was restored by Dr. Thomas Viner who donated it to the Hartford Auto Museum.

Mr. H. C. Bradfield was head of the Bradfield Motors Company. His experience was in taxicab production with the Yellow Cab Company in Chicago, Illinois.

These were introduced in 1928 as the 67-B model with the 6-55 engine. There was the option of the smaller engine as was in the 6-70. These were sold in Milwaukee as

The seven-passenger Sedan, 1929.

The All-Year Coupe-Roadster, 1929. (Folding Top)

The Coupe-Roadster, 1929. (Solid Top)

late as 1931.

The 1929 models were all White Eagles, the six-cylinder models having been phased out in 1928. The new big offering was the model 8-126 where the 126 stood for its horsepower. Tests on the Indianapolis Speedway track showed this model to be capable of a speed of 100 miles an hour.

The Brougham Sedan, 1929.

New Kissel White Eagle Speedster, 1929, 115 hp, 100 miles an hour.

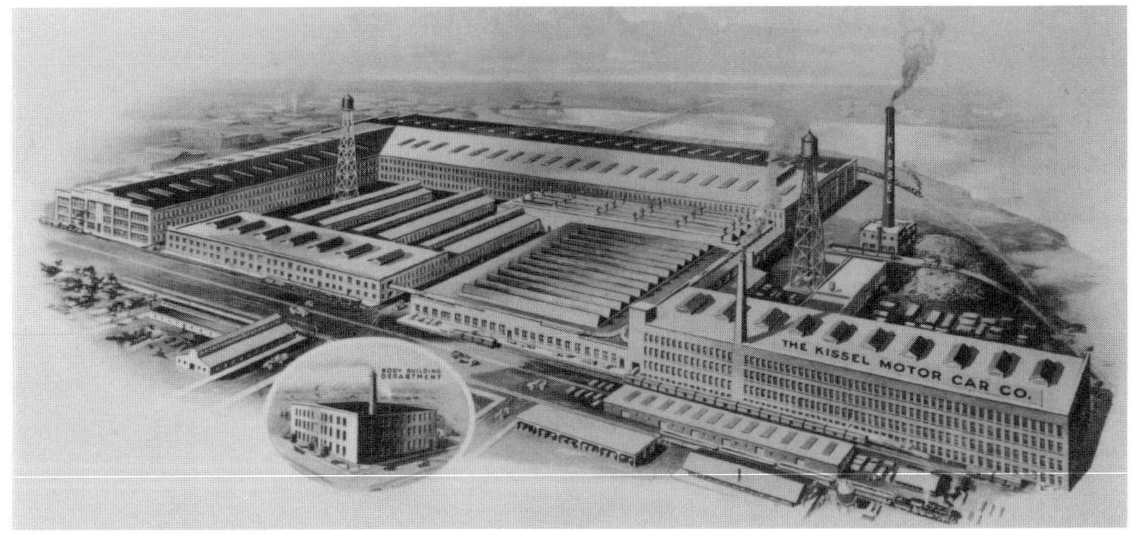

The Kissel Motor Car Company plant, as it looked in 1929.

Kissel 1930 White Eagle Touring. Manufactured by the Kissel Motor Car Company. This vehicle was sold new in Argentina. Donated by Dr. Frederick Simone to the Hartford Auto Museum.

Kissel 1930 model 8-95 White Eagle Brougham. Manufactured by the Kissel Motor Car Company. On loan from John and Jerry Kissel to the Hartford Auto Museum.

Sales were down in 1929. Early 1930 was a difficult time for Kissel when they were unable to meet interest payments on loans. As late as August of 1930 Kissel was engaged with Mr. Archie Andrews of New York to produce the front-wheel-drive car, the Ruxton. At most, Kissel produced 26 Ruxtons with touring bodies. The Moon Motor Car Company of St. Louis, Missouri, produced perhaps several hundred. They were also in difficult financial straits in late 1930 and went under in December that year.

The Kissel cab, introduced in 1929 is shown in a model featuring an open front driver compartment. The Bradfield Motors division of Kissel found its market for these in the taxi trade of New York City and Milwaukee.

Kissel manufactured Bradfield taxicabs, ready to be shipped out of Hartford, Wisconsin, to cab company in Milwaukee, 1930-1931.

A friendly receivership was arranged in September of 1930 and the Kissel Motor Car Company was now out of business after 25 years. As mentioned, a few taxicabs were assembled in 1931 from leftover parts. The plant space sat mostly unoccupied except for a few small businesses there until 1935.

After the demise of the Kissel Motor Car Company, in the following year, Kissel was reorganized as Kissel Industries. The previous owners continued to run this new entity. One of their early products was the manufacture of kitchen chairs. Kissel had wide experience with the use of wood in fabricating its wood frames in all the Kissel vehicles.

By late 1934 Kissel was manufacturing outboard engines for Sears and Roebuck of Chicago, Illinois. Under owners consisting of Kissel Industries, the West Bend Company, Chrysler Marine, and Bayliner, the plant produced outboard engines for over 50 years. The plant, often enlarged, exists today as Mercury Marine, division of Brunswick.

William Muller And The Ruxton
By Val Quandt

The Ruxton story began with designer William Muller. During the latter part of the 1920s, Muller was working at the Edward G. Budd Manufacturing Company in Philadelphia. There he had the opportunity to do experimental work in developing his front-wheel drive. Muller wished to use the Budd Company to manufacture bodies to go with the front-wheel drive concept; some as-yet-undesignated auto manufacturing company would build the entire car. The Hupp Motor Car Company in Detroit was soon selected as the manufacturing plant for the car.

William Muller, an engineer, conceived the design for the front-wheel-drive Ruxton, in the 1928 to 1930 period.

Later, in a communication from New Orleans, where Muller was working in 1963, he described his professional background. From 1909 to 1920, he spent his time as a race mechanic, driver, and engineer. He mentioned associations with some automotive and racing greats, such as Fred Duesenberg and Ralph dePalma. By 1920, he was with the Willys Corporation in Elizabeth, New Jersey, as a road-test engineer. Later in that year he had joined Budd in Philadelphia. He was there in 1926 when he began the first experiment with front-wheel drive.

Muller placed the first front-wheel drive transmission with a six-cylinder Studebaker engine. His second car, which became his private transportation, had an eight-cylinder Continental engine. He nicknamed it "The Alligator" because someone, on seeing it for the first time, remarked that it reminded them of an alligator.

Early in 1929, Archie Andrews, then of New York took notice of Muller's work. He began a liaison with him to produce the car which would be called the Ruxton. Ruxton was the surname of a gentleman who worked as a partner in an investment banking firm in New York City. When Hupp turned down the invitation to produce the Ruxton, Andrews set about to form his own company, called New Era Motors. Among the directors of the new company were Frederick W. Gardner of the Gardner Motor Car Company, and C. Harold Wills, designer of the Wills Sainte Claire automobile. Andrews again needed an automobile manufacturing company to produce the car, so he turned to a succession of firms, Gardner, Peerless, and Marmon, before getting the Moon Motor Car Company of St. Louis to take on the project. Moon was having management and financial difficulties at the time. Moon management desired to keep the New Era officers locked out of the plant. Andrews and Muller literally stormed the factory, took over, and installed their own officers, with Muller as president. This was on April 12th, 1930. By November 1930, Moon was in receivership. Presumably what Ruxton cars were produced were built in the few months between June and November of that year. Some sales lagged into 1932.

At this time, Andrews was also making contact with George Kissel, president of the Kissel Motor Car Company in Hartford, Wisconsin. He wanted Kissel to do some assembly work, and also to make the transmission for the Ruxton. He advanced a $100,000 loan for this purpose, with a promise that another $150,000 was to follow. The Kissel Company was feeling the economic downturn in 1929 and 1930, and could not meet a pre-existing mortgage payment in April of 1930. That problem, and pressure from Andrews that he might take over the plant if Kissel could not live up to the agreement regarding Ruxton production, caused Kissel to ask for, and arrange for, a friendly takeover of the plant by a receiver in September of 1930. Several months later, in November, the Moon Motor Car Company asked for receivership, and New Era Motors was to follow the next month.

The first prototype Ruxton in 1929 bore a radiator emblem consisting of a question mark. Considering the subsequent difficulties of the firm, this seems almost prophetic.

The Ruxton was a striking automobile. It weighed 4,000 pounds, and was about ten inches lower than the customary sedan of the time. Because of this low height it needed no running boards. It sported the vertically oblong Woodlite head lamps. The body had pin-striped painted bars. The radiator mascot was now the griffin, the Greek mythologic half-lion, half-eagle. This figure was repeated on the wheel covers and the hubcaps. The engine had a three-speed transmission with the front-wheel drive.

The Ruxton roadster bodies came from the Baker-Raulang Company in Cleveland, Ohio. Sedan bodies were manufactured by Budd in Philadelphia. The several Phaeton bodies were produced by Kissel. Two of these became the personal cars of George and Will Kissel.

The Ruxton, in 1930, showing its low profile compared to a conventional sedan of the time.

The handsome, low-slung, front-wheel drive Ruxton, as it appeared in 1931. The portrait appeared in the "Automobile Quarterly" in 1969.

The 1931 Ruxton, in Roadster body style. Low slung and featuring "cat eye" head lamps.

In a letter from the engineering department of the Moon Motor Car Company in St. Louis, dated July 11, 1930, help was extended to Kissel regarding their work on the Budd bodies. These were reported as "having blemishes requiring labor and material to prepare these bodies for priming and painting by removing deep scratches, solder, and repairing cracks if located." Under the same July 11th date, Moon listed 24 items of concern under the heading of "transmission." Moon again was instructing Kissel "while you have instructions as to just exactly how these transmissions should be set up and we have sent you the fixture for testing these transmissions under load, I question if the fixture will be received in time for you to test before making your first assembled car." So it would have been necessary for Kissel to do their transmission work and vehicle assembly during the few weeks between the middle of July and September when the company folded.

In spite of the relatively short life of the Ruxton enterprise, Muller continued to persevere with his attempts to produce a front-wheel drive car. There is on record in an 11-page patent disclosure filed on November 25, 1931, and a patent was granted by the US Patent Office on July 23, 1935. In it, he described plans for a front-wheel drive sedan. The car shown is a very plain one, especially so compared with the elegant Ruxton. This particular car was never produced.

Again in 1940, William Muller was actively trying to market a front-wheel drive car. This time he was working with Cameron Peck, a businessman of Evanston, Illinois, and head of the Cord Owners Club of Illinois. Also active with the effort was Douglas Van Patten of Ontario, Canada. There were reams of communications between these individuals. Plans called for Muller to make 25 cars for Peck. Some distant overtures were made to General Motors. Muller had written to Will Kissel at this time inquiring whether Kissel might make transmissions for the proposed cars.

In a reply to Muller in January of 1940, Will Kissel referred to the fact that Ruxton transmission patterns and tools were shipped to St. Louis, and that Kissel Industries were then making outboard engines. He also commented that he had a four-passenger Ruxton Phaeton that he drove occasionally, and that "the car still looks very good even though it is old fashioned." After much maneuvering, and ultimately a strained relationship between Muller and Peck over remuneration that Muller wished from Peck, the whole effort was dropped.

There are not a lot of Ruxtons left today. The Classic Car Club of America lists in its roster only about a half dozen. What are undoubtedly exaggerated figures generally list the Moon output of Ruxtons at 200 to 500 and Kissel output at 26. If a federal judge were to be believed, Ruxton, in November of 1930, had a very small number of Ruxtons. The newspaper quote at the time stated "application for a federal receiver for the Moon Motor Car Company was denied by a federal judge who saw no reason to appoint a federal receiver to sell thirty-five to forty Ruxton cars."

Herman Palmer, the Kissel motor and chassis engineer, is quoted as the source of the Kissel production figure on Ruxton. Will Kissel, in his scrap book entries in 1951, made the comment that Kissel made no Ruxtons. This might be explained, however, as representing his view that Kissel made no entire Ruxton cars, but did some assembly work. With Fred Werner at work heading the body department, Kissel had the skills to make beautiful bodies, and did so for some Phaetons. In the last hectic days of Kissel their recordkeeping suffered. In a succession of events after the Kissel Motor Car Company and Kissel Industries (1932-1944) sold out to the West Bend Company, the outboard motor companies threw out all the earlier Kissel parts and records. Thus, office records and Kissel parts that would be of inestimable value to researchers and restorers were lost forever.

In 1931 there was some hope of return to car production in Hartford, when Kissel was asked to build several Lever engine cars for the A.L. Powell Company. Powell had been involved in an earlier attempt to build the Elcar with a Lever engine. Several of these engines were reported to be fitted to left-over Kissels from testing. There was even an attempt to build an eight-cylinder Lever-powered car on an updated Ruxton chassis.

Chapter Six
FOX RIVER VALLEY
and Environs

The Wausau Flyer
By Michael E. Keller

Many strands make up the rich tapestry of American automotive history. Since its earliest days, there have been literally thousands of inventive and energetic entrepreneurs who knew that they could build a better automobile. These pioneers in the fledgling motor car industry came not only from the larger metropolitan areas, but all parts of the nation.

The lumber town of Wausau, Wisconsin, was one of those more rural areas that was quick to follow the development of the horseless carriage, and later to become involved directly.

The first appearance of a self-propelled vehicle within the city limits of Wausau was the steam-powered Locomobile in 1901. The automobile was displayed as a companion attraction of a traveling minstrel show, and was said to have garnered a great deal of attention.

It was shortly after the show in 1901 that one W. H. Mylrea purchased a single-cylinder Winton for his personal use. As the first automobile owner in Wausau, Mylrea reported that the lever-steered vehicle with the engine under the seat and sans windshield was reliable and safe. Just as a multitude of earlier owners were to report, however, the area farmers were very much against his new "contraption" as it scared their horses.

The acceptance of the automobile by the nation as more than a passing fad or plaything of the rich made it inevitable that Wausau would be involved in these early automotive developments. The first automobile dealership in Wausau, and indeed one of the earliest in the state, was begun by Mark Ewing and Lewis H. Hall. In 1906 the first carload of automobiles was delivered to the still-thriving lumber center.

That first carload consisted of three Ford automobiles. One was to be retained by Hall for personal use, the second sold to well-known photographer I. A. La Certe, and the third was to be delivered to Burley Hoar. Mr. Hoar was a laundryman in Rhinelander. Hall reported that the 60-mile trip to that northern city was most arduous, in that there were no roads, paved or otherwise, to make their trip easier. Trees needed to be felled and brush was used to cover the stones which would regularly strike the differential. Leaving Wausau at 7 a.m. Hall would not reach Mr. Hoar's laundry until 5 p.m. that night.

When Hall and Ewing founded their automobile dealership, it was in conjunction with Hall's already established bicycle shop. Located at 308 S. First Avenue, the successful west-side shop had been the scene of much activity since Hall came to Wausau in 1904.

Originally a building contractor in rural Marathon County, Hall had become successful in that endeavor, just as he had while employed as a millwright at the Sawyer Brothers sandpaper company, now 3M. With his mechanical background, it was natural that he would be intrigued by the new machines and become involved with their early evolution. Hall continued as a Ford dealer until 1908. At that time he began negotiations with a representative of the Chalmers Detroit Motor Car Company and accepted shipment of the first Chalmers cars in Wausau in 1909. A higher-class automobile than the Ford, the Chalmers representative considered Wausau to be a prime market with its plethora of wealthy lumbermen. The prediction came to fruition as Hall was able to sell a respectable 22 six-cylinder Chalmers for the spring season.

As the first dealer in the area, the Hall shop on First Avenue also became the first repair shop in that area. In that factory

This is the Wausau Flyer in 1910, which had a very short existence.

repairs and assistance were near nonexistent. The repair of the pioneer vehicles was done "at need." Priding himself on being well-equipped and supplied, this repair service naturally tied into Hall establishing the first drive-in gasoline service station in the city. Later this was expanded to retail gasoline outlets in several Marathon County communities, in addition to bulk oil sales in Wausau and Athens.

Not satisfied with simply being a successful automobile dealer, Hall felt that he could better the product now being produced in the Motor City. Hall entered into an agreement and partnership in 1910 with Wausau businessman, Joseph A. Plier, to build a prototype automobile of a new design. According to Irv Hall, Lewis' son, the idea was to build a better car for less money.

The plan was ambitious. The prototype, dubbed, the "Wausau Flyer" utilized a chassis built by Wausau Iron Works and featured a power plant built by Waukesha Engine. A three-speed transmission was used, as were mechanical brakes. Bearings were by Timpkin. Chalmers fenders were grafted onto a body created and produced by the Wausau Veneer Company. Three acres of land on Wausau's west side were optioned for factory construction, and the plan had the backing of the Wausau business community.

It was not long before other test drives were conducted for the purpose of sales and backing. The Wausau Flyer was exhibited at the Wisconsin Valley Fair and created a great deal of interest. Having seen the prototype in action, three orders were placed by civic-minded citizens, one by a Dr. Solh, the other two not recorded.

It was at this point that financial difficulties began to spell the end of the Wausau Flyer. Although there was a functioning prototype being used daily in the city, an eager and enthusiastic manager and small work force in place, land available for a factory, and orders for automobiles on the books, the directors of Citizens Bank balked when approached for start-up funds. As many entrepreneurs were to learn in the early decades of the century, the banking establishment was conservative beyond scope and money was not freely allowed for such a speculative endeavor. Hall's personal finances were responsible for all expenses thus far and Citizens Bank deemed it would continue that way.

The Wausau Flyer had died because lack of funds disallowed actual manufacture, not an uncommon cause of death for a multitude of proposed makes in the first two decades of this century.

In an attempt to recoup a bit of his substantial investment, the prototype was sold to a Marshfield physician for $2,000. The one and only Wausau Flyer has been lost to history.

Undaunted, L. H. Hall and his family continued to prosper in the automobile industry. When the Chalmers line of automobiles was discontinued in 1924, Hall became the first Maxwell dealer in the state. This relationship was successful as well. When the Maxwell firm became a part of the Chrysler Corporation in 1925, Hall became the first Chrysler dealer in the state of Wisconsin.

At least in a tertiary sense, the Hall dealership was cast into the national spotlight when President Calvin Coolidge came to Wausau to address the Wisconsin American Legion convention. The trip from the train station to the convention hall, as was all his transportation during the brief visit, was provided by Hall. The President rode in a Chrysler Phaeton, driven by L. H. Hall.

In addition to this one foray into automobile production, Hall designed and built a 20-ton stake body trailer to be used for the transportation of logs. The logging industry was still very much viable in the 1920s when this special trailer was produced. Designed to negotiate the rough terrain encountered in the logging environment, the trailer was extensively used locally and was considered a success.

The long and prosperous automotive career of L. H. Hall came to an end with his death in 1961. But the Hall legacy continued with the surviving family members.

His widow, Evelyn Hall, took over the reigns of the Chrysler and Dodge dealerships until their sale in the early 1980s. Irv Hall, their son, was involved with the dealership and automotive interests his entire life.

Although mass production of the Wausau Flyer never materialized, the efforts of L. H. Hall and Joseph A. Plier deserve to be noted. That "Wausau thread" in the tapestry of automotive history makes it that much more interesting and full textured.

Update On The Harding Automobile

By William T. Cameron

This is the history of a mysterious automobile named the Harding Steer-Safe, thought to have been built in Oshkosh, Wisconsin, somewhere around 1915, by a nephew of President Warren G. Harding.

The writer of this article volunteered to research the Harding automobile and he reported on the result of his efforts in a summer issue 1983 of the "Spark" magazine, which is the official organ of the Wisconsin Society of Automotive Historians.

This description also included his research into the histories of other vehicles which in the early part of the twentieth century had their origins in the cities of Neenah, Menasha, and Oshkosh, Wisconsin.

It is done in the context of first person reporting, as Bill Cameron did in writing to his "Spark" magazine audience.

One of the cars on a list compiled by the Wisconsin Society of Automotive Historians, the Harding was said to have been built in Oshkosh, but my research at the Oshkosh library revealed no trace of such an automobile. There was a Samuel B. Harding, but we don't find him in a city directory until 1919 and then only as a proprietor of a foundry producing boilers and steam engine equipment.

My report in "Spark" told of my visit to the Stanley G. Reynolds collection of mostly unrestored automobiles in Wetaskiwan, Alberta, Canada, and finding a Harding automobile jammed in between two other antique vehicles in the loft of an old barn where I could photograph only the front end of the car. These pictures are on the following page. Attempts to secure more information from Mr. Reynolds about the car, both in person and by subsequent letters proved fruitless. It was not until some time later that I was able to obtain some meager information about his purchase.

Over four years have elapsed. Spasmodic research has continued and we now have more of the story. But much more still remains a mystery.

Additional research began when Chet Krause sent me a page from Harrah's September 1981 auction brochure picturing and describing a 1915 Harding roadster, designated as Lot No. 73.

Chet's note reads: "Built by Harding Machine Company, Oshkosh - may be only one built (the roadster) but have a report that a coupe was also made."

A letter to Harrah's brought an 8x10 glossy of the 1915 Harding roadster showing a boxy rumble seat protected by a separate windshield. The oversize front wheel hubs apparently contained the "Steer-Safe" unit. The caption repeated the same misinformation about the Harding Machine Company of Oshkosh, Wisconsin, and the fact that the car was built by a nephew of President Warren B. Harding. A letter accompanying the picture stated that the car was sold at the September 1981 auction for $7,500 "present owner unknown."

The Harding "Steer Safe" as seen in 1915, and reported by Bill Cameron.

Keith Marvin, who loves to solve car mysteries, agreed to secure some kind of a response from Stanley G. Reynolds and after several months delay received what appears to be a work sheet or set of instructions to an employee on what to look for when picking up the car at Harrahs - as it was now clear that he was the successful bidder. This apparently solves one mystery: There was not both a Roadster and a Coupe still in existence, only the former.

The next information to surface on the Harding was Beverly Rae Kimes' write-up in the "Standard Catalog of American Cars 1805-1942." In addition to what now seems to be an unlikely claim that "two of these cars are known to exist" we find this sentence, "A reference from 1950 reported the discovery in Green Bay, during that year, of a Harding Roadster bearing 1924 license plates; another Green Bay old-timer remembers seeing a Harding Coupe."

Acting upon this Green Bay reference I wrote to Jeff Gillis, an automotive historian in northern Wisconsin, asking if he would help run down this particular reference; could it be that Hardings were built in Green Bay, not Oshkosh?

Jeff writes to Bev asking her to see what additional information might appear in her files, which of course, I should have done in the first place.

Beverly came up with two interesting items. The first a very faint copy of a letter written by a Mr. Ted Pamperin on June 27, 1960, offering to sell to Harrahs - what do you suppose? - a 1915 Harding Roadster. The letter, postmarked Green Bay, Wisconsin, June 27, 1960, mentions the fact that "the car was designed by Samuel B. Harding, a cousin of President Warren G. Harding and also a personal friend of my grandfather." Mr. Pamperin goes on to say "the car has been partially restored by me but because I am attending the University of Wisconsin and have practically no time to devote to it, I am interested in selling. The car is a one-of-a-kind automobile - we have the original plans and know that no more than 73 were built. Mine was Mr. Harding's personal car."

In Beverly's report to Jeff she says that that "reference" about a Harding having been seen in 1950 in and around Green Bay appeared as an article in the *Green Bay Gazette* early in July 1950. Through the Inter-Library Loan program I obtained a microfilm tape of the newspaper of that date, but could not find the article in question.

Jeff checked the address on that 1960 letter and found that Pamperins were listed and upon phoning found that they were Ted Pamperin's mother and father. Upon receiving this information I wrote to Mr. and Mrs. Pamperin. Several days later I received a letter from Ted's mother stating among other things: "We did know Mr. Harding as an older man. He came from Chicago to Green Bay. In Chicago he had been an architect and inventor. He was hired by the WPA to supervise construction of a shelter and a bandshell on some property donated by the Pamperin family for a Brown County public park. It was he who told us of the presidential connection. We never heard that the car was built in Oshkosh. Mr. Harding borrowed some money from our family and gave the car as security. It was abandoned by him later and given to our son and friends to restore." (Signed, Doris Pamperin.)

Mrs. Pamperin supplied son Ted's address, but a letter to him has not yet elicited a reply. Similarly a letter to the Brown County Historical Society has not been answered. However, Jeff Gillis is in touch with the research librarian at Society headquarters who promises a reply shortly.

I have also written to President Harding's home, a Division of the Ohio Historical Society, asking if President Harding had a cousin rather than a nephew Samuel B. Harding. No reply to date.

This concludes Part II of the Harding Story. Hopefully the next and final chapter will answer such questions as: If the car was not built in Oshkosh, where? Ted Pamperin says his car was the "first of 73" - what became of them? "We have the original plans" - does he still have them? Was the "Steer-Safe" front end unit patented? Just who was this Mr. Samuel B. Harding, when and where did he live?

The Harris Six
By Keith Marvin

When G. D. Harris left the automobile business in Menasha, Wisconsin, late in 1923, he left an historic legacy of having produced a handful of sporty Phaetons bearing his name, having manufactured these cars as a sideline of a tractor company and having built the cars only after bankruptcy proceedings had enveloped his business.

The Harris Six was one of those cars which was sort of known locally for a brief period and which almost never got any publicity at all outside its own bailiwick, which in this instance happened to be Menasha, Wisconsin. The Harris cars appeared to be well designed, used proven components where the make of these components are known, and were aesthetically attractive cars. What more, one might have asked then, could one ask?

The answer to this, as it turned out, could have been “The car itself.”

The Harris Six was the by-product of the U.S. Tractor Company, which moved to Menasha from Chicago in 1919 and which produced the Uncle Sam Tractor, an export piece of machinery. Shortly after its arrival in the Badger State, the company changed its name to the U.S. Tractor and Machinery Company.

Somewhere between that time and 1923, the decision was made to market a passenger car to be sold both domestically and for the export market. In those days, several automobiles were being manfactured in this country for sales overseas and the idea was a popular one.

The first public announcement of the new car appeared in the *Menasha Record's* April 30, 1923 edition, the ad including an excellent drawing of a cycle fendered, individual doorstepped, disk-wheeled sport Phaeton, complete with side-mounted spare wheels, glass wind wings, spotlight, front and rear bumpers and trunk. The picture looked almost exactly like the contemporary Winther car which had been built in Kenosha, Wisconsin, up until a few months before. This is hardly surprising, as the Winther Company had folded up and its assets had been taken over by none other than Mr. Harris.

The ad heralded the new car as “A Beautiful Car Embodying Remarkable Qualities At A Very Moderate Price,” and they weren't fooling either. Price of the seductive Phaeton was listed at $1,485.

The Harris Six of 1923.

The other more standard looking varieties were cited, the five-passenger touring car and the five-passenger "All year," which was apparently the same with the California top treatment. These models were to sell at $1,275 and $1,675 respectively. Plans approached the grandiose. "We are prepared to furnish these cars with special built Coupe and Sedan bodies," ran the advertising copy. The ad made clear that the disc wheels would be exclusively available on the touring Phaeton only.

Specifications were few and far between, although the car was described as having a 3¼ x 5-inch engine, the highest priced Warner transmission with a multiple disc clutch and a 120-inch wheelbase. By this time the U.S. Tractor and Machinery Company had undergone a further metamorphosis and the company was now billed as the Wisconsin Automotive Corporation. It even had a cable address, "Ustraco."

If the idea of manufacturing an export car wasn't so much of a novelty in those days, being a spin-off of a tractor company was. There were a few examples of this, however, notably Case, yet another product with its factory in Racine, Wisconsin. There would be another, too, operations having almost exactly coincided time wise with Harris by the Cletrac Company of Cleveland, Ohio. Cletrac, an amalgam of Cleveland and tractor, was chancing the introduction of an economical four-cylinder car, which after the first few prototypes were supplied with the Cletrac nameplate, became the Rollin after Rollin White, a company official. Whether this change was the result of honoring Mr. White or the realization of the harsh, unlovely sound of Cletrac, is open to speculation. The Cletrac/Rollin survived into 1925 and its ultimate failure was presumable due to not being quite as economical as it had set out to be.

But that's another story. The Harris Six ads continued to appear in the local press and the name of the car became a household word in Menasha and the neighboring city of Neenah.

The *Menasha Record* of July 23, 1923 announced that the company was undergoing "financial improvement." What the paper was talking about wasn't exactly clear, but a very short time later, in what was one of the rare instances of the Harris Six obtaining national notice, "Motor Age" reported, in its August issue, that the company had been reorganized with the same personnel, e.g. Christ Walter, a Menasha business man, the president; Mr. Harris vice president; Dr. A. B. Jensen, treasurer and Mr. Joseph G. Sailer, secretary. The article also stated that the firm would also engage in the manufacture of buses. An earlier rumor that the corporation would also make trucks had been vigorously denied.

But for all the promotion and all the dreams, the whole idea ended up with some petty ads, a handful of components and a number of disappointed and somewhat less affluent citizens who had invested in the venture. By the time the corporation moved into bankruptcy courts, not one prototype car had been assembled from the parts on hand.

To settle the case, the courts ordered the construction of as many of the cars as might be possible from the existing components and an estimated six to ten units were built.

According to Dr. R. A. Jensen of Menasha, who recalls the fiasco, all actual Harris Six cars were of the disc-wheeled sport Phaeton type which leads the writer to believe that these would have been the initial promotion cars for which the parts had been purchased. Apparently things moved a bit too swiftly for even a token "production."

Mr. Harris subsequently went into the production of snowplows, which, according to Dr. Jensen, proved successful in Appleton and other Wisconsin communities where they were sold and used.

As for the cars, he theorizes that both Continental and Waukesha engines were used in the few that were built. The cars were sold locally and ran for several years. None are known to survive.

This article is as written by Keith Marvin for "The Upper Hudson Valley Automobilist, Autumn 1974."

Little-known Autos Built in and Around Oshkosh, Wisconsin, Early in the Twentieth Century

By Bill Cameron

Quickly, what comes to mind when I say Oshkosh? Overalls, "Bigosh?", Trucks, maybe? Rafting on the Fox River? Sailing on Lake Winnebago? But if you asked that question in 1890 your answer would be - "Oh, that's the sawdust city," famous for it's sawmills, custom-made doors, windows, maple flooring, fancy launches, work boats, steam-powered marine engines." Not by the furthest stretch of the imagination could anyone have guessed that within the next dozen years or so Oshkosh would be the birthplace of eight automobiles, along with the cities of Neenah-Menasha, and one of the countries larger manufacturers of trucks and gasoline engines that found their way into other makes of automobiles.

While most early horseless carriages were being built by bicycle manufacturers and carriage makers, it is strange to find similar activity taking place in a city where there were neither. But remember, sawmills are powered by steam engines and motor boats were equipped with some type of motive power long before similar engines were installed in road vehicles. So it is reasonable to assume that the sawmill and marine mechanics and blacksmiths of Oshkosh would respond to that same urge that swept the country in the middle 1800s and apply their skills to building a self-propelled road vehicle.

The Ballard

The first car built on the shores of Lake Winnebago was the handiwork of a Mr. A. W. Ballard who was born in 1845 and died in 1922 at the age of 77. Originally from Whitewater, Wisconsin, he moved his gunsmithing business to Oshkosh in 1882, and soon had gained a reputation as a "fixer" of anything mechanical. It is reported that he put together his first horseless carriage in 1894 which would appear to put him right up there with the Duryea brothers and others as among the "first" designer and builder of a functional, gasoline-powered automobile.

The Ballard was essentially a buggy with high wooden wheels, hard, leather covered seats, a wooden body shell with mudguards and dashboard of leather. It was equipped with a two-cylinder unknown make of gasoline engine mounted over the rear axle; the wheels driven by bicycle chains. The car had wheel steering and cranked from the side.

A second Ballard car was quite similar to his first, except that it had smaller diameter wheels and lever steering. He drove the car to the nearby Chilton Fair where he was greeted with ridicule, sarcasm and laughter by the crowd. This so angered Mr. Ballard that he issued a challenge to race any horse-drawn vehicle at the fair around Lake Winnebago, a distance of over 100 miles. Two dandys took the challenge and to everyone's surprise, Mr. Ballard's contraption came in first.

This event came to the attention of a Wausau physician, Dr. Sauerherring, who asked Mr. Ballard to build him a four seater. This third Ballard had lever steering, heavy-duty bicycle-type wire wheels and kerosene headlights. It is said that the good doctor found this vehicle far superior to his horse and buggy rig, especially when the call came to deliver a baby at three o'clock in the morning.

It is not known why Mr. Ballard did not continue making automobiles as he was only 50 years of age in 1895 and lived another 27 years pursuing his gun and fix-it business and handling difficult mechanical problems anywhere they arose in and around the city of Oshkosh.

The Doman

The next automotive activity in Oshkosh occurred some three years later with an announcement in "The Horseless Age" of October 18th, 1899, which stated "H. C. Doman, Oshkosh, Wisconsin, has designed a gasoline carriage which he intends to manufacture." Research has turned up very little information on this alleged automobile. However, the Oshkosh City Directory of 1898, lists Mr. Doman as the proprietor of the Union Iron Works and Foundry at 118 Marion Street, and in 1900 his company is listed as "manufacturers of engines." To add to the mystery, articles published some twenty years later in the "Weekly Northwestern" referring to the Ballard car states: "The first car ever built in Oshkosh was made by H. C. Doman." There is no further reference to Mr. Doman's automobile until 1903 when the City Directory states that the Union Iron Works is a "manufacturer of marine gasoline engines and complete launches, marine and stationary engines, dowel door machinery and steam pumps." Nine years later, in 1912, we find that Harry Doman and Herman C. Doman are listed as mechanics employed by the Doman Motor Car Company - but containing no evidence that an automobile was being manufactured at this time.

The Radford Automobile

Although listed as an Oshkosh built car in "The American Car Since 1775," no record of such a car was found. The City Directory of 1895 lists the Radford Brothers (Stephen, William, and Charles W.) as manufacturers of lumber, sash, doors, blinds and other wood products. If they built an automobile it probably was a single experimental model not offered commercially.

The National Automobile

"1775" also carries a reference to an automobile called the National, reportedly built in Oshkosh in 1902-03. The City Directories of this period list a National Automobile and Motor Company, 18 Light Street, H. H. Muggley and Charles Jameson, proprietors. However, efforts to learn something of the alleged car were fruitless.

As mentioned earlier, Oshkosh at the turn of the century was a bustling boat building center and this included the manufacture and sale of marine engines which were not only used to equip Oshkosh built boats but were sold throughout the United States. One of these engine manufacturers, first listed in 1903, was the United States Engine Works, Samuel Sutton and Gustaf Boak, proprietors, "machinists and manufacturers of stationary and marine gasoline engines." This company survived until 1916 but there is no evidence that they built engines for road vehicles.

Another company with a similar name - United States Manufacturing Company - is listed in 1900 and subsequent years as "manufacturers of bicycle sundries, gasoline engines and glue applying machines." (This latter machine was undoubtedly utilized by the Diamond Sticky Fly Paper Company, the manufacturer of a familiar product emanating from Oshkosh in the early 1900s.)

The TMF High Wheeler - 1909

The exception that proves the rule that most automobiles were designed and built by bicycle or carriage manufacturers is the unlikely contribution of J. T. Termaat, a portrait photographer of some prominence in Oshkosh from 1898 until at least 1910. Before the turn of the century Termaat joined forces with Louis J. Monahan, a machinist with J. A. Barnes Company to form the Monahan and Termaat Company, a manufacturer of "gas engines." The listing was changed the next year to "manufacturers of marine gasoline engines" and very quickly the company began advertising nationwide in both the commercial and pleasure boating magazines. For some strange reason the names were reversed in 1905 when the company moved to a new address at 34-36 River Street, manufacturing a one-cylinder, two-cycle, water-cooled engine with make-and-break ignition. Each year saw the addition of additional cylinders and by 1908 the company was advertising a four-cylinder engine, designed for boats but also manufacturing stationary engines, electric light outfits and pumping engines with all sizes from 1½ to 100 hp.

In 1909, photographer Termaat and machinist Monahan approached H. Homer Fahrney, a wealthy resident of Oshkosh who had financed many a manufacturing venture in the city, to put some of his wealth behind the building of an automobile. The result was a car called the TMF (Termaat-Monahan-Fahrney) High Wheeler. At this point the partners sold out their interest in the marine engine company; however, the new owners continued to do business under the name of Termaat and Monahan. The automobile company was called the Badger Manufacturing Company and in 1914 built a narrow-tread, cut-down two seater called the T-M Cycle Car. However, little is known of either this or the original TMF High Wheeler.

In 1916, a new company was formed called the Universal Motor Company with Louis J. Monahan as president and J. D. Termaat as vice president. This company lasted for three years but confined their activities to engines and other auto-related products, one of which was a device for supplying air and water for automobiles at street corners, several of which were in everyday use in Oshkosh in the middle teens. The apparatus kept the air hose up out of the way by suspending it from an iron arm or crane hinged to a heavy spring of the type we now see at RV sanitary dump stations.

Zeibell Cycle Car

There are several references in early automotive literature to the Zeibell Cycle Car, presumably manufactured in 1914 by A. C. Zeibell. Although little is known about the alleged automobile, there is considerable information on the Zeibell family and Arthur C. in particular, from 1900 to 1920 and beyond. Of the 20 or so Zeibells listed in the Oshkosh City Directory in 1900, only two appear to have been associated with gasoline engines and possibly the manufacture of automobiles. Early in the century, Arthur Zeibell is listed as a pattern maker for the Termaat and Monahan Company. Also listed is Robert L. Zeibell, a foreman for the same company. Apparently the brothers were loyal employees for when, in 1914, J. D. Termaat and L. J. Monahan left the original company bearing their name, to form the Badger Manufacturing Company, both brothers are listed as working in the foundry at 39 Ceape Street. The company is listed as manufacturers of "auto engines." When Messrs. T. and M. started a second business called the Universal Foundry Company, Robert Zeibell was appointed president and Arthur C. as secretary. The product at this point is listed as "patterns and castings."

It seems logical to believe that the alleged Zeibell Cycle Car and the reported TMF Cycle Car, both produced in Oshkosh in 1914, were the same automobile as no reference to either could be found in either the Historical Society or the Oshkosh Public Library.

Badger Automobile Company
By John Gunnell

An entry in "The Standard Catalog of American Cars 1805-1942" seems simple enough. It says that, in 1909, in Clintonville, Wisconsin, "the Badger Four Wheel Drive Auto Company was organized for the manufacture of vehicles utilizing the Zachow-Besserdich patents."

Where is Clintonville? What was the town like in 1909? And what are the Zachow-Besserdich patents? The answers to these questions are available. They tell us additional facts about a company that still exists today; a company that is still producing Wisconsin-built motor vehicles.

Clintonville is a small city located to the northeast of my hometown of Iola. Locals in this area tell people, "draw an 'X' through the state of Wisconsin and you'll hit Iola." Clintonville lies in the northeast corner of our county. Therefore, if you move slightly northeast of your 'X', you'll find Clintonville.

The city has one main highway and dozens of tree-lined residential streets. Highway 45 travels north-south, and becomes Main Street in the heart of Clintonville, a stretch of no more than ten blocks, if that. Traveling down Main, you'll see a hardware store, furniture store, a Hardee's, a feedmill, a used-car lot and other buildings. You'll probably have few hints that the FWD Corporation, where FWD trucks and Seagrave fire engines are built, lies just a few blocks off the main drag.

Ninety years ago, the town of Clintonville was little more than a few clapboard dwellings and shops clustered on the banks of the Pigeon River. Main Street had not yet been paved and the biggest building in town was Folman's Department Store. It provided clothing and other necessities to the village's 480 families and 1,837 residents. Other "big fish" in this "small pond" were county clerk Frank Gause, Joe Cotton, owner of the *Clintonville Gazette*, and attorney Walter A. Olen. Somewhat further down in the pecking order were Otto Zachow and his brother-in-law William Besserdich. They operated the local machine shop.

As machinists, the pair developed an interest in horseless carriages. The state of Wisconsin had about 3,000 of these contraptions when the year 1905 began, and at least 3,001 by early the next year. The new one was a Reo that Zachow and Besserdich obtained, as a result of becoming agents for the Michigan automaker. The maroon, four-place touring car was delivered in February of 1906.

1912 FWD, touring.

Newspaperman Cotton described the car as a four-seater runabout weighing 975 pounds and featuring an 8-hp engine capable of 26 miles per hour. After it appeared in town, interest in automobiles rose and, before very long, Dr. W. H. Finney purchased a car from the machinists. Three more automobiles were sold before the summer ended.

The new-fangled contraptions impressed local residents with their advantages and disadvantages. Both the demonstrator and Dr. Finney's car were involved in horse-frightening incidents, with resulting damages and lawsuits. This, of course, was not uncommon. Wisconsin, like many states, would soon pass a right-of-way law, requiring motorists to stop to let horse-drawn vehicles pass. Still, the movement to put Americans on wheels was unstoppable, in Clintonville, as in every other locale.

As Clintonville's new auto enthusiasts put their machines to the test, certain limitations of automobiles became obvious. On a 20-odd-mile trip to the town of Waupaca, Dr. Finney and attorney Walter A. Olen got stuck at the bottom of a sandy hill. They ground the cogs off the Reo's sprocket, while trying to extract the vehicle. On a late spring trip to the village of Marion, Finney and Zachow ran into mud, caused by a thaw, and sunk the car in up to its axles. Such experiences prompted the two machinists to look for ways to perfect motor travel over unimproved roads.

Otto Zachow had been raised on a farm, where inventiveness and adaptability played important roles in daily life. He knew how to make things with his hands and understood basic mechanical principles. He had not yet, however, stumbled upon the principle that would help make him famous. Instead, his first thoughts leaned in the direction of more power. He guessed that a car with a bigger engine than the Reo would do better on wet, sandy, snowy, icy, or muddy unpaved roads.

Later, Zachow would reveal that the idea for his four-wheel-drive system sprung up during a longer journey to the city of Appleton, about 60 miles south of Clintonville. On that trip, he carelessly drove his car down a hill, into a ravine with a flat bottom. At first, he continued to the bottom and turned the car around. Then he attempted to climb back up the hill going forward. He could not. The front wheels would not climb. Instead, they merely dug into the hillside. Eventually, Zachow turned the car around and tried again. This time, the powered wheels climbed the hill. It was then clear to the machinist that a car with powered wheels at both ends would have superior climbing power.

Zachow then devised a double-Y-shaped universal joint encased in a drop-forged ball-and-socket that permitted the front wheels of a car to turn without interfering with the transmission of power. Next, he approached Walter A. Olen to help him organize and patent his idea. His son, an apprentice machinist with the Northwestern Railroad, in Fond du Lac, helped him create patent drawings. Patent applications were filed on August 1, 1907, but there were numerous delays in obtaining them. Many others were working on similar inventions at the same time. So, it took almost a year before the patents came through.

After they arrived, the machinists started work on a new automobile chassis of their own design. It featured four-wheel-drive and a center-mounted "transform" (transfer) case that could direct power to both the front and rear axles A cross-compound steam engine was used as its power plant.

In tests, the new car performed quite well. The *Clintonville Gazette* noted, "They have plowed through drifts three-feet-deep, pushed huge billows ahead of them, gone over the roughest and most slippery roads and climbed the steepest hills at 25 miles an hour... There is talk of organizing a company. The car should be a winner from the word go."

That was an exaggeration, however. The boys had bills to pay and the steam engine proved to be less suitable than a gasoline power plant. They had also neglected their business somewhat. So they set to work catching up with their backlog, to raise enough to pay the lawyers, buy an engine and pay for a new body they had ordered for their car. Nevertheless, Zachow had faith in his idea and felt that a fortune could be had if it was perfected.

With the help of Dr. Finney (who agreed to bankroll a one-third share), the sum of $35,000 was raised to capitalize an automaking venture. Together, the three men organized the Badger Four Wheel Drive Auto Company "for the manufacture of vehicles utilizing the Zachow-Besserdich patents."

The deal called for Zachow and Besserdich to give up exclusive rights to their patents to Dr. Finney, in exchange for his financial backing. The machinists were to continue their normal work, while providing the labor required to manufacture the new four-wheel-drive car. Both of them mortgaged their homes to pay off back debts. Other problems evolved, such as the beginning of a used-car market that held down demand for new cars. By the end of the year, Dr. Finney was discouraged. He had spent $5,000 and not a single car, beyond the test vehicle, had been built.

At this point, it was lawyer Walter A. Olen who was called to the rescue. Otto Zachow visited him to discuss the problems of the Badger Four Wheel Drive Auto Company. His strong belief in his four-wheel-drive principle inspired Olen to start making the rounds of local businessmen. He broached the idea of raising capital through the sale of stock to them and through a city-wide fund-raising effort in conjunction with the Clintonville Advancement Association. He pushed the concept of building up the company for the benefit of the city, rather than tearing it apart.

Olen's ideas, backed by a lot of hard work created some positive initial results. Dr. Finney was reimbursed. Zachow and Besserdich received stock in exchange for their patent rights and a board of directors was established to create a new company. Walter A. Olen was elected its president. In August 1909, a factory site was secured. In September, the Badger Four Wheel Drive Auto Company became the Four Wheel Drive Auto Company.

This new firm was far from an immediate success. In fact, serious problems and squabbles would continue to plague it for over a year. Sales of cars were few and far between. But, it would eventually make the grade and immortalize the initials FWD in the truck manufacturing industry. The Badger part of the name would pass into oblivion, without a single "production" car having been built. However, the Badger Four Wheel Drive Company was the springboard for FWD Corporation.

Chapter Seven
WISCONSIN-BUILT TRUCKS

On Our Own!
From Winther Truck to Pullman
By Martin P. Winther

This article was submitted by Vincent Ruffolo, as written by Martin P. Winther in 1976.

In retrospect, with many years of experience in the business world, I look back upon the formative period of the Winther Motor Truck Company to try to pinpoint what went wrong and how it could have been made successful. Even now it is difficult to see how it could have succeeded in the face of circumstances not foreseen nor under control. I am telling the story for the first time in this narrative and providing a synopsis of the events that made up the life and demise of the Winther Motor Truck Company, later known as Winther Motors, Incorporated.

The action started in 1916 when I was almost 28 years old. In considering a merchandising force for the Winther Company the possible availability of many of the best men from the disbanding Jeffery-Nash truck group was a factor of real interest. Walter D. Rightmire, the Jeffery truck sales manager, offered his services which were later accepted.

First, the group that expected to control the corporation was agreed upon. Forming the nucleus were Martin P. Winther; William Martinson, former division manager of the Jeffery Company; W. D. Rightmire; and William Hinricks, treasurer of Wisconsin Bridge and Iron Company in Milwaukee. Their respective responsibilities were as follows: president and general manager, Martin P. Winther; vice president of manufacturing, William Martinson; sales manager, W. D. Rightmire; and treasurer, William Hinricks. Later the following were added: chief engineer, Virgil Downing; secretary, Charles Abbott; and accountant, H. Hagman.

A budget for three years of operation was prepared by the group based upon the known overhead costs and estimated volume of the one and one-half, two and one-half and three ton trucks scheduled ahead for three years. The five and seven ton truck line would come in production after three years. Capital requirements were calculated to be $300,000 at the start with another $100,000 to be added in two years.

The Corporation was formed in 1916, and a group of men made the original cash subscriptions. The first stockholders included Dr. E. W. Timm, George P. Mayer and William Hinricks, all of Milwaukee; and Martin Winther, William Martinson, and Louis H. Bill, all of Kenosha. This group supplied the bulk of the $300,000. A total of over 40 were holders of the original shares. A substantial portion of the $100,000 stock issued later was held by C. I. Sykes and Charles Lynch from Ardmore, Oklahoma.

The budget indicated that the company would be operating in the red for the first year. The red ink was calculated to disappear in the 15th to 18th month from the start. Actually, the company was making a profit 12 months from the date of incorporation.

The motor truck industry in these years consisted of about 300 small, assembly-type plants. The items they actually manufactured were the frame, driver's cab, and controls. Complete engines were supplied chiefly by Continental, Hercules, Wisconsin Motors and several others. Fuller, Spicer, Cotta and others made transmissions. Axles, front and rear, were supplied by Eaton, Timken, Clark Equipment Company and others. Wheels, tires, springs, steering gear and universal driveshafts were supplied from numerous sources.

A few motor truck companies manufactured some of their own components and were, therefore, more solidly rooted to weather the financial storm that lay ahead. The strongest of these were General Motors, White Motors, Mack, Autocar, Ford and Dodge. These manufacturers were able to survive the chaos that followed the ending of World War I. The "assemblers" were not and collapsed.

Once the Winther Truck Company was in operation, it became apparent that there was an urgent need for special application equipment that we could and should supply as truck manufacturers. Engineering development and sales promotion concentrated efforts in that direction, resulting in a definite increase both in sales volume and profitability of the product.

The four-wheel drive feature was added to the line. The free steering arrangement used in the four-wheel drives was developed by Anthony and me, and is still used on similar drives in production today although the patent has long since expired.

The Long Lines Division of American Telephone and Telegraph was in the market for a four-wheel drive truck to carry an engine-driven posthole digger. The Winther Company designed and built a number of such posthole diggers for the Long Lines Division before World War I interfered. After the war ended, the posthole digger continued as a standard piece of equipment for telephone line construction, but, of course, manufactured by others.

Automobile shipments to Australia had come to be almost nonexistent at this time. A group of financiers from Australia selected J. W. McGee to come to the United States to find someone with capacity and know-how to assemble a specific number of automobiles to be made from standard components then available on the open market. They hoped to buy 5,000 cars to be assembled and shipped to Australia as quickly as possible. The credit was established, and the body design was furnished by the group. The proposition they made to me was too lucrative to pass up, and there was sufficient space available in the plant to make these assemblies.

A body builder in Indiana agreed to make the body, completely finished, ready to assemble to the chassis. Orders were placed for frames, engines, transmissions, springs, wheels, steering gear, and other accessories on the basis of releases of 500 cars guaranteed. The balance was to be released on 40 days notice to complete the 5,000 order at a production rate of ten per day. After the first 500 automobiles were completed, priorities for war material interfered with completion of the total order, and component suppliers accepted cancellation of 4,500 units.

J. W. McGee saw the last car of the original 500 shipped off to Australia. Shortly thereafter he went to Columbia, South Carolina, where he had originally lived, to visit with his mother. While there he succumbed to a heart attack, and thus ended the saga of the Winther automobile, for that was the nameplate on the cars.

FWD/FWD Corporation
By John Gunnell

The FWD truck was the outgrowth of a crucial invention by Otto Zachow who, with his brother-in-law William Besserdich, ran a machine shop in Clintonville, Wisconsin. This invention was a double-Y universal joint encased in a ball-and-socket joint which allowed power to be applied to the front-driving wheels of a car that could still be steered.

After the initial formation of the Badger Four Wheel Drive Company to utilize the Zachow/Besserdich patents, an automobile manufacturing company called Four Wheel Drive Company was formed through the sale of stock to local businessmen and other investors. Zachow and Besserdich were given stock shares in exchange for patent rights to the invention. Attorney Walter A. Olen, who conceived the plan to save the original company, became the first president of the firm.

The first Four Wheel Drive Car, built under the original Badger name, was known as the "Battleship." To promote its unique abilities, the company offered an award of $1,000 to any automobile that could follow the Battleship for ten minutes. In the summer of 1911, some 116 rear-drive cars accepted the challenge and all failed. In 12,000 miles of testing, the performance of the Four Wheel Drive Car was never surpassed by another vehicle. It was virtually worn-out proving its capabilities. During the early years, the company's test drivers, such as Chauncey Williams, Frank Dorn and Luella Bates, played a big role in promoting its products.

Still, things did not go well at first. The original general manager quit the company and Walter A. Olen made three important decisions. The first was to halt the practice of law and devote all his energies to being the company's president. The second was to hire Peter Batenburg as factory superintendent. The third was to offer Otto Zachow a $450 bonus to complete construction of a Four Wheel Drive Truck by February 1912. Most historians use 1912 as the current truck company's starting date. The original plan was to produce passenger cars. However, the two-ton truck became an important addition to the company's early production run of seven cars.

One of the early FWD cars was given an express-like body to haul mail to the factory. Eventually, it was sent, by the U.S. Army, along with several other makes of trucks, on a 1,500-mile cross-country test from Washington, D.C., to Atlanta, Georgia, to Indianapolis, Indiana. It proved very successful in operation over difficult terrain.

As a result of this and other tests, with World War I as a catalyst, orders for three-ton and five-ton FWD trucks mushroomed. The first order for 50 trucks to be sent to England, was received in the fall of 1914. At that point, the company was in such bad shape that the entire factory had to be mortgaged to raise $200,000 to build the trucks.

By 1915, FWD stockholders were suddenly earning $30 per share and a stock dividend of 100 percent was granted to raise the capitalization of the firm to $500,000. About 400 trucks were manufactured that year. The allies in Europe had also placed standing orders for 200 more vehicles per month. There were now FWD trucks being sent to countries throughout the world.

On February 25, 1916, the U.S. Government chased the bandit Pancho Villa into Mexico. To make their 500-mile raid 200 miles into Mexico, an order for 147 FWD trucks was placed. Trucks already bound for England were repainted and sent to Mexico. By 1916, production was reaching into the thousands.

Late that year, it was clear that America would soon be entering the war in Europe. FWD made a decision to cancel its European contracts in the case of such action. That July, the U.S. Army placed a $12 million order for 3,750 three-ton trucks. Things improved steadily thereafter, to the point where three other manufacturers (Mitchell, Kissel and Premier) were eventually licensed to produce FWD trucks, in addition to those being made in a greatly expanded factory at Clintonville. Ultimately, 15,000 of the three-ton Model B trucks were produced for the armed forces. The company had easily become the largest producer of four-wheel-drive trucks in the world.

The famous Model B cab-over was powered by a Wisconsin four-cylinder engine with a two-speed Cotta constant mesh transmission and FWD's own front- and rear-driving axles.

With the end of the war, the military found itself with some 30,000 trucks and nearly half of them were FWDs. Sales of the surplus trucks glutted the markets in Europe and America. Eventually, the majority were sent to state highway departments to use in a postwar road-building program. Providing needed parts for so many trucks kept the company busy after the war.

Eventually, the old trucks wore out and new ones were needed. By this time, FWD had a good reputation and was able to grow. A factory in Canada was opened in 1919 and the Menominee Motor Truck Company of Michigan joined the FWD family in 1921.

The Model B, which weighed 6,400

pounds, sold for $4,000. It remained in production through the early 1930s, with many refinements, such as pneumatic tires. A conventional type FWD truck was developed in the late-1920s for both civilian and military use.

FWDs were used in many specialized fields, from snowplowing to oil field work and mining. Engineers from the firm worked with various industries to modify trucks for their specific needs. A range of lighter, two-ton class trucks was developed in the mid-1930s. They featured modernized cabs, one-piece windshields and V-type radiators. Cab-over-engine (COE) models bowed in 1937 with streamlined cabs and V-windshields. A four-door COE truck was also introduced for use by utility crews ... an industry first. By 1938, Cummins diesel engines were available.

FWDs were never well-known for the popular pontoon fender styling, but there was one heavyweight conventional series that did have them in the late 1930s. It included the T-40 and T-60 models and, possibly, others.

A restyled COE model called the T-32 was announced in 1940. It had a 40,000 pound GVW and a 98-hp six linked to a five-speed transmission, with overdrive optional. Full-floating front and rear axles were of the single-reduction, spiral-bevel type, with manually-locking differential for use on slippery roads. A conventional TT32 was also offered at this time. It had a rounded grille and a V-windshield.

Other conventional FWDs included SU. SUA, CUA and MJ5 models in the four-to-six-ton range. Generally, 80-hp FWD and Waukesha sixes were used in gas-engined FWD trucks of 1½ to 15-tons, with four models offering diesel. The 1940 prices ranged from $2,440 to $12,225.

During World War II, FWD supplied the armed forces with heavy-duty civilian-style trucks (noticeably COE models), plus special SU-based open cab COEs, made for the U.S. Marine Corps, with individual windshields for the driver and mate. A series of postwar 4x4 conversions were added to the line for light-duty work, along with some medium-duty high-frame models built for road scraping. There was also a long-nosed heavy-duty version of the Model U with a GVW of 44,000 pounds.

In the 1950s, FWD adopted new cabs for conventional models. A popular offering was the "Chicago" cab, shared with IHC and other truck companies. Two types of COEs were marketed, one using a conventional Chicago cab that was widened and the other using a 1958 Ford C-series cab with grille and fender modifications. Several other new models also appeared at this time. A very short wheelbase model was specially designed to go anywhere off the highway to do earth boring for utility poles. The cab was of a forward slanting type. This BXU model was nicknamed "The Blue Ox."

FWD's "Tractioneer" line first appeared in 1958 and lasted well over 20 years. The initial flat-nosed COE model was soon joined by conventional, some of which had the front axle set back to a position under their Dodge-type cab. In addition to 4x4 models, there were 6x6s, 10x8s (some with tandem front axles) and 12x10s (also with tandem front axles). Tractioneers are used mainly as concrete mixers and in other construction industry applications.

Perhaps the most sensational vehicles ever produced by FWD were the "Terracruzer" 8x8 off-highway carriers. These were used in Pakistan's Pak-Stanvac project to haul full loads of oil well drilling equipment into monsoon regions where no other trucks could go. The chassis alone weighed 22,000 pounds, but ground pressure was lowered by using unique, watermelon-shaped tires. The Terracruzer's capacity was eight tons and it was powered by a 250-hp turbocharged Cummins diesel driving through a 10-speed Fuller gear box and FWD transfer case.

Another FWD development of the late 1960s was the 8x8 CRF (crash-fire-rescue) truck for airport standby emergencies. These P-2 models are enormous heavyweights at 65,000 pounds. They are powered by two 340-hp engines driving through an FWD-designed collector box to dual transmissions. Either engine can be used to power the trucks or their pumps, or both may be used to power the truck to 55-miles-per-hour, in less than a minute, with 2,200 gallons of water and 200 gallons of liquid foam on board.

The company changed its name from Four Wheel Drive Auto Company to FWD Corporation in 1960. In 1963, it bought the fire apparatus division of the Seagrave Corporation of Columbus, Ohio.

In the mid-1960s, a series of "Forward Movers" with non-powered front axles and 6x4 drive was introduced for highway service. Conventional, such as the B5-2178 model, looked much like Tractioneers with their Dodge-type cabs, but had smoother fenders and, in some cases, forward-slanting windshields.

Crane carriers have been a regular part of FWD's lineup for years, the majority being one-man COEs with drives up to 10x8. Even as early as 1939, FWD removed the right half of some conventional cabs to use that space for shovel booms when in transit.

Diversity has always been part of FWD's purpose-built marketing program. In 1970, for instance, the company offered 93 models in five different drives, with conventional or set-back axle arrangements, various engines, conventional or COE cabs, many transmissions and a wide range of rear axle configurations, plus choices of vacuum, air or hydraulic brakes. Production in certain years may go into the thousands of units, while in other years, just a few hundred are built.

Oneida of Green Bay
By John Gunnell

The Oneida Truck Company was located in Green Bay, Wisconsin. There are three distinct phases in the company's history. From the beginning in 1912 to 1923, it was known as Oneida Motor Truck Company. From 1924 to 1928, the name Oneida Manufacturing Company was used. From 1928 to the end in 1930, it was the Oneida Truck Company.

The Oneida name comes from a tribe of Native Americans which migrated from New York state to Wisconsin. Today, the Oneida Nation still has a reservation in the Green Bay area. One of the regions popular attractions is a casino run by the Oneida Nation.

The first Oneida trucks were made in four sizes from one-ton to three and one-half-tons. All of them were powered by four-cylinder Continental engines. A three-speed Cotta transmission was used with Timken worm-drive rear axles.

By 1919, a five-ton truck was added to the range, along with Hinkley engines and Wisconsin axles. For a time, the company produced an agricultural tractor, in addition to trucks. This was, most likely, the motivation for the name change in 1924.

From 1920 through 1922, a two-ton electric truck was offered. This was of a cab-over-engine design, like most electrics of that time.

Financial difficulties caused two reorganizations of Oneida during the 1920s, but construction continued on a small scale despite the problems. Trucks in the one-ton to five-ton range were turned out, as well as 25-, 30- and 42-passenger buses. Continental and Hinkley engines were used until 1927, when a second reorganization brought a switch to Hercules power plants.

Other Wisconsin-Built Trucks
By John Everitt

The land called Wisconsin lies within those borders known as the "Cheddar Curtain." The first European to set foot here, landed in Green Bay in 1634. His name was Father Nicolet. The fertile, thickly-wooded and well-watered country he found would ultimately spawn a growing, industrious society, and one that was skilled enough to exploit the native materials to advantage and create their own powered wagons of commerce that we have come to call trucks.

America's "Third Coast" is the Great Lakes. The coastline of the Great Lakes was explored and settled long before America's interior. Ships and canoes enabled the early traders to bypass native Indians and impassable terrain. By the

1850s there was a lively shipping industry on the Great Lakes. Wisconsin's agriculture and industry was shipping valuable grain, lumber, and lead ore eastward and receiving coal, pig iron, and immigrants on low cost back haul. The ships' owners were so eager to get back to Wisconsin's ports that they would haul any cheap freight to subsidize the trip back west from Cleveland, or Buffalo. Finished implements and machinery from the East were prohibitively expensive, yet the demand for plows, wagons, and sawmill equipment was intense. With such a ready source of coal and iron on the docks and so much demand from the expanding interior, the immigrant craftsman leaped into foundry and manufacturing work. Green Bay, Manitowoc, Sheboygan, Milwaukee, Racine and Kenosha are some of the lakefront towns to put their names on machinery before the time of the Civil War. Every one of these towns had a shipyard, too.

The railroad boom of the 1870s and the 1880s brought commerce and prosperity to the towns of the interior, forever dimming the prospects of lake ports. The prosperity of a railroad town was dependent on the monopolistic whim of a single carrier, unlike that of a lake port where any ship may call. The state government was ill equipped to control the clout of the railroads and their free-spending lobbyists. Wisconsin's voters were mostly farmers who did not prosper from the predatory freight rate structures imposed by the railroads. The Grange movement was a political force then, and sought an alternative route to market for the produce of Wisconsin's farms, and that was better roads.

In 1873 a clergyman and physician named Dr. Carhart built a light, steam-powered buggy and drove it on the streets of Racine. In 1875 his success inspired the state legislature to post a $10,000 prize for any vehicle that could traverse the 200 miles from Green Bay to Madison at an average speed of five miles per hour. Perhaps it was for this competition that William Sternberg, of Sterling fame, built his steam wagon in that same year.

Vehicle technology was moving ahead, but the roads of Wisconsin were impassable six months out of a year. A given stretch of road may be clear for most of its length, but one snowdrift, mud hole or steep grade could render its whole length useless. The dairy farms and dairy industry were especially dependent on regular pickups and deliveries year around and bad roads were proving costly.

It is the turn of the century in Milwaukee and the companies whose names are household words are in full swing or just starting up, such as Allis-Chalmers, Harnischfeger, Fairbanks-Morse, Evinrude, Harley-Davidson and Briggs & Stratton. Easy access to ice, grain, and wood for barrels has made Milwaukee lager beer nationally famous.

A smaller company called Johnson Controls started building a line of trucks in 1901. Already a high technology company in their day, Johnson-built trucks alongside their core business of heating controls and communication systems for large buildings, a field that they still lead today. Their first truck, a one ton, was steam powered with an underfloor boiler and chain drive. Later models were gasoline powered with an engine built under license from Renault. In 1907 the Johnson Company discontinued vehicle manufacture, but not before building the first U.S. postal truck fleet.

There were at least 26 other truck manufacturers who started in Milwaukee prior to 1912, but the only picture evidence found so far are of the Brodesser, the Progress, the Smith-Milwaukee, the Stegeman and the Sternberg. One may recognize some of these more prominent component makers who made the truck assembly business so easy to get into: LeRoi, Wisconsin, Waukesha, Wisconsin (Timken) Axle, and A. O. Smith.

The Sternberg truck was the predecessor of the Sterling, the truck that is second only to the Mack. The same William Sternberg who built the steam wagon 30 years earlier came to Milwaukee in 1904 to look for manufacturing space after his Davenport, Iowa, shop had burned to the ground. He leased two floors in the Brodesser Elevator factory. One of his

Johnson Controls, 1st truck, 1901, one-ton

sons, Ernst, became partner with Robert G. Hayssen, later president of Sterling, and together they built the Hay-Berg roadster and raced it at the West Allis State Fair Park where the Indy cars still race today. Their gear ratio was too tall to accelerate quickly and they could not keep up. Ernst, who was driving, become so frustrated that he drove the car through the fence and left the race. The winner was Henry Ford.

In 1906, the same year that his father's landlord, Brodesser, built his first truck, William Sternberg Jr. was working at the Meiselbach Motor Wagon Company in North Milwaukee. Meiselbach had a two-ton model and a one-ton express. The two Sternberg brothers discussed with their father the possibility of building their own trucks. Within a year the first Sternberg was completed with a friction-type variable speed drive and chains for the final drive. This 1914 Sternberg, now owned by Lloyd Van Horn, was found in a Wisconsin barn in 1938 or 1939 and was then restored in the Sterling factory. It is believed to be the only one left.

Brodesser, 1912, later called Juno

Progress, 1912

Smith-Milwaukee, 1912

Stegeman, 1914, model 1526

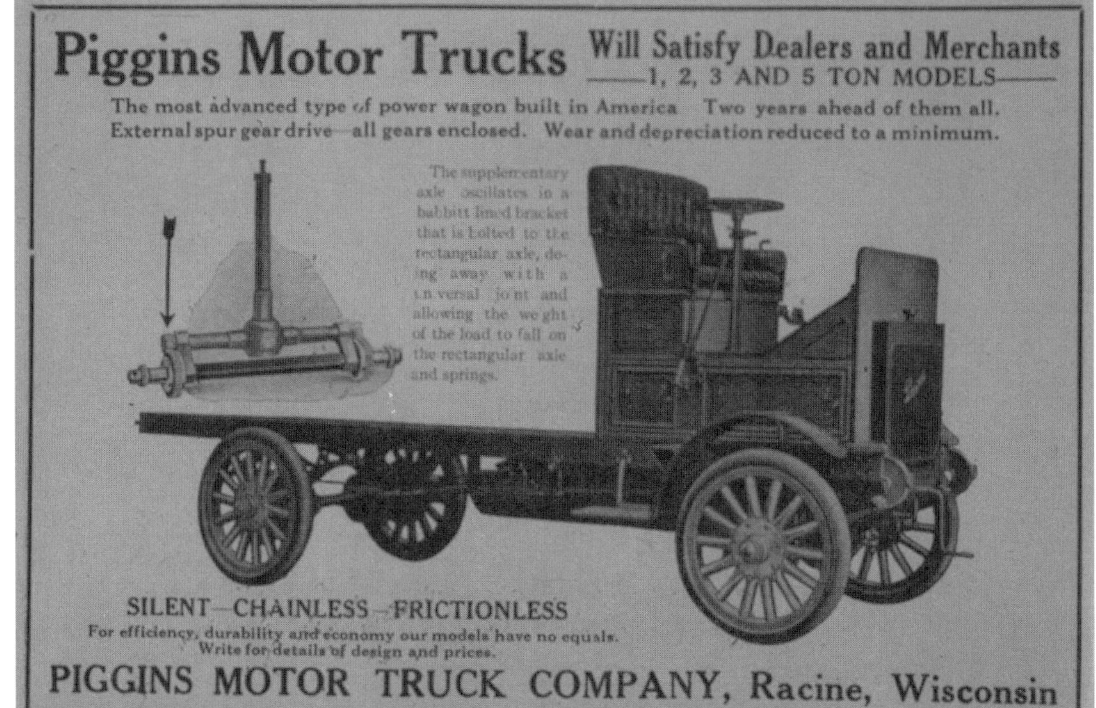

Piggins, 1912

Sternberg, later Sterling, 1st truck, 1907

When the Great War began in 1914, the market for heavy-duty trucks took off overnight. Well-made trucks found eager buyers in the French and British governments. The export agents working for Sternberg could not overcome the objections raised by the Allies over the German origin of the Sternberg name. The name "Sterling" was sufficiently Anglicized yet still resembled the original name enough to maintain recognition. The Sternbergs were two years ahead of their German-American neighbors in erasing the "old country" flavor of their enterprise, no matter how painful. With America's entry into World War I the print, film, and music media whipped up an anti-German hysteria campaign that hung like a dark cloud over cities such as Cincinnati, St. Louis, Chicago and Milwaukee. Sauerkraut became "Liberty Cabbage." Up until that time German culture and language were widely celebrated. However, German-Americans were at best ambivalent about the war if not outrightly pro-Kaiser. Sterling built 489 class B Liberty trucks for the war.

Sternberg, later Sterling, 1914, two-ton

The "trucks with the wood-lined frame" were well-positioned in the marketplace to weather the postwar glut of trucks and truck makers with modern, handsome styling and high quality, heavy-duty construction.

In 1932 Sterling became the first U.S. manufacturer to install Diesel engines as factory equipment. The model FD 195 5H's were sold to Valley Freight Lines of Fresno, California, and were equipped with Cummins H6 engines. Sterling had another first with a supercharged model going to a mining company in Argentina that operated at the 12,000- to 14,000-foot elevation. Originally designed for 18-ton payloads, these trucks eventually carried 30-ton payloads when equipped with a semitrailer and 93,600-pound gross weight in 1935. In 1936, Sterling was first with a true tilting-cab truck because it left no obstructing sheet metal in the way of the mechanic.

Sterling, 1928

Sterling, 1923, model WB, 2 1/2 ton. Photo courtesy of the Hays Antique Truck Museum, Woodland, California.

Endorsed by none other than George Raft of gangster movie fame, the model J was meant to keep Sterling users loyal to Sterling though their heads may have been turned by Diamond T's or Kenilworths. The odd grill treatment resembled an old Wurlitzer jukebox, perhaps.

The U.S. government paid the Sterling Company a supreme compliment during World War II by using so many trucks, both chain and shaft drive, with little or no modification to the running gear. Although exclusively non tactical in their deployment, Sterling trucks served nobly in construction, rescue, recovery, and transport roles.

Military vehicle collectors might wish that the war had gone on long enough that some of these Sterling tactical prototypes would have gone into production. The 12 ton, 8x8, the model T26 was powered by the American LaFrance 275 hp, V-12 and could climb over a 42-inch-high vertical wall or negotiate a 53-inch mud pit with a gross weight of 85,000 pounds. This armor transport version hauled a T26 heavy tank for a gross weight of 180,000 pounds. Later prototypes were equipped with the Ford GAA 1,100-cubic-inch V-8 tank engine that provided 525 hp and twice the torque of the American-LaFrance V-12.

On June 1, 1951, the ownership of Sterling passed to the White Motor Company in a stock swap. Production continued in Milwaukee for two more years with the new nameplate as the only difference. On July 1, 1953, the operations moved to the White factory in Cleveland. Another 128 Sterling-Whites were built in Cleveland. Except for some Bucyrus-Erie crane chassis, that was it.

Sterling was the last truck manufacturer of any note to build chain drive trucks. These are the main advantages of chain drive:

1. Direct application of power
2. Straight driveline (no U-joints)
3. Better ground clearance
4. Ease of changing drive ratios
5. Less torque concentration on individual components

Juno, 1913

Juno, 1913

This single differential tandem drive was strength and simplicity itself. This unit, however, had three torque proportioning differentials to make turning easier, promote better traction and reduce wheel spinning.

Parker trucks were built in Milwaukee starting in 1918. They used Wisconsin engines at first, but later used Continentals and Waukeshas. They appear to have built a good, heavy truck. There is a Hayes survivor to be found at the Hayes Museum in Woodland, California. It is a 1919 three and one-half-ton truck.

The Titan was another assembled truck built in Milwaukee with a Buda engine.

We heard of the Brodesser truck early in the Sterling story. William Sternberg had rented space in his building. In 1912 sales of the Brodesser must have been sufficiently strong for them to leave Milwaukee and build a complete factory 50 miles northwest in the small town of Juneau. To break with the past, and perhaps to cultivate commitment in the local market, the truck was now named Juno. Somewhat obsolescent with its cab-over-engine configuration, the Juno had dropped its friction drive in favor of the three-speed sliding-gear transmission. A 1912 ad claims "A Juno truck can be bought from our replacement department in separate parts at exactly the same price as a finished chassis." Furthermore, "Juno parts are all interchangeable." By mid-1914 they had closed their doors.

The Kissel Motor Car Company of Hartford, Wisconsin, was one of the two established truck manufacturers that actually built some of their own engines. Better known for their touring cars and roadsters, like the famous Gold Bug and the White Eagle, Kissel made a full line of trucks from as early as 1910. Kissel engineers were among those truck industry leaders who met in 1917 to design the standard three and one-half-ton Class B Liberty truck for the U.S. war effort. For all their contribution to that crash program, they ended up building FWDs under license for the duration of the war. Substantial subassemblies must have come from Clintonville. After the war Kissel resumed civilian production of trucks, including many fire trucks. Kissel went into receivership in September of 1930.

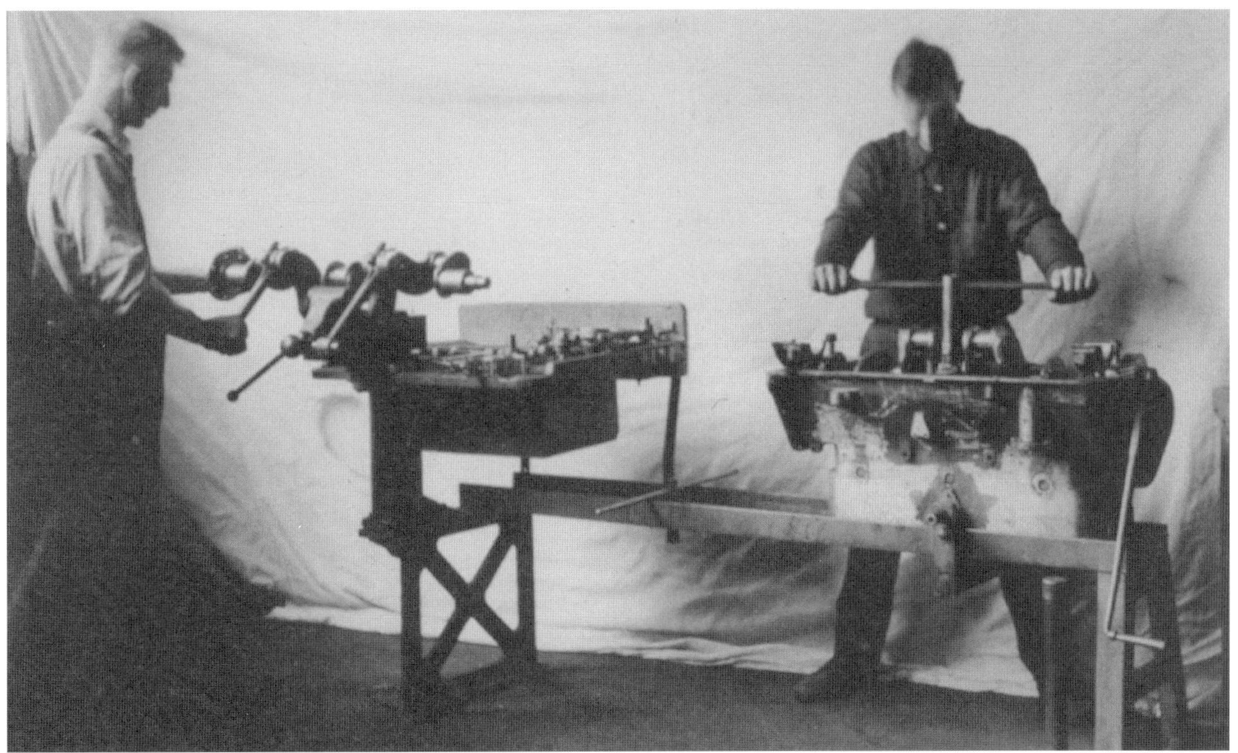

Kissel, 1917, production FWD Model B engines

Kissel, 1923, Model 1127

General Pershing, and 1915 Quad

In 1900 Thomas Jeffery bought the old Sterling Cycle Company building in Kenosha. When the Rambler hit the market in 1902 it was a huge success. Later the Rambler chassis was popular for fire trucks, hearses, and express bodies.

In 1913, apparently at the request of the U.S. Army Quartermaster Corps, a four-wheel-drive, four-wheel-steer and four-wheel-brake truck was developed of one and one-half-ton to two-ton capacity. Using a Hayes Buda built engine and a configuration not unlike the Model B Clintonville FWD, the Jeffery Quad was a success. The U.S. Army took delivery of the Jeffery Quads immediately. The allies in World War I took delivery of 11,490 Jeffery Quads.

Charlie Nash left General Motors in 1916 to do things his own way. He acquired the Jeffery Company, changed its name to Nash Motor Company and made plans for his new line of luxury cars and commercial vehicles. In 1918 a more modern, conventional line of trucks was introduced in one-, two-, and two and one-half ton capacities. The early locking differential was an option on Nash's Clark built rear axles.

Truck production was suspended in 1929 and resumed briefly in the late forties for export and to supply Nash dealers with tow-truck chassis.

The Winther motor truck was also located in Kenosha and in 1918 started out building a heavy-duty spur-drive truck in capacities of from one and one-half to seven ton. Built under license or as a joint venture the Winther-Marvin was a four-wheel drive, Wisconsin-powered truck. Winther developed some specialized uses for their chassis to encourage purchases as a package.

Nash, 1919, Model 4017F, Quad

Nash, 1920, Model 2018, one-ton
Photo courtesy of the Hays Antique Truck Museum, Woodland, California.

Nash, 1949, two-ton

Another Kenosha truck producer is Peter Pirsch and Sons. Pirsch originally made hand and horse-drawn ladder trucks, and built his first motorized ladder truck on a Rambler chassis. The first complete Peter Pirsch fire engines came in 1926 and in 1928 Pirsch was the first U.S. manufacturer to build a pumper with a fully enclosed cab. Pirsch still builds on commercial chassis in addition to their custom fire apparatus.

The Fox Valley region of Wisconsin encompasses many counties, but the ones where there is a history of truck production are: Brown, Outagamie, Winnebago and Waupaca. The best known makes are the FWD at Clintonville and Oshkosh.

In 1905 Otto Zachow and his brother-in-law, William Besserdich expanded their machine shop business to become the Clintonville agents for the Reo. On a trip to Appleton, Otto inadvertently drove his Reo down into a ravine. He told the story of how the front wheels were pushed into the soft bank by the action of the rear wheels, sticking the car. It occurred to him that if he backed up the bank, the wheels would lift themselves up instead of becoming buried. "Who is it? Who ever heard of a mule walking around on two legs?", Otto said to William. He then began working on a FWD car. Otto had not yet finished his handmade prototype when he knew he needed the protection of a patent. Walter Olen, then a young attorney in Clintonville, advised Otto to get mechanical drawings made and to finish his prototype.

In 1908, after a year-long wait, the patent was approved. By the middle of winter, the steam-powered four-wheel-drive car was ready for testing and the secret was out. The newspaper proclaimed that "They have plowed through drifts three-feet deep, gone over the most slippery roads, and climbed the steepest hills at a 25-mile-an-hour clip. There is talk of organizing a company."

Winther, 1917, Model 128 six-ton logging truck. Photo courtesy of the Hays Antique Truck Museum, Woodland, California.

Winther-Marvin, 1920, Model 459, one and one-half ton, 4WD. Photo courtesy of the Hays Antique Truck Museum, Woodland, California.

However, the steam engine was heavy and undependable and after they paid Walter Olen his $3 and the patent attorneys their $17 how could they afford a gasoline engine? The car, later known as "the Battleship" got built with investors' money, which was money raised by their new associate, Walter Olen. By 1911 they had enough invested to build a factory, and on December 20 the factory whistle

1st Four Wheel Drive, FWD, steam-powered prototype, 1908

blew for the first time.

In 1912 Captain A. E. Williams of the Quartermaster Corps conceived of a field trial for cross-country operation that would prove the motor truck's value as a replacement for the six-mule wagon. The route went from Washington, D.C., to Fort Benjamin Harrison, Indiana, by way of Atlanta, in February. The roads were a sea of mud and only the FWD made it. For the occasion of the army's test that next summer of 1912, newly-hired superintendent and engineer, P. J. F. Batenburg designed a three-ton truck. A Dutch immigrant, his favorite expression was "The faster it goes, the better how is it?" This was run from Dubuque, Iowa, to Sparta, Wisconsin, by way of Madison, in the company of a complete regiment and again the FWD truck outperformed the competition. Despite the two well-publicized successes in army trials, gloom settled over Clintonville and the FWD Company. The much anticipated army orders never materialized.

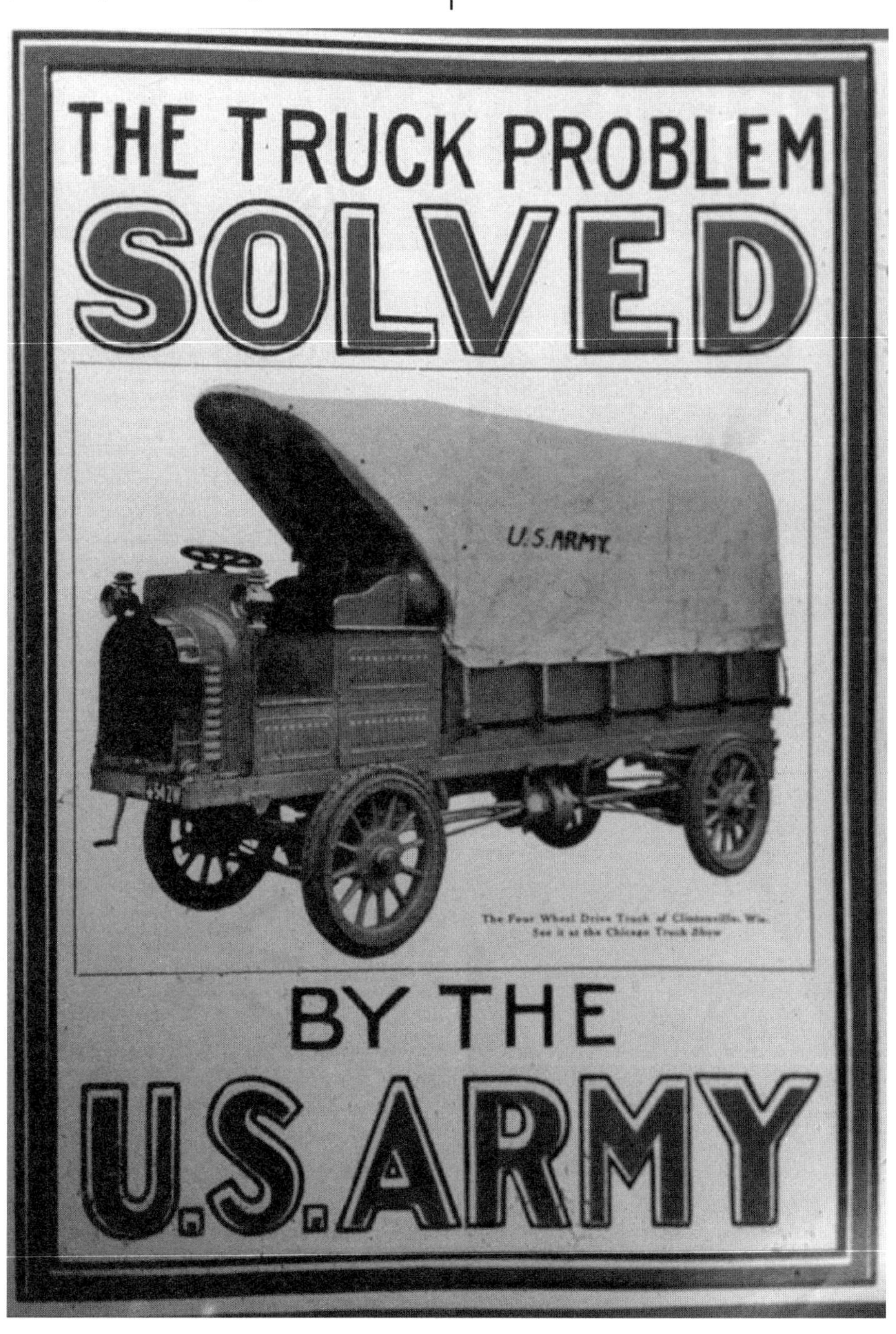

FWD, 1913, three-ton Army prototype

The guns of August of 1914, signaled a resurgence for the FWD. In the fall of that year a three ton and a five ton were shipped to England with a driver and a salesman. Within a month of their departure from Clintonville an order was received for 50 more. By the end of 1915 FWD had shipped nearly 400 trucks and had standing orders for 200 per month. Walter Olen got a $1,000 bonus and every one of the 450 employees got a live goose for Thanksgiving.

On April 6, 1916, the FWD Company was ordered to ship 147 trucks to General Pershing at Columbus, New Mexico. A diplomatic squabble then erupted between the U.S. and Britain over the 44 trucks ready for war in Europe. They were painted and repainted three times before the U.S. government settled for a shipment in May. Captain Williams, organizer of the 1912 trials, wrote that "...the FWD is proving its superiority to all others in the Mexican service."

FWD, 1918, Model B

FWD, 1918, Model B, 1922 picture

America's entry into World War I brought an order for 3,750 trucks to be delivered to the U.S. Army at the rate of 175 per month. Ultimately, 16,000 of these Model B's were built for the allies during World War I.

With railroad service too scarce in 1918, most FWDs were driven in caravans to the embarkation point in Baltimore, picking up supplies and equipment along the way. A contingent of Doughboys from Georgia and South Carolina composed a verse to commemorate their long-awaited departure in the fierce winter of 1918:

Farewell to the city of Clintonville,
We bid thee a fond adieu;
We may go to hell in an FWD.
But we'll never come back to you.

Otto Zachow had given up his shares in 1911 to spend more time at the machine shop that his brother-in-law and partner, William Besserdich had left. As early as 1913, Besserdich had been selling shares to his associate B. A. Mosling and by 1914, he was out. He and Mosling later went off and organized the Oshkosh Motor Truck Company in 1917. Another section of this book describes the Oshkosh Motor Truck Company. Then in 1919 FWD purchased the Menominee Motor Truck Company in the Michigan Upper Peninsula town of Menominee.

Menomonee, 1917, Model HT, one-ton.
Photo courtesy of the Hays Antique Truck Museum, Woodland, California.

The post war truck glut hit FWD hard and in spite of every effort sales declined every year until 1925 when employment bottomed out at 500. In 1918 there had been 1,600. Taking advantage of their skills acquired during the wartime buildup, women like Luella Bates and Margaret Sawyer ably demonstrated the features of the FWD at shows. FWD developed many specialized applications to generate sales. These included a ten-ton semi-tractor, oil-well-cementing rigs, road-building trucks and snow-removal equipment. So many war surplus Model Bs were still going strong ten years later that various upgrade packages for suspension, steering, and starting improvements were offered to bolster revenue.

FWD still worked closely with the U.S. Army between the wars, but budgets were tight and the Quartermaster Corps was building its own trucks in the early '30s under the direction of Arthur Herrington. However, some commercial models like the five-ton model M7 and the two-ton CU 6s were purchased for special applications.

As in World War I, the late entry of the U.S. in World War II found FWD already hard at work supplying the allies. Although 7,000 of the model HAR-1 were sold to the U.S. Army, many more than that went to the British Army. Employment during World War II rose to over 3,000 people. FWD trucks had unearthed unexploded bombs in London with their boring equipment, gone ashore on D-Day, and helped build the Alcan Highway, a noble record of achievement.

FWD continued its strategy of selling into specialty markets with unique designs. Their four-wheel-drive semi-tractor was operated by Clarence Meyer's Petroleum Transport Company when Phillips 66 featured it in one of their late 1960s print ads. Also, their V-12 Deutz-powered semi-tractor was shown by Don Chew a number of times. FWD has never gone out of business, but other companies could copy the 4 x 4s and 6 x 6s that were once the bread-and-butter of the company. They now subsist by building Seagrave fire engines, the most handmade fire truck in America.

Oneida, 1918, Floyd Dorn collection

Oneida, 1928

The original Zachow and Besserdich machine shop is still there in Clintonville as the FWD Museum. The same Margaret Sawyer we saw in the 1920s is the part-time curator. The original "Battleship" is there as well as some pieces of the original steam engine in the very first experimental car. It is well worth the trip 100 miles north of Milwaukee.

Oneida trucks were built in Green Bay from 1917 until 1930.

The contiguous south central counties of Sauk, Dane, and Rock are the last we shall explore in the story of Wisconsin-built trucks and it begins with the man, Fred Kohlmeyer. Brought from Germany as a boy, he moved to Loganville with his parents in the 1880s. He joined the Alaska gold rush briefly and on his return the name "Klondike" stuck. While helping his brother on the threshing crew, his extraordinary mechanical ability was used to refine the machinery and operations.

His portable sawmill and well-drilling operations needed trucks to be efficient and in 1911 he built a pickup. By 1915, he was building trucks for Ninnamin's dray line and the Loganville fire department. These vehicles were called "Klondikes." His other accomplishments included the 1912 to 1915 trucks called Wisconsin. Built in Baraboo were circus wagon chassis for the Ringling Brothers Circus. They built a fifth wheel for semitrailers that the Fruehauf people in Detroit were interested in, and came to see, and promptly patented. Fruehauf then got an injunction against him from using his own design. His housecar was driven to and from California on winter vacations. Gilbert Burmeister's 1930 Klondike was built for Phil, Ed, and Martin Thieding and was the last one built.

Klondike, 1929, 1 1/2 ton

In 1917, Loganville's A. Leicher had a building constructed for two of his boys, Bert and Frank, to build another line of trucks called "Wisconsin." Their older brothers, Fent and Ed, were doing well with their Luverne fire truck and auto business in Luverne, Minnesota, and transplanted their know-how back home to Loganville. The new firm faced war time material shortages and specialized in the conversion of passenger cars into trucks.

Meanwhile, Wisconsin tractors were being built in Sauk City, Wisconsin's second oldest settlement. John Westmont and Earl McFarlane built the 40 hp Wisconsin with Climax, Waukesha, and Beaver engines and kept the weight under 6,000 pounds, an accomplishment for the day. They are listed as truck manufacturers in the 1923 "Commercial Car Journal." These trucks may be Sauk City Wisconsins rather than Loganville Wisconsins, but neither Chuck nor Bob McFarlane remember trucks being built by their father, Earl.

In the year 1923, John Westmont and an uncle of Gene Olson organized yet another Wisconsin Truck Company, this time in Madison. In two years they built trucks and at least one bus, a six-wheeler called the "Badger." After their bankruptcy in 1924, they reincorporated as Wisconsin Truck and Equipment for the manufacture of oil burners for many years, one is still in use in Madison.

Another truck bearing the name of Wisconsin was built in Sheboygan from 1915 to 1918, but little is known about it.

Back in Sauk City, in 1923, the Wisconsin Tractor had been discontinued and ex-employee Henry Grass wanted to build trucks. His capital came from a Chicago dweller named Bill Stoltz who frequented Sauk City's resorts during the summer. They built a factory that still stands, for the moment, and produced a well-made line of trucks that were ahead of their time. Grass-Premier stretched their customers' Depression-Era dollars by featuring Lycoming engines over the more expensive Waukesha.

Grass-Premiers with Lycoming straight eights would outrun anything on the road. The history is told of a bootlegger whose liquor tank was concealed within a stack of live poultry cages. The straight-eight powered hootch truck would roar through the night in a cloud of feathers with always the same skinny chickens on board.

Grass-Premier, 1928

Stoughton, 1926, Model B-Jr $1^1/_2$ ton.
Photo courtesy of the Hays Antique Truck Musuem, Woodland, California.

One of the last Grass-Premiers was a V-8 Ford-powered cabover with the engine mounted on a sliding subframe where it was possible to remove the engine in 15 minutes, and replace it in 17 minutes. UPS was so impressed with the Superior Roadmaster that they wanted it built for them in New York. Being naturally suspicious of people from back East, the owners turned down the deal. After building some 150 trucks, an average of two a month, they closed their doors in 1937.

In southern Dane County, the Stoughton Wagon Works had been in business since the time of the Civil War. Named after the town, they are still going strong as Stoughton Trailers. From 1920 to 1928 they had their own line of trucks with a variety of engines, Waukesha, Midwest, and Hercules.

Our last city, Janesville, in Rock County, may someday be the only city in Wisconsin still building trucks with their Chevrolet plant. It started in 1918 when Billy Durant's General Motors bought the Samson Tractor Company to counter Henry Ford's fantastic success with the Fordson line of farm machinery. The odd-looking, forward-control Samson truck was not selling well and by 1923, the Janesville plant was producing Chevrolet cars. It is not known how many or what kind of Chevrolet trucks were produced in Janesville over the years, but they continue to be a Wisconsin favorite.

The one major truck manufacturer in Wisconsin today is Oshkosh Truck Corporation, detailed in the next chapter.

116 Samson, 1915, 3/4 ton

Chapter Eight

MAJOR CAR AND TRUCK MANUFACTURE IN WISCONSIN TODAY

Brooks Stevens Automotive Contributions

By Val Quandt

The writer had the privilege of interviewing Mr. Brooks Stevens at his auto museum in Mequon, Wisconsin, in August of 1993. The content of this account is the result of this interview and written materials furnished by Brooks Stevens.

Stevens credits his father, William C. Stevens, executive vice president and director of design and development with the Cutler Hammer Company in Milwaukee, with interesting him in the automobile. The senior Stevens was the inventor of the preselective steering wheel gear shift in 1916.

In the late 1930s, Stevens designed land yachts which functioned as mobile homes and sales offices for William Plankinton, the Western Printing Company of Racine, Wisconsin, and the Johnson Wax Company of Racine.

The volume one, issue one of the "Automobile Quarterly" in the spring of 1962 had a two-page spread of a sketch by Brooks Stevens of a huge and luxurious land cruiser, a motor home called the "Gondola Terra." It advertised 101 built-in features for the comfort and convenience of the sportsman and executive. It was intended to be a "futuristic" and "tomorrow" vehicle.

In 1946 Stevens designed the Jeep station wagon, and the Jeepster Phaeton for Willys Motors. Between 1948 and 1955 he collaborated with Kaiser and Frazer with their line of passenger automobiles.

In 1951 Stevens designed a race car using a Henry J chassis and a Willys F engine. These cars were raced for several years at the tracks at Road America at Elkhart Lake, Wisconsin, at Janesville, Wisconsin, at Sebring, Florida, and throughout the United States.

Stevens saw the need for a new kind of racing car against the only racing car existing in America at the time, the Cunningham car, which was an expensive one. The first two of these Stevens designed cars were called Excalibur J, with one having a Henry J, L head engine of 2½ liter displacement and the other being a Willys F head engine. These cars raced in competition against more exotic vehicles and competed well in races across America.

David Stevens sits in the cockpit of his design of an Excalibur J race car.

From 1952 through 1954, using the F head engine they won 13 first place trophies, 9 second place, and 7 third place trophies. There were further racing events annually through 1957 with yearly Sebring race participation.

Brooks Stevens and his Excalibur J cars received their strongest accolades for their performance in the Sebring 12-hour endurance race on March 7, 1954.

As Stevens noted, the demise of the Kaiser automobile ended their participation in the Excalibur development. But these cars reappeared on the racing circuits in 1983 as vintage racing became "de rigueur." They were driven by his son David, grandson Tony, and friend Robert Shaw.

Between 1953 and 1956, Stevens designed a succession of cars which had a limited production of some three to six vehicles of each design. These were the Valkyrie in 1953, the Gaylord in 1956, and Scimitar in 1956.

Stevens traced his interest in the Mercedes Benz SS 180 Phaeton to when he acquired one from the estate of singer Al Jolson. He was then an engineering consultant to the Kaiser-Frazer Corporation. In 1966, while a consultant to Studebaker he used the Mercedes radiator appearance for his redesign of the Studebaker Hawk.

In the late 1950s and early 1960s Stevens designed for Willys including some vehicles for the Brazilian market, and from 1963 to 1967 for Studebaker. In 1969 and 1970 Stevens contributed designs for American Motors Corporation for their Hornet, Gremlin, AMX, Javelin Landau, and Ambassador.

Stevens and his sons David Brooks, and William C., known as Steve, developed the Excalibur I in 1964. This was based on a 4/5 scale of the Mercedes Benz 1927/1930 SS doorless roadster. The SS Automobile Company was born in August of 1964 for the manufacture of these cars. It became the sixth largest manufacturer of automobiles in America at that time. By 1966 some 100 Excaliburs had been built. Stevens was searching for some designation of the word "sword" and came up with the Arthurian legend sword, the "Excalibur." The vehicle used a Chevrolet Corvette engine, and a Studebaker Daytona chassis. By 1970, approximately 1,000 vehicles had been manufactured. The models prior to 1970 were the Excalibur I cars together with the original Excalibur racing cars.

This is the famous Excalibur I roadster, made from 1964 to 1969, Brooks Stevens designer.

Excalibur I series, of 1964, a Brooks Stevens creation. Vehicle on loan to the Hartford Auto Museum, where it is on exhibit.

In its first two years the Excalibur was offered only in the two-passenger roadster. Then starting the third year, both a roadster and a four-passenger Phaeton were offered. Series II existed from 1969 through 1974 and the series III was built from 1975 through 1979. Then there was a change with the series IV, which came out in 1980, and was styled after the larger 1937/1938 Mercedes 500/540 K and ran through 1984. The series V ran from 1985 to 1988 and was offered in a four-door sedan. The total produced from 1965 through 1988 was 3,608 automobiles.

These are examples of the Excaliburs made by Brooks Stevens, the II series from 1969 to 1974.

This is a model of the Excalibur, series three, Phaeton.

In middle 1986 the company filed chapter eleven bankruptcy. Later that year Henry A. Warner became president of the acquisition company that purchased the assets. The company management has gone through several German interests since that time.

The Stevens brothers also were responsible for the development of the Excalibur Jr., all aluminum go-cart, put out by the Gilson Manufacturing Company from 1960 to 1968.

Briggs and Stratton in Milwaukee, Wisconsin, in the early 1980s devised an experimental car utilizing gasoline and electric battery power. This was called the Briggs and Stratton Gasoline/Electric Hybrid as an energy saving design concept. It was developed with the assistance of the automotive craftsmen of Brooks Stevens Design Associates. In a descriptive and pictorial leaflet it shows a handsome vehicle which could seat two adults, two children, and some luggage. An additional two wheels in the vehicle rear supported the added weight of the 12 batteries.

Briggs and Stratton clearly stated that they were not intending to get into the manufacture of automobiles, but rather to demonstrate an alternative to the standard gasoline-driven automobile.

The gasoline engine in this vehicle was an 18-hp model 42 of the Briggs and Stratton line. It was small for the job but adequate, when amplified with the battery power, for low speed travel and low to intermediate distances of travel.

Stevens also did design work for AMC with their 1980 XJ100 Wagoneer, and the Cherokee station wagons.

The foregoing is a compendium of the activities of Brooks Stevens and his sons in the automotive field. For the former this spans more than 40 years.

The design work of Mr. Stevens goes much beyond the automotive field. His fertile mind designed Steam-O-Matic irons, the Petipoint iron, the Hamilton clothes dryer, outboard motors including Outboard Marine, lawn and garden equipment including Lawn Boy rotary mowers, for the Milwaukee Road, the Hiawatha and Olympian trains 1941 to 1946, Allis Chalmers farm tractors in 1934, machine tools, furniture, office buildings, sales and show rooms, and a myriad of other designs for industry including the medical fields. Mr. Stevens lists having had 585 clients during his career.

It is recognized that this last listed paragraph describes work outside of the automotive field, but it gives a measure of the design influence of Brooks Stevens through a long career.

The present Excalibur Automobile Corporation is located in Milwaukee in the suburb of West Allis, on South 106th Street.

A visit in July of 1994, found a specialty automobile plant busy at manufacturing and assembling Excalibur and Cobra automobiles. The Excalibur presently being offered is called Limited Edition 100, referring to the 100 vehicles to be manufactured for this series. They are still styled after the 1937/1938 Mercedes Benz 500/540 K. The engine is a Corvette, with 300-hp and a four-speed automatic overdrive transmission.

This vehicle is equipped with 17-inch wheels, and four-wheel disk brakes.

It has a soft top and removable side curtains. As with all the Excaliburs that preceded it, this Excalibur has a striking appearance. On the factory floor was an

An Excalibur sedan convertible, in 1994, being readied for shipment from its West Allis, Wisconsin, plant.

Above, the 20th Anniversary Signature Series Excalibur Phaeton. Below, the 20th Anniversary Signature Series Roadster. The Excalibur Automobile Corporation in West Allis, Wisconsin, is presently engaged in the manufacture of these elegant Anniversary Signature Series of Excalibur phaetons, roadsters, and limousines. They are style based on the Excalibur IV series.

Excalibur limousine of truly mammoth size, with a steel top, and ready for delivery.

The other product in this specialized auto plant is the Cobra. The Cobra styling is based on the 1962 Shelby English bodied AC-Ace vehicle. Shelby had used this style until 1965 when he went to the new Mustang fastback.

The present Cobra is designed as the JAC 427 Cobra. This vehicle is somewhat larger in overall size than the classic 1966 427 Cobra. It has a Ford 5-liter V-8 engine and coupled with a weight of just 2,500 pounds gives it a high performance capacity. It is 165-inches long with a 94.5-inch wheelbase.

The body is made of fiberglass and with both a soft and hardtop, together with a roll bar. The interior is lined with leather. It has 16-inch wheels. The transmission is five-speed manual. It possesses a top speed of 145 mph. Available exterior colors are red, metallic blue, black, British racing green, and yellow.

At this visit in 1994 the plant was working at full capacity to fill its orders.

The Cobra, a modern version of an earlier English vehicle, is also manufactured at this West Allis Excalibur plant. It has a Ford V-8 engine.

A replica of the 1966 Cobra sports car, being assembled at the Excalibur plant in West Allis, Wisconsin. The body is fiberglass.

THE DUESENBERG II AUTOMOBILE

By Val Quandt

The following account is based on a visit to the Duesenberg automobile manufacturing plant in Elroy, Wisconsin, in 1994. At the time, it was called the Precision Classics.

Richard Braund Sr. started the company in 1975. He still has an interest in the company, now run by his son, Richard W. Braund.

Here approximately ten artisans put in about 6,000 hours to produce one Duesenberg automobile. These are called Duesenberg II, and are presently made in five models. There is a Duesenberg II Torpedo Phaeton, a Duesenberg II Royalton each with a 153½-inch wheelbase, Duesenberg II Murphy Roadster with a 142½-inch wheelbase, a boattail Speedster, and a Torpedo Roadster.

With the exception of few items such as tires, electrical wiring and such, these are all manufactured by hand at this plant including an immense and sturdy chassis. They are in every way the equal of the original Indianapolis Duesenbergs, with the added modern day antipollution devices and some of the electrical gear such as power windows, brakes and steering.

When visited in late summer of 1994, this plant had about ten vehicles in shop, some being finished and readied for customers as new cars, and some in shop for necessary refurbishing for present owners. These vehicles weigh in at 5,000 pounds and the bodies are steel reinforced fiberglass construction.

The original Duesenberg J, of which these are replicas, came out in 1929. As mentioned, Braund started up in 1975 and had ready for sale his first vehicle in 1978. There have now been built in his plant, 60 cars with present prices from $140,000 to $170,000, and with Braund

The Duesenberg Estate Golf Car, noted to be a car and not a cart. It is powered by a 32-volt battery, and has the frontal Duesenberg appearance.

The Duesenberg II, model Murphy Roadster.

feeling that they are underpriced for value.

The Duesenberg II has been featured in the State of Wisconsin highway map, where in recent years it has featured our Wisconsin Governor Tommy Thompson and his wife standing alongside one of these beautiful vehicles.

The earlier Duesenbergs were the result of designs by Gordon Buerhrig working for the Cord Motor Company. This company went out of business in 1937.

The Duesenberg II Royalton, 5-passenger, based on the Gordon Buerhrig designed Derham Tourster.

This is the Duesenberg II automobile, the Speedster boattail model, based on the original Duesenberg J models manufactured between 1929 and 1937, designed by Gordon Buehrig, and backed by the legendary E.L. Cord.

The assets of Precision Classics, Inc., were purchased by David Hartje and his wife on December 19, 1996. Richard W. Braund and his wife stayed on with the company. This company, called Duesenberg Motors, Inc., has been continuing to offer the five models that had already been developed, and an additional product in 1997, the Duesenberg Estate golf car to the golf industry. This is a reduced scale version of the Duesenberg II, built on a Columbia ParCar chassis.

This company wishes to produce up to ten vehicles per year, and also 30 golf cars per year.

The Duesenberg II Torpedo Phaeton was inspired by a letter from Mark Lawrence, a young man from Washington, D.C., addressed to Gordon Buerhrig, in which he suggested "a car having the appearance of an open Phaeton, but the physical enclosure of a convertible sedan." The Duesenberg II features a rear seat instrument panel, and folding front and rear windshield frames, and twin Lorraine spotlights.

The Duesenberg II Murphy Roadster is a replica of the bodies from the Walter Murphy Company of Pasadena, California, which produced 55 for the 480 Duesenbergs built. This included a rumble seat, access step plates, and an optional removable hardtop.

The Duesenberg II Royalton is a five-passenger vehicle, where less than 50 of the originals were ever built. This featured a dual cowl, with folding rear windshield, side curtains, and a folding convertible top.

The Duesenberg II Speedster was an E. L. Cord inspiration and out of the racetracks of the time. This vehicle did 160 mph on the Bonneville Salt Flats. Only one was built and it featured a boattail trunk.

The Duesenberg II Torpedo Roadster offers conventional classic styling with running boards, large wire wheels, and side-mounted spare wheels.

The Duesenberg II Torpedo Roadster, embodies the spirit of the Speedster, and more conventional classic styling.

The Duesenberg II Torpedo Sedan is scheduled for production in 1999. It was inspired by the show car of the 1933 Chicago World's Fair. This was the ultimate of elegance. It was built on an SJ chassis with 320 bhp and 130 mph.

All of these Duesenberg II automobiles are of full-scale design, on a $153\frac{1}{2}$-inch wheelbase, and the Murphy Roadster shorter at $142\frac{1}{3}$ inches. Virtually all of the manufacturing details are handled at the plant, and hand done. The engine used is the 5.5 L EFI engine, from the Ford Motor Company. The electronic overdrive automatic transmission is also by Ford.

The Duesenberg II Torpedo Sedan, built on the original SJ chassis.

Part of the company's first factory.

Oshkosh Truck Corporation "... Anywhere The Wheels Can Touch The Ground"

By Ray Scroggins

In the early days of motoring, when paved roads were rare, and mud and ruts were the rule rather than the exception, William R. Besserdich and Bernard A. Mosling founded the Wisconsin Duplex Auto Company at Clintonville, Wisconsin, in 1917. Some years earlier, Besserdich had helped develop the FWD truck and was a firm believer in the need to deliver power to all four wheels to cope with the poor road conditions of the time.

William R. Besserdich

Bernhard A. Mosling

The Four Wheel Pioneers, early picture, c. 1917

This is the manufacturing area of the first Oshkosh factory.

Later that year, the new company moved to Oshkosh, where it still exists as the Oshkosh Truck Corporation. The firm added the name of its new hometown in 1918, when it became Oshkosh Motor Truck Mfg. Co., a name that was changed to Oshkosh Motor Truck, Inc. as part of Depression-Era reorganization in 1930. The company's identity took its current form in 1967.

The prototype Oshkosh truck, built in late 1917 by a Milwaukee machine shop, was a stake-bodied unit of one-ton capacity.

Known affectionately as "Old Betsy," the 3,280 pound truck is owned by the company today and is still operational. Among its features are a LeRoi gasoline engine driving through a three-speed transmission, and standard 32" x 4" pneumatic tires. As a prototype, it helped sell stock in the company by demonstrating the advantages of all-wheel drive and patented components that included an automatic, positive-locking center differential, as well as front-axle steering pivots equipped with roller bearings.

Old Betsy, the first Oshkosh truck.

The Model A

The first production Oshkosh truck was the two-ton Model A, introduced in 1918. It used a 72 hp Herschell-Spillman 4-cylinder engine that heated the fuel at three different points before ignition to get better performance from the era's low-grade fuels. Other features included thermo-siphon cooling, a Brown-Lipe 4-speed transmission, and a cab that had a door on each side, rather than just the passenger's side entry found in most trucks then. Built on a frame fabricated by Milwaukee's A. O. Smith Company, the Model A used 36" x 6" pneumatic tires on demountable rims and included an electric generator and starter for a price of about $3,500. In 1921, according to a report in the *Oshkosh Daily Northwestern*, a local woman drove a Model A up the steps of the local high school as part of an advertising firm. The newspaper reported, "Miss Blanche Rahr of this city at the wheel piloted the big machine ... in a fashion that won the applause of spectators who had gathered to witness the stunts." At the time, the company advertised with the slogan that an Oshkosh truck "Goes Anywhere the Wheels Can Touch the Ground."

The Oshkosh Model A.

The Model F

More Early Models

In 1920, Oshkosh expanded its line with the 3½ ton Model B, followed by the 5-ton Model F in 1924. These had the same setback axles and artillery wheels as the Model A and played an important role in building and maintaining the nation's growing system of roads after World War I. Production began in 1925 on the Model H, a 6-cylinder truck with double-reduction axles.

The Model H

The Model TR

About this time, Oshkosh trucks started to gain popularity for the emerging municipal service of snow removal. Earlier, cars often spent the winter on blocks due to poor roads and ineffective alcohol antifreeze. Improved road surfaces brought increased winter traffic, and with it, the need to keep roads passable.

For a short time, the company attempted to compete in the mass-produced rear-wheel drive market with its Express models, including a $1\frac{1}{2}$ ton Model R available with a 4-cylinder Hercules or 6-cylinder Wisconsin engine. The experiment was short-lived, however, and it soon returned to concentrating on its primary focus of all-wheel drive vehicles.

During 1932, at the bottom of the Depression, Oshkosh Truck introduced its FC and FB trucks. Powered by 6-cylinder Hercules engines rated at from 102-hp, they had GVW (gross vehicle weight) capacities up to 44,000 pounds. Double-reduction axles were standard, with transmissions from 4- to 12-speeds available. A Cumins diesel engine, the first diesel in an Oshkosh truck, was offered in 1935.

Diversifying into markets other than snow removal and municipal uses, the company introduced the first-ever rubber-tired earthmover in 1933. Known as the Model TR, it was a large four-wheel drive vehicle

The J-Series

designed for use with bottom-dump semi-trailers and self-loading scraper bodies. With four-wheel drive and steering, the big rigs had a turning circle diameter of only 31.5 feet and soon became popular on the nation's big dam, airport, and canal projects.

In 1935, Oshkosh broadened its truck line with the J-Series, with 1930s automotive styling that included a one-piece windshield and slight rounding of the V-type grille and fender lines. J-Series capacities ranged from 2 to 3 1/2 tons.

World War II and the Military Market

The introduction of the W-Series in 1939 proved to be fortuitous, as the country soon entered World War II. These trucks featured increased power, greater capacity, better driver comfort and better styling. Gasoline or diesel power choices were now available on all models, with GVW ratings from 18,000 to 44,000 pounds. After the U.S. entered the war, the W-Series trucks were in demand by the military for use with dump bodies and snowplows.

The war experience also set the scene for the company's growing presence in the military and airport markets that continues to the present. Through the 1980s and much of the 1990s, contracts for military vehicles and airport crash trucks still made up a major part of the company's business.

Runway snow removal was a big job for the W-Series trucks, which were often equipped with rotary snowblowers powered by 175-hp Climax engines mounted on the back, in addition to their standard 112-hp Hercules engines. Snow removal was also an important assignment for Oshkosh trucks on the homefront, where they kept roads open so that wartime production schedules could be met.

The W-Series

Postwar Growth and the Ready-Mix Market

As World War II drew to a close, the company was able to move its W-1600 into production. These 6x6 vehicles were designed for off-road service in oil fields and for heavy hauling. In 1947, the W-2200 was introduced as a larger, faster, more powerful 4x4 than offered by the competition. They were available with 6-cylinder Hercules, Cummins, Buda, and Hall-Scott engines ranging from 139- to 295-hp. In addition to snowplowing, these units were popular for hauling sugarcane to processors and iron ore at mines.

After the war, the large-scale influx of returning troops settled down to jobs and families. The demand for housing and streets fueled a building boom that led Oshkosh to introduce the gasoline-powered Model 50-50 concrete carrier. With its 4x4 configuration, it could be counted on to deliver ready-mix concrete to the job site without getting stuck. As the first truck created specifically for concrete delivery, it featured a set-back front axle that enabled it to carry 50 percent of the weight on each axle, thus its model designation. Following the success of the 50-50, the company introduced the Model 45-55, a similar diesel-powered truck that used a rear axle rated at 23,000 pounds instead of the 50-50's 18,000 pounds capacity.

The following year, 1956, saw the introduction of the Model 1832, a tandem-axle 6x6 based on the 50-50 design with an 18,000 pounds front axle rating and 32,000 pounds on the tandem. All of the 50-50 derivatives were recognizable by their extreme front axle setback that put the front wheels directly under the cab. These became known as the C-Series when the Model F was introduced in the early 1960s.

The front axles on the Model F were moved slightly forward to achieve maximum payloads in states where certain weight distribution requirements were in effect. As the demand for larger concrete carriers grew in the 1960s, larger front axles were added, with capacities that eventually grew to 23,000 pounds. Other factors also favored the Model F design. A revised mixer design changed the weight distribution and made the extreme front axle setback less advantageous. Federal braking

The Model 50-50

The Model 1832

standards also were tightened, which added to the benefit of moving the axle forward where it could accept more weight transfer during braking.

F-Series trucks were available in configurations that included 6x6, 8x6, 10x6, and 10x8 drives, which were popular for delivering both ready-mix and concrete blocks. The design also evolved into the D-Series, with tandem driving front axles and 16 cubic-yard capacity.

More diverse markets were the target of the heavy-duty R-Series introduced during the 1960s. These 6x4 trucks and tractors were designed to stand up under marginal road conditions in places like Australia, Africa, and the Middle East.

Also from the 1960s into the 1980s, Oshkosh sold its A-Series chassis to fire apparatus manufacturers such as Pierce,

The F-Series

The J-Series

Ladder Tower, Inc., Snorkel, and Van Pelt. This five-man, cab-forward design was built on a 6x4 chassis and supplied to these customers, who often marketed the outfitted truck under their own trade name. Except for the A-Series and a series of conventional trucks built between 1956 and 1966 using International cabs, Oshkosh trucks have always used flat glass all around.

In 1975, the company introduced the B-Series, a forward placement concrete carrier that eliminated the need for a driver to back into a congested job site. With a one-person cab located over the front axle and the engine in the rear, the driver could now discharge the concrete exactly where it was wanted. The chute was controlled from inside the cab, eliminating the need for wheelbarrow and permitting safer and more exact placement.

An improved forward-placement vehicle, the S-Series, came out in 1982. It was a complete package that included both an Oshkosh-designed mixer, for single-source delivery and field support.

Expansion into Broader Markets

New and unusual markets that began to develop in the 1970s and 1980s often called for innovative designs. In 1974, the J-Series was developed, based loosely on the F-Series. These large vehicles were used in desert oil field applications, particularly in the Middle East and China. Two monstrous six-wheel drive trucks, the Desert Prince and the Desert Knight, had diesel engines of 325-hp to 485-hp, with 2,000 square foot radiators and huge balloon tires for the desert environment. An unusual feature on some models was a tubular front bumper that held fresh drinking water.

A departure in style and mission was the cab-over-engine E-Series introduced in the 1970s. Designed primarily for use with semi-trailers, the flat-fronted, tilt-cab truck had a full-width grille and was available in 4x2 and 6x4 versions. It was assembled in kit form in Australia for a time, and was manufactured at the company's South African plant into the early 1980s.

The H-Series, of about the same vintage, was designed for heavy-duty snowplowing. It had a forward-slanting windshield and was powered by a 225-hp Caterpillar diesel, with a second Cat diesel providing 425-hp to a two-stage spiral ribbon rotary plow.

Snowplowing was one of the major areas where Oshkosh shone in the military market as well. Since the early 1960s, military and governmental customers were a significant factor in driving the company's growth and product development.

The Model WT-2206

One example is found in the WT-2206 that was developed in the 1950s to keep runways open at the Air Force's Strategic Air Command (SAC) bases. Located solidly in the snowbelt, these bases had to be ready for action at all times, no matter how heavy the snowfall. These innovative trucks, with 325-hp Hall-Scott engines and Allison automatic transmissions, featured a unique rollover plow design that allowed the driver to roll it over to the other side and plow the snow in the same direction on the return pass back up the runway. Formerly, it was necessary to lift the plow and return to the starting point to keep the plowed snow moving the same way, so the new plow doubled the efficiency of the operation. Teams of the trucks operating in tandem at 55-mph made quick work of keeping the runways open.

After these vehicles had seen 10- to 20-years of service, the company worked with the air force to develop a remanufacturing program that would upgrade the trucks for less than 60 percent of the cost of a new unit. While the rugged vehicles had long service lives and needed few repairs, the program provided an opportunity to upgrade from gasoline to diesel power and obtain a new warranty while producing considerable savings for the taxpayer. The program was extended to other vehicles, some built as long ago as the 1940s, which were remanufactured and upgraded several times over a 30-year period.

All Wheels Driving Into The Future

In the 1970s and 1980s, military vehicles continued to make up a substantial portion of the Oshkosh product mix. The U.S. Navy MB-5 was one of the vehicles that launched the company into its leadership position in this field. An aluminum-bodied aircraft rescue and fire fighting (ARFF) truck, the MB-5 carried 400 gallons of water that expanded to 5,000 gallons of extinguishing foam when mixed with a foam concentrate. The foam was delivered from a roof turret, making it quick and easy to aim at a fire. Several hundred of the units were built for the navy, including a dozen that saw service on the flight decks of aircraft carriers. A similar version, known as the M-Series, was available for civilian service as well.

Additional crash truck versions ranged from the smaller MB-1, a 1,000-gallon ARFF truck, to the huge 66-ton P-15, a 6,000-pound capacity, eight-wheeled unit powered by two 492-hp Detroit Diesel V-8s and able to deliver 60,000 gallons of foam. Expertise in manufacturing vehicles for the military soon led the company to introduce several other vehicles. These included an articulated 8x8 DA airport rescue and fire

The U.S. Navy MB-5 Aircraft Rescue and Fire Fighting (ARFF) truck.

The U.S. Navy MB-1

The U.S. Air Force P-19.

fighting vehicle, derived from articulated, high-mobility tactical cargo truck originally built for the U.S. Marines. Other military vehicles included a series of aircraft tow tractors for the U.S. Air Force, the M-911 Heavy Equipment Transporter (HET) used to pull heavily loaded equipment trailers, and the Air Force 40K aircraft loader.

The 8x8 DA Aircraft Rescue and Fire Fighting vehicle.

The U.S. Air Force U-30.

The U.S. Army M-911 Heavy Equipment Transporter (HET).

When the company won its largest government contract in 1981, it had no idea of the critical role its trucks would play in Operation Desert Storm ten years later. More than 13,000 of the 8x8 Heavy Expanded Mobility Tactical Trucks (HEMTT) were built in the first ten years, in five models: two cargo trucks, a tanker, a tractor, and a recovery vehicle. These are powered by a 445-hp Detroit Diesel V-8, driving through a four-speed Allison automatic transmission.

As this is written in the mid-1990s, the company continues to supply the military market with a diverse range of heavy-duty transport and service vehicles, as well as serving commercial markets for ready-mix transit, snow removal, road maintenance, recycling and refuse collection, motor home chassis, and transport trailers.

U.S. Army HEMTT model

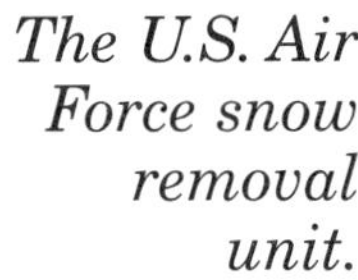

The U.S. Air Force snow removal unit.

The recycler/refuse collector.

General Motors Corporation, Janesville Plant

By Val Quandt

Janesville, Wisconsin, a city of 52,000 population, is the home of a General Motors assembly plant.

This is a sprawling plant situated on 137 acres of land on the south edge of this city. It is located on Industrial Avenue, a fitting name for this large enterprise.

At the present time this plant is run by a total of 5,055 workers, with 4,697 being hourly employees, and 358 are salaried.

The U.A.W. Local 95 was formed there way back in 1937 and exists there today.

A tour of this plant displays a combination of industrial activity, both with the use of robots especially for welding procedures, strategically placed computers, and above all workers doing what only human hands and decision-making can provide.

The output of the plant is listed at 192,000 units in a year. At the present time, that is July of 1994, the plant was busy assembling Chevrolet Blazers, Suburbans, and Crew Cabs. It also assembles a variety of trucks on various chassis extensions.

Assembly parts are mainly trucked in to the Janesville plant. But some of the larger and heavier items such as frame members and axles are frequently brought in by rail. Some 500 suppliers within a 75-mile radius of Janesville furnish a substantial quantity of materials and services for the production of these vehicles.

The Blazers and the Suburbans ride virtually as comfortable as the passenger cars. It may be a matter of semantics, but they are considered to have a truck chassis.

GM Janesville had its beginning right after World War I, in 1919, when they purchased 54.5 acres of land at the present site to construct the Samson tractor. This was a William Durant enterprise intended to compete with the successful Ford tractors. It lasted only a few years. Already in that first year GM had expanded to a new building measuring 225 x 545-feet.

Chevrolet first started making vehicles in North America in 1912. For most of the years it has also had an assembly plant in Canada.

In 1920, GM Janesville began production of a 3/4 ton M-15 truck. Then in 1922, this plant started building Chevrolet passenger vehicles which it continued through the years until 1990. Exceptions would have been the 1942 to 1946 World War II years. There also was limited production during the depression years of 1932 to 1935. In 1933 Janesville moved its operation to the site of the Chicago World's Fair where they assembled 3,200 cars where the assembly could be viewed by the visiting public.

During these war years Janesville was under military contract to make Howitzer 105 mm and a variety of smaller shells for the military. Also during these years GM Janesville supplied Chevrolet parts and services for army and navy vehicles.

Through the years, beginning in 1922, GM Janesville has built Chevrolet passenger cars in addition to GM trucks, utility vehicles, panel trucks, motor homes, and school bus chassis. By 1925, the 100,000th vehicle had been assembled in Janesville. By 1929, and the beginning of the economic depression, Janesville GM had produced a total of 500,000 vehicles.

In its early years Fisher Body occupied part of the plant, and Chevrolet the other. But by 1968 Fisher Body and Chevrolet were combined into the GM Janesville Assembly Division.

Janesville was one of around nine assembly plants in North America, including one in Oshawa, Canada. Later this number would swell to about 17. The GM plants have been strategically placed across the breadth of the United States.

A portion of the serial number of each vehicle would designate the origin of the assembly plant. In the case of Janesville the numeral designation was "21." In some other years the designation was a "J." The serial numbers could be found at areas of the vehicle such as the dash, door posts, and others.

Right into the depression years and into the early 1930s Janesville GM was producing top-of-the-line Chevrolet cars, in those days selling for around $725. In 1931, Janesville produced 115,409 of these cars out of a total Chevrolet production in America of 619,554.

A high of 5,600 employees were working at the plant in 1973. Between that time and

This is a series of pictures taken at the General Motors Assembly Plant at Janesville, Wisconsin, in 1994. The tour was conducted by an official of the plant, which was found to be in an immaculate condition. The workers were engaged in assembly of light and heavier models of General Motors trucks.

December of 1990, when production of the Cavalier passenger car ceased, the plant made a variety of Chevrolets, Oldsmobiles, and Cadillacs. The Cadillac was the Cimarron which came out in 1982 and shared the Chevrolet chassis.

Production then went to truck assembly, a continuation that exists today.

The plant is working at full capacity, with many ten-hour shifts, producing products which have been well received by the buying public. Constant improvement linked to quality control is the stated effort of the plant.

Chrysler Motor Car Company of Kenosha

Chrysler manufacture of vehicles in Kenosha spanned a relatively short period of time from February of 1987 to early in 1988. More recently Chrysler is using the plant for building engines and is undergoing building additions of over 250,000,000 square feet.

When Chrysler took it over, the plant was one of the oldest in America. Since then much of the old plant has been torn down. It dated back to 1902 and the Jeffery Rambler. In succession it became Nash in 1917 and in 1954 with the merger of Nash Kelvinator and Hudson it became American Motors Corporation. This existed until 1988 and the takeover by the Chrysler Corporation.

In chronological order the following offers the skeleton of the dates in the history of Chrysler in Kenosha during this period.

This history begins in the year 1986 when on September 25, American Motors and Chrysler signed an agreement under which AMC would build M-body cars at Kenosha, beginning in late February of 1987. On February 23 of 1987, M-body production was launched at Kenosha.

Two weeks later on March 9 of 1987, Chrysler announced plans to buy the Renault interest in the AMC corporation contingent upon the approval of the AMC shareholders to sell their stock to Chrysler. On August 5, 1987, the AMC shareholders did approve the sale of the company to Chrysler.

A month later on September 8, 1987, L-body Chrysler production was launched in Kenosha.

Six weeks later on October 24, Kenosha employment hit the peak of 6,106 active hourly and salaried employees. This surge of activity was short-lived, however, when on January 27, 1988, Chrysler announced that it would phase out the assembly and stamping operations at Kenosha later in that year, with the L-body in June and the M-body in late September.

On February 16, 1988, chairman Lee Iacocca, announced the establishment of a Kenosha trust to provide an estimated $20 million to Kenosha employees who lost their jobs and were faced with possible loss of their homes or the inability to continue the education of their children.

On April 2, 1988, Mr. Iacocca announced that Chrysler would continue L-body and M-body assembly and stamping operations at Kenosha through the end of 1988.

After an early suit by UAW Local 72, begun in February of 1988, it was dropped on May 11, 1988, after reaching a new contract agreement with the company.

It was essentially over in September, when Kenosha city and county officials voted to accept Chrysler's closing agreement and Governor Tommy Thompson announced the state would also accept the agreement and not pursue legal action against Chrysler.

The Chrysler plant, begun in 1902 under Jeffery had expanded to 935,000 square feet under roof of 23 acres and another 65 acres of property outdoors.

But on a smaller scale, some activity did persist at the plant, making engines. This was for the 2.5 liter four-cylinder engine and the 4.0 liter six-cylinder engine for Jeeps and trucks.

Presently, the plant is building these engines and in 1997 was undergoing a plant expansion of 365,000 square feet, at a cost of $44.4 million for its 2.7 L V-6 engine. This is slated for a 1998 model year introduction. Plant statistics include a plant of 1,285 million square feet and a lot of 65 acres. Employment lists 1,500 union, and 156 salaried.

Chapter Nine

MANUFACTURERS OF COMPONENTS

The A. O. Smith Corporation

By Val Quandt

The company of A. O. Smith is synonymous with automobile frames. Charles Jeremiah Smith was an Englishman, who at the age of 22 years, sailed to America. As was the case with many other Europeans at that time, he was infused with the spirit of hope and adventure in moving to America with its land of new opportunities.

C. J. Smith was a trained machinist. After arriving in Milwaukee and marrying a woman whom he met on the passage ship he applied his skills running a machine shop with the aid of his sons.

Smith (top left)*, his sons and his employees pose in front of C. J. Smith and Sons Carriage Works and Machine Shop on Second Street in this circa 1876 picture.*

At age 33 years he went to work for the newly formed Milwaukee Railroad. Later at the age of 54 years he went back into business for himself making machine parts for industry such as baby carriages, and bicycles, which in the last decade of the last century were flourishing.

By 1895, he was the largest manufacturer of steel bicycle parts in this country. He and his workers were innovative in producing tubular frame parts for bicycles.

A. O. Smith imported the design for the Smith Motor Wheel from England. The company manufactured Motor Wheels—an antecedent of the moped—from 1914 until 1919.

1921 Briggs and Stratton Flyer, they had purchased this machine from A.O. Smith. It was a Model D, buckboard with Motor Wheel. Vehicle is in the Hartford Auto Museum.

Of the several sons of C. J. Smith, Arthur O. Smith was an engineer in Chicago. He rejoined his father in the bicycle supply business. By 1902, with the national interest in the latest means of locomotion, the automobile, he was experimenting with and then producing his early automobile frames. In 1903, orders came from Cadillac, Studebaker, Packard, and Locomobile.

On August 24, 1904 the A. O. Smith Company was incorporated in the State of Wisconsin for the manufacture of automobile frames.

In 1906, an early customer was Henry Ford needing frames for his model K Fords. A. O. Smith was making ten frames in a day. Henry Ford announced that he needed 10,000 frames, and these in four months. Undaunted, Arthur O. Smith met the challenge and indeed had this number of frames ready in this period of time.

A. O. Smith has always been staffed with sufficient engineers to promote technology generally ahead of its time and its competition.

When A. O. Smith died in 1913, his son Lloyd R. Smith took over as president of the company at the age of 30 years.

L. R. Smith and his company bought the rights to the "Motor Wheel." This sold widely during the years of 1914 to 1919 and led to its use in the Smith Flyer, a buckboard where it was truly a fifth wheel. This vehicle would be comparable to a modern day go-cart, with little semblance to an automobile. In the same years, 1915 to 1919, A. O. Smith manufactured the Silent Smith truck, its only ever foray into the auto or truck manufacturing field.

During World War I, A. O. Smith, as virtually all of the automotive and related industries, was called into service to manufacture war-related materials. In their case they made bomb casings. A. O. Smith in 1917 was developing a coated weld rod which was a boon to improved electrical welding. The idea for this came from a high school student then in the employ of the company.

With World War I over, A. O. Smith began again to concentrate on its automobile frame business. It set its engineers to making a block-long production line which was heavily automated, with only employees to tend the machines. They had produced the "Mechanical Marvel" which could perform 552 separate operations in making a car frame. The demand for frames was so great that it opened a second plant at Granite City, Illinois, just across the Mississippi River from St. Louis, Missouri.

During World War II, A. O. Smith was again making bomb casings and also torpedo casings. While outside the scope of this writing on automotive history, it will be noted that A. O. Smith in all the years following 1917 was active in many applications using their perfected welding techniques. These were for brewery tanks, the gas and oil industries using their line pipe, and home and commercial water heaters. In the latter and in their Harvestore silos, A. O. Smith had perfected bonding glass lining to steel.

L. B., "Ted", Smith at the age of 30 years, took over the company in 1951. He retired from direct management of the company in 1984.

In the 1960s the auto market was veering away from the full frame and in many cases going to the welded frame. But General Motors was a consistent purchaser of full frames. In 1976 GM bought A. O. Smith frames for their three new vehicles, the Chevrolet Monte Carlo, Cadillac Coupe de Ville, and Oldsmobile Delta 88 Royale.

In February of 1980, GM announced that it was switching over to the front-wheel drive. When other automotive companies were doing the same thing it devastated the market for full automobile frames.

But the automakers were beginning to sell more light trucks and vans still using full frames. This tended to pick up the slack in the frame industry.

In 1980 A. O. Smith opened a new plant in Milan, Tennessee. This was for the production of axles for front-wheel drive cars. This plant made the axles for the Chrysler Corporation K cars for the next 12 years. At the same time the Milan plant began

"The Quadrille of Dragons," the automated riveters in A. O. Smith's South Plant. Businessmen and engineers world-wide were stunned when the company unveiled its Mechanical Marvel in 1921.

The A. O. Smith stored collection of their automobile frames awaits shipment at its railroad yard, it being the largest supplier of standard automobile frames for the industry.

making axles for GM front-wheel drives.

Then in the early 1980s Ford Motor Company began experimenting with an engine cradle for their world-class cars, the Taurus and the Sable. When these automobiles came into the market in 1985 they had the A. O. Smith engine cradle. In time, A. O. Smith made more than one million of these cradles for the market and with excellent quality records.

Going into the 1990s A. O. Smith was responding to its market by realizing the necessity for "Just in Time" delivery of its automotive products. They followed up with this idea by developing five regional assembly plants close to the assembly plants of the Big Three auto manufacturers. This would be for full frames, cradles, and modules.

Roger S. Smith is an official of the A. O. Smith Corporation, of the fifth generation, and son of L. B., "Ted", Smith. In a recent book he has written with Charles S. Wright, he concludes with the statement that the A. O. Smith Corporation is "Retooled for the nineties, and beyond."

In the 1980s, the A. O. Smith perimeter frames were in demand in the GM truck chassis. As the pick-up grew in popularity as a family vehicle, demand for full frame assemblies increased. By the late 1980s, light truck frames for vehicles such as the Ford Ranger had become A. O. Smith's largest single product line.

JOHNSON CONTROLS AUTOMOTIVE HISTORY 1901-1912

The early history of Johnson Controls, from 1885 to 1912, was characterized by inventive genius, by clear-eyed practicality, and by great diversification of products. While temperature control systems were always central, this formative period saw such diverse products as gigantic tower clocks, church chandeliers, steam couplers for trains, puncture-proof tires, pneumatic bicycle seats, beer carbonators, push-button toilets, and automobiles. When Professor Warren S. Johnson, founder of the company, built his first truck in 1901, a one-ton steam-powered flatbed truck made expressly for a Milwaukee sheet metal dealer, Theodore Roosevelt was in his first term as president. Milwaukee, home office of Johnson Controls, had a population of 150,000, and the city was still rebuilding after the disastrous 1892 fire. Streets were illuminated by gas and roadbeds were surfaced with cobblestones. Omnibuses were horse drawn, and there was one blacksmith for every 350 Milwaukeeans. It was in such an era at the turn of the century that Professor Johnson entered the new, struggling, but highly competitive automotive industry. Already there were 17 Milwaukee and over 150 other Wisconsin automotive makers in business in 1901. Professor Johnson established his new automotive division in the old Johnson factory building located at 118-120 Sycamore Street; Michigan Street between Third and Fourth Streets. After 1903 the automotive division moved to the company's present site at Jefferson and Michigan where it took up parts of the third and fourth floors.

Johnson Roadster, c.. 1910

Express truck

Stake body truck

This jitney and the two preceding pictures show the Johnson steam-driven trucks of the 1901 to 1905 period. Their vehicles from 1905 to 1912 were conventional gasoline powered.

1905 Johnson, limousine

1906 Johnson, auto-carriage

1910 Johnson, touring

1911 Johnson, Silent Four special touring

1912 Johnson, model B, touring

The Revolution in Transportation

Initially, Professor Johnson entered this field, as he told his board of directors in December 1901, "to take our part in the coming revolution in American transportation and to assist the company to continue to build volume and to expand factory production." Professor Johnson, an avid automobile enthusiast, brought one of the first steam-driven automobiles to Milwaukee before the turn of the century. He also developed a new design for an improved steam-powered automobile engine, one that relied on a specially-made boiler whose coils were imported from Scotland. This new engine design was patented before the turn of the century. It was so well-made and so practical that in 1913, a period well into the era of the gas driven internal combustion engine, the patent was sold to the White Motor Company of Cleveland, the biggest manufacturer of steam-powered cars in the country at the time.

Standardized Trucks and Custom-Made Pleasure Cars

Between 1901 and 1912, several distinct standardized truck and car designs were developed. Some of these included a line of heavy-duty work trucks, a line of fancy commercial delivery trucks, a line of quick service (fire, police, and ambulance vehicles), and a line of roadsters, runabouts, five and seven passenger limousines and touring cars, and the famous Johnson line of pleasure cars. These pleasure cars the 1909 Johnson catalogue described as "high-class family automobiles that were easily managed, readily kept in repair, yet sensible and safe; they would insure comfort and pleasure rather than sport and excitement." In addition, any kind of car or truck could be custom-made. Johnson was especially well-known for their beautiful car interiors and their finely crafted wood-paneled vans.

Merchandising and Sales

Existing company sales records for the period 1909 to 1912 indicate that automotive sales averaged up to 15 vehicles per month. Trucks out sold cars two to one, and custom-made vehicles accounted for one-quarter of all sales. These vehicles were manufactured only in Milwaukee and sold from the garage showroom located at number One Grand Street. Company records also showed that vehicles were sold to dealers and to private buyers throughout the United States and Canada. The sales success, especially of the custom-made pleasure car line, stemmed from their luxurious interiors and imported accessories. 1906 company ads in the *Milwaukee Sentinel* asserting that Johnson "sold the best made vehicles to the best people" was no idle claim. Customers were often enthusiastic about their new vehicles. For example, a Chicago man bought a roadster, and after paying the required 25 percent down payment, he demanded that a Johnson employee drive him back to Chicago, as he did not know how to drive. The employee was instructed to teach the owner how to drive, and when the owner appeared competent to drive on alone, the employee was to catch a train back to Milwaukee.

Conversion From Steam to Gasoline-Powered Engines

All Johnson vehicles manufactured before 1906 were steam powered, as were most American-made vehicles of the period. This American propensity for steam-driven cars stemmed from the tight control George B. Selden had over a 1895 patent for a gasoline-powered internal-combustion engine. Few early American automakers wished to work under Selden's license due to its unprofitable restrictions. Several factors caused Professor Johnson to convert his vehicles from steam to gasoline after 1906. Henry Ford, who began business two years after Johnson established his automotive division, formed a group that successfully overturned Selden's internal-combustion engine patent in court. This legal development, combined with the great admiration Professor Johnson had for the gasoline-powered cars he saw in Paris and in London during his 1905 European business tour, caused him to order all future Johnson vehicles to be manufactured with gasoline-driven engines. The first Johnson gasoline-driven cars appeared in late 1906.

This engine conversion closed a colorful but precarious era in early automotive history, one filled with stories about how the old steamers sometimes came to grief. The famous comic actor Raymond Hitchcock, appearing in Milwaukee in 1905, visited the Johnson showroom where be bought a luxurious Johnson steamer and had it shipped back to New York. During a motor parade down Broadway, Hitchcock's kerosene-burning boiler caught fire, making him the object of unwanted public attention. An angry and image-conscious Hitchcock immediately returned the car to Milwaukee.

Johnson Controls Automotive Firsts

Such accidents, quite common to all steamers, disappeared with the introduction of the internal-combustion gasoline engine. From 1906 to Professor Johnson's death in early December 1911, Johnson Controls manufactured some of the best made gasoline-powered cars and trucks in the country, and can proudly claim a number of automotive industry firsts. For example, Johnson built the first successfully motorized United States mail trucks in 1906, a service the government commemorated in 1912 when it issued a 15-cent parcel post stamp with a Johnson mail truck on the stamp face. In 1910 Johnson built the first fleet of railway line trucks. A dozen of these trucks were used by the Milwaukee Electric Trolley Car and Railway Company to maintain and to repair electric power transmission lines and trolley wires. The first truck to operate in Death Valley was sold in 1910 to Whiting and Meade of Los Angeles. And the first automobile hearse manufactured in America was built for the Pierce Brothers of Los Angeles in 1910.

Johnson Controls and Specialization

By 1912, it was clear that diversification in business was giving way to industrial specialization. The flamboyant era in which colorful inventor businessmen like Thomas Edison, George Westinghouse, Henry DuPont, Charles P. Steinmetz and Warren S. Johnson launched successful businesses by creating as many different practical products from their scientific theories as possible, evolved into a new era where companies specialized in one line of products. Multiple product firms reorganized and consolidated themselves as single line specialist companies, just as family-owned joint stock companies were streamlined into the present public-owned national corporations. Professor Johnson's hand-picked successor, Harry W. Ellis long envisioned this new business direction and when elected president in 1912, he ordered the end to all but the temperature control systems line in the field Johnson Controls soon came to dominate. The significance of Johnson's part in early automotive history was that in the era of the quality custom-made cars Johnson made some of the best. Their line of standard design trucks can be seen as an early step towards mass-produced assembly-line vehicles built to a standard design. In all of this Professor Johnson demonstrated inventiveness, concern for constant technical improvement, and imaginative vision in design in production and in merchandising techniques, qualities central to present-day Johnson Controls operations.

Warren Johnson died on December 5, 1911. The 1912 Johnson automobile was to be the last manufactured by the Johnson Company. The automobile business was sold to the White Truck Company of Cleveland, Ohio. Their efforts at temperature control systems, which started in 1885, were now to continue as their main business.

In 1978, the company merged with Globe Union, the largest U.S. manufacturer of automotive batteries. The merger doubled Johnson Controls' sales and in 1981 Johnson Controls became a billion dollar enterprise. Globe Electric of Milwaukee and Union Battery of Chicago had merged in 1929 to form Globe Union, Inc.

Further diversification in Johnson Controls occurred in May of 1985 when it purchased Hoover Universal in Michigan, which made plastic products and also automobile seats. Then in June of 1992, Johnson Controls bought EAH Naue in Germany, a manufacturer of foam and other interior components for automobiles. In December of 1995 Johnson Controls bought Roth Freres SA of France, thus further expanding its automotive interiors business.

Major Acquisitions in 1996

Johnson Controls made two huge acquisitions in the year 1996. In February of 1996, it agreed to form a joint venture called Intertec Systems with the Inoac Corporation of Nagoya, Japan. They will produce instrument panels and other interior components for major automakers. Inoac is a recognized technology leader in the interior systems industry supplying instrument panels, door trim and polyurethane foam products. Inoac is the largest independent supplier of instrument panels to the Japanese auto market, making products for almost every automaker based in Japan.

Then in July of 1996, Johnson Controls entered into an agreement with Prince Automotive of Holland, Michigan. Prince is a major supplier of interior systems and consoles, door panels, floor consoles, visors and armrests. Prince is best known as a leader in the integration of electronics into the vehicle interior. Testimony to this is the recent introduction of the HomeLink (TM) transmitter allowing remote operation of garage doors, gate, security, and lighting systems in the home.

At this point, Johnson Controls is the world's largest seat system supplier and a major producer of interior components including headliners, door panels, instrument panels, and parcel shelves, operating 113 facilities in 18 countries.

Johnson Controls products were much in evidence at the North American International Auto Show at Detroit, Michigan, in January of 1997. Here on January 20th they taped a segment drawn from their battery division and automotive interiors by Prince. This gave a look into the next decade and century with its futuristic offerings.

Under the heading of new battery technology, Johnson Controls showed its new "Thin Metal Film Battery." This is about 20 pounds lighter than their standard Motorcraft battery and with the same starting capacity.

Seat belts will be integrated into the seats as with the air bags. With the press of a button presently seats can be warmed and in the future likewise they can be cooled. Seating will be self adjusting to the user, so called "comfort seats."

A model showed a sun visor that moved along an overhead track adjustable to the movement of the sun rays.

Floor and overhead consoles would be modified to include a compass and temperature gauge.

The floor console would include space for storage of a car phone, and speakers could be moved out of the dash to a console as to free up more space for storage in the dash. On the passenger side a pullout ledge could be used to hold a laptop computer or to be used as a work surface for some other activity.

If a vehicle were stalled on the road an electronic switch could be activated to call a central station to locate the stranded vehicle and secure roadside assistance. Further-more, a similar switch could be used to call in to an 800 number to state the location being sought and receive point-by-point instructions on how to arrive at this location.

An open swing-out door handle is often out of reach of the occupant for door closure. Here a door handle strap would bend out increasingly as the door retreated away so as to assist the occupant in grasping the door for closure.

A tiny innovation would be a clip attached to and a part of a sun visor to hold accumulated papers that presently fall onto your lap when the visor is lowered.

The Waukesha Motor Company
By Val Quandt

This company had its beginning in 1906. It occupied a small space on North Street in Waukesha, where it was known as the "Blue Front Garage," and later in this year becoming the Waukesha Motor Company, managed by Henry L. Hornung, Fred Ahrens, and Allan Stebbins.

One of its first products, in 1908, was a fire engine truck for the city of Chicago. But through the years, commercial vehicle engines were only a part of their production which was in the fields of engines for mining, oil drilling, logging operations, and later air-conditioner units.

Hornung was a prominent man nationally during the First World War with President Woodrow Wilson who solicited his help with the design and production of the Class B Liberty three and one-half ton trucks. After this war and until World War II the company was doing experimental work in developing better gasolines that were less knock prone, and likewise engines, in this case the L-head engine with a research designed anti-knock combustion chamber. This was known as the Ricardo Head.

In World War II Waukesha went to wartime production with a variety of engine applications including land transport vehicles.

In 1968, the company was acquired by Bangor Punta Corporation of Greenwich, Connecticut. It then became known as the Waukesha Engine Company. Then, further in 1974, it was acquired by the Dresser Industries Company of Dallas, Texas.

In 1974, Waukesha had withdrawn from the truck engine market, which by then had gone almost exclusively to diesels.

By the late 1980s Waukesha had phased out the last of the engines for other types of engine-powered mobile equipment. This ended Waukesha's over 80 years of continuous manufacture of engines for trucks, tractors, and other mobile equipment.

The History of Midas Mufflers

By Val Quandt

This history goes back to 1918, and at the termination of World War I. At its onset this new company was called the International Steel Products Company with its factory location in Hartford, Wisconsin. Its originator and guiding force was Mr. Joseph Marx, who then headed it for decades. Their plant was on three and one-half acres of land immediately adjacent to the Kissel Motor Car Company. Some 50 local persons bought stock in the firm to produce a muffler then called the Uvee.

At its beginning, the plant consisted of just six employees who manufactured 30 mufflers a day. By the 1930s the plant had grown considerably. Some of their early mufflers were made for the Model A Ford, a product that is still manufactured today.

Marx formed a business relationship with International Parts Company of Chicago, the forerunner of Midas International Corporation. In 1956 Nate H. Sherman founded Midas and introduced the Midas guarantee, a revolutionary

Joseph Marx, in late 1940s.

International Stamping Company employee picture taken in December of 1945.

The 1961 plant fire that totally destroyed the manufacturing facility.

The aftermath of the fire was a heap of destroyed mufflers, machinery and a burned to the ground building.

Picture taken in the summer of 1977 in front of the office of the International Stamping Company. In the foreground to the left is Joseph Marx, and to the right is Nate Sherman.

concept in the industry.

In 1961 the International Stamping Company was purchased by the Midas International Corporation. In that same year, on July 7, 1961, the 50,000 square foot manufacturing plant was totally destroyed by a fire. The fire started in a paint spray booth, where lacquer was sprayed electrostatically onto muffler surfaces. A spark caused this to ignite and explode. After cleanup some temporary space was set up for resumption of manufacturing. But the main manufacturing facility was moved to 17 acres west of this location that had been purchased in 1949 by Joseph Marx from the JorMac Corporation, which name was a contracture of its owners, Jordan and MacIntosh. Prior to this time the Stamping Company had used this building for overflow and warehousing. Now it became their main plant, which with additions, exists today.

In 1972 the Midas International Corporation was purchased by the IC Industries, later to become the Whitman Corporation, a diversified Chicago based holding company. Around the same time, Daubner Manufacturing Company, also based in Hartford, was purchased for their related automotive exhaust components including saddle clamps, cut pipe, and U-bolts.

By this time muffler production had risen to 3,000 units in an eight hour shift. Joseph Marx had now retired and appointed Gerald Hayes as the new plant manager.

In 1988 and 1989 Midas consolidated manufacturing operations in Bedford Park, Illinois, together with its Canadian operations, into its Hartford, Wisconsin, facility. In 1993 Gerald Hayes retired and management was taken over by Rick Ahern.

The Hartford facility today consists of 360 employees in a 200,000 square foot plant, which produces over 30,000 mufflers in a day. It also produces resonators, saddle clamps, hangers and pipes. Products are shipped to 13 Midas warehouses throughout the United States and to five in Canada. From the warehouses the products are distributed to over 1,800 Midas shops across the States.

The Midas International Company today, comprising 200,000 square feet of manufacturing space with its 360 employees.

This is a Model A Ford muffler, still made at the present time.

Many procedures today, such as this seam welding operation, are done by robot.

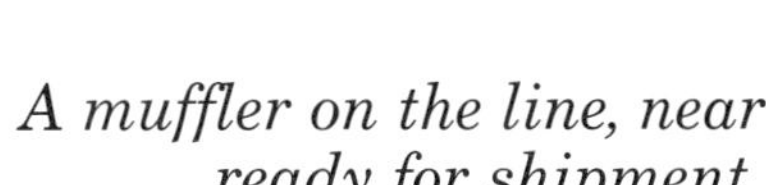

A muffler on the line, near ready for shipment.

The Rajo Cylinder Head

Early Model T Street Mod For Only $57.50

By Chad Elmore

For a mere $57.50 in 1922, readers of "The Saturday Evening Post" or "Collier's" could give their Model T Ford the strength that Henry hadn't.

With the Rajo Valve-in-Head installed, the driver would no longer be forced "to the side of the road to let larger, more expensive cars pass by" or experience a "pick-up speed that's too slow to let you beat a street-car to the next corner."

The rajo cylinder head could be installed on the Model T engine within five hours, with no extra machining. It added up to 14-hp instantly. An average coupe could travel a blazing 80 mph.

For racers and casual drivers, the Rajo meant dependability and high speed. In September 1921, a Rajo-equipped Ford driven by Glen Schultz took first place in the small car class in Colorado's grueling Pikes Peak Hill Climb, and placed third, overall.

In the early 1920s Frank Gegoux announced his intention to set a record seven-day trip from coast-to-coast.

Documentation could not be found to ascertain whether or not he made it, but his confidence in the Rajo head warrants mentioning.

His modified Ford, nicknamed "Desert Pal," was equipped with the original 1913 block that had logged more than 360,000 miles during Gegoux's many previous cross-country trips.

"I equipped 'Dessert Pal' with what I thought to be the best type of overhead valve system procurable for a Ford - a Rajo head," Gegoux was quoted in a press release. "With the aid of this marvelous attachment I am confident that my object will be successfully reached."

The Rajo head, which would make any Model T perform "as wonderfully as any $3,000 automobile," helped create the hot rod movement that would become popular following World War II.

The name "Rajo" was derived from a combination of the name of the city where it was made, Racine, Wisconsin, and its inventor, Joseph W. Jagersberger. Jagersberger, a veteran of the first Indianapolis 500 and the brutal, turn-of-the-century European racing scene, knew more than a little about speed and performance.

Jagersberger was born in Vienna, Austria on February 14, 1884. Not even 14 years old, he was hired as an apprentice in the Daimler Motor Works in Stuttgart, Germany, where Daimler cars and eventually Mercedes were produced.

In 1897 Jagersberger participated in his first race, riding as mechanic for Camille Jenatzy, a famous racer from Belgium. The team won the 90-mile cross-country race (they were the only ones to finish). Jagersberger was one of three people in Vienna who knew how to drive an automobile at the time.

Jagersberger rode with Jenatzy again in 1900, his second big race, a cross-country run from Paris to Berlin. They didn't fare so well this time, as the nature of racing had changed.

"Anything short of cold-blooded murder was considered legitimate in that race," Jagersberger said in a 1927 "Literary Digest" interview. "It was part of the game to run the other fellow in the ditch, regardless of consequences." Jenatzy was in the ditch a dozen times before finally breaking down for good in Frankfort.

Jagersberger's first big race as a driver came in the infamous 1903 Paris-Madrid road race. There were more than 100 entrants at the start of the race, which offered a mix of dusty, winding roads, and careless spectators. Before Bordeaux was reached, 32 entrants had been killed or badly injured.

"In this race I personally saw three men lose their lives," Jagersberger remembered. "I witnessed one very unfortunate accident when Marcel Renault, brother of the French automobile manufacturer, shot off a turn into a deep gully." Renault died from his injuries.

Due to the number of serious accidents, authorities stopped the race at Bordeaux, less than half the distance. Jagersberger was credited with fifth place. The Spanish government refused to allow the mess into its country, and the cars were parked under military guard. Drivers could get their cars only under the condition that they would be returned home by train, and were to be towed by horses to the station.

Two months later, Jagersberger once again rode as mechanic with Jenatzy, this time in the Gordon Bennett race in Ireland. James Gordon Bennett, owner of the *New York Herald*, had started the international series in 1899, in which countries competed against each other in domestic-made cars. The Gordon Bennett trophy, an expensive, ostentatious work of art, was awarded to the winner.

Jenatzy would win the trophy, one of two accomplishments he would be best remembered for. (At the controls of an electric car, Jenatzy had become the first man to drive over 65 mph - not by much, though, at 65.79 mph - in 1899, a record that would stand for three years.)

Jagersberger came to the United States in 1903 at the request of John Jacob Astor, a New York City fur baron. Jagersberger's granddaughter believes Austria's mandatory military service requirement may have played a role in his decision to come to the U.S., too. Jagersberger acted as chauffeur for Astor in between building race cars, which he did for him as well as for millionaire sportsman Harry Harkness.

Jagersberger, or the "Flying Dutchman" as he was often called, began dirt-track racing around this time in New York and Boston. He also coached and rode with Harkness, who owned several Mercedes, and was with him when he set a record in the "Climb to the Clouds" hill climb held at Mount Washington, New Hampshire, in 1904.

Jagersberger's racing success caught the attention of J. I. Case of the Case Threshing Machine Company of Racine, Wisconsin, who was preparing a den of race cars under the direction of J. Alex Sloan. At the request of Case, Jagersberger moved to Racine in 1911.

A three-car Case teamlined up for the first Indianapolis 500 in 1911. On the pole in the #1 Case was Louis Strang, a talented former Buick team driver and nephew of front-wheel drive pioneer J. Walter Christie. Jagersberger, in the #8 Case was in the next row beside 21-year-old Will Jones in Case #9. (Car numbers and starting orders for that first race were according to the order officials received the entries.)

The steering knuckle in Jagersberger's car broke on the front straight during lap 87, spreading the front wheels apart at 75 mph. Robbed of any control, Jagersberger hit the brakes. Jagersberger's mechanic, C. L. Anderson, either jumped or fell directly into the path of Harry Knight's Westcott. Knight swerved into the Case and then slid broadside into the pit area, where he took out Herbert Lytle's Apperson. The most serious injury was sustained by Knight, who fractured his skull. For the cars involved it was the end of the race.

History would record Ray Harroun as the race winner, but Ralph Mulford would claim for the rest of his life that a scoring error had been caused when the accident occurred on the starting line, and that he was the actual winner of the race.

On lap 109 Strang retired with the same steering failure that had affected Jagersberger. Case officials, fearing an incident with Hones, retired his car also.

With Jagersberger at the wheel, Case would score wins in several hill climbs in Illinois the same year. While its success in major speedway events was limited, the Case car was popular at country fairs where the name was well-known for farm equipment.

Strang had once prophetically said that he "would never be killed in a race. If I get it at all it will be on the road." In July 1911 he was killed, while driving a technical car for the Wisconsin Automobile Association reliability run. A dirt approach to a bridge caved in, causing the car he was driving to role down the bank and "turn turtle" near Blue River, Wisconsin. His passengers, including Jagersberger, were able to jump clear. Strang's death hit Jagersberger and the Case company hard, but both continued racing.

In November 1911, tragedy once again hit Jagersberger. While traveling faster than 60 mph in practice at a Columbia, South Carolina, racetrack, a tire suddenly lost its air, sending Jagersberger and his car off the course and through a fence. Jagersberger was thrown from the car and pinned under it. His riding mechanic jumped clear, receiving minor injuries.

Jagersberger was seriously injured, and spent eight months in the hospital. Although his right leg and an eye had to be removed, the *Columbian Record* reported that he was designing a new race car in the hospital.

Case was eager to have him back. "The bunch up here are counting up the days until you get back and when you do we will have a nice, new wooden prop, painted all over with automobiles, waiting for you," read a letter from a Racine friend.

In 1912 Jagersberger attempted to race a specially designed car in the Milwaukee Vanderbilt Cup race - becoming only the second one-legged driver in history to race - but the strain was too much, and Jagersberger retired from active racing. He would remain a fan with wife, Amanda, with whom he eloped in 1913, for the rest of his life.

Jagersberger stayed with Case as a consultant until 1914, when he left the company to form the Rajo Manufacturing Company. In 1918 he developed a high compression head for Model Ts. Sales of the Rajo head, like the cars they were installed on, took off, and by 1924 they were all over the country, in use on everything from race cars to tow trucks. During the company's peak, Rajo shipped 500 heads a month. Jagersberger built almost 30 racing engines during this time, along with producing various engine parts for Ford trucks and Fordson tractors.

When the T was supplanted with the Model A in 1928 the Rajo's popularity quieted but did not die. Rajo sold tens of thousands of heads for stock and racing applications during its life.

Jagersberger retired after World War II but continued his association with Rajo, now called the Rajo Automotive Research Company. Production costs forced the company to suspend the manufacture of cylinder heads.

In February 1947, M. H. Colombe, an exporter in Chicago, wrote Jagersberger, after discovering the heads were no longer made when trying to secure an order bound for Turkey: "I shall appreciate it if you will advise me when you start making these (cylinder heads) again. I am quite sure I could get a very large volume of business for you, on a cash basis...."

Jagersberger was working at the drawing board up to the time of his death. In the March 1952 issue of "Motor Trend" Griffith Borgeson tested what would be his last creation, a high-performance head for the Chevrolet.

The new Rajo head offered a unique dual intake system, in which the second system would come into play at any throttle opening chosen for extra acceleration. It also allowed the engine to breathe easier and run at a lower temperature. The new head took three seconds off the zero-to-60 mph time of the Chevrolet in 1951.

"The smoothness of the modified engine is uncanny," wrote Borgeson, "but the strangest thing of all is to sit at the wheel of a car that was never intended to go like a jackrabbit and have it do just that."

Unfortunately few of the new Chevrolet heads appear to have been produced, owing to a defect in the molds. In October of 1952 Jagersberger died of a heart attack. Jagersberger's partner, Dick Miller, who operated the financial side of the business, sold the company after Jagersberger's death. The Rajo name lived on as a machine shop into the 1960s.

Chapter Ten
RELATED AUTO TOPICS

Wisconsin State Fair Park; There and Back Again

By Phil Hall

This article on the Wisconsin State Fair Park does not obviously refer to Wisconsin automotive manufacturing. However, it might be of interest in the context of automotive activity in Wisconsin.

While the Indianapolis Motor Speedway is looked on as the grandfather of auto racing tradition in the United States, it is six years the junior of the oldest continuously operated national championship auto racing track, the Wisconsin State Fair Park Speedway in the Milwaukee suburb of West Allis.

The mile oval was first stirred up in competition by powered tires instead of horses hoofs in 1903, while the Indianapolis two and one-half mile bricks were not raced on until 1909. Except for the war years, both have been the scene of major auto races ever since, although admittedly the Indianapolis 500 far outranks the offerings at the Milwaukee Mile in national and world importance.

The beginnings of the Fair Park track can be traced back to 1891 when the state of Wisconsin bought land for a new fairgrounds in North Greenfield, taking 120 acres of the McPhetridge farm. The track was completed the next year and harness racing events were part of the state fair slate into the twentieth century.

Motorized racing events were being held at various locations across the country and the fair officials decided to give it a try.

The first official race was held on the dirt mile on September 11, 1903. A five-mile open event was held and was won by William Jones of Racine, who wheeled a Mitchell. He averaged just short of 36 miles an hour. While there were problems with the events that day and the day that followed, including a fatality, officials saw the attractions of racing, and decided to continue it along with horse racing. However, for the cars, it was determined that the name drivers of the day would be needed to draw good crowds.

Among those attracted early in the century were the legendary Barney Oldfield, who brought the famed Peerless Green Dragon to the track for the 1905 event.

Racing continued to prosper into the teens, but a tornado caused extensive damage to the grounds in 1914, and a fire destroyed the main grandstand shortly thereafter.

There was no question that the facilities would be rebuilt. The new improved grandstand was used for the first 100-mile contest in July of 1915, and won by Lou Disbrow in a Case entry out of Racine.

In order to get good fields of cars, various promoters were tried over the years from the teens into the twenties. Some did the job and some ran off with the purse.

Stability was sought and found in 1929. Tom Marchese, who along with his brothers, had built up a good reputation in local business, was hired to promote a race. Helping in choosing the Marchese name was his brother, Carl, who was a race driver and just finished fourth in the 1929 Indy 500.

Tom promoted his first event on July 21, 1929, which was headlined by a 50-mile contest, won by Gus Shrader. Just short of 6,000 fans were on hand. The fans were busy cheering for Tom's brother, Carl, who finished second.

Tom Marchese continued to promote races in the Depression years, but did not have exclusive rights until September, 1946. Tom's Wisconsin Auto Racing Association promoted events on the mile, as well as midget events on the inner quarter-mile dirt oval.

After WW II, stock cars grew in popularity with the fans. They showed up as jalopies on the short track and as late models on the mile. The first race was on August 22, 1948. After a protest the event was awarded Paul Bjork, who drove a 1948 Kaiser from a thrill show.

Stock car racing has been a part of the schedule ever since. The AA Contest Board started sanctioning the races in 1951, and the United States Auto Club (USAC) took over in 1956 and continued into the early eighties.

A tough decision was made in 1953 when it was decided that the horses, which still ran at the track, had to go. The track was paved for the 1954 schedule. The inner quarter mile was recontoured. A paved road course was also mapped out in 1954 and eventually used for many smaller class sports car events over the years.

The quarter mile continued to host modified and sportsman stock car events on week nights through the 1966 season. The paving of the mile's pit area eliminated the front stretch of the short track.

At the end of the 1967 season, Tom Marchese sold Wisconsin Auto Racing to John Kaishian, who promoted short track events in the Milwaukee area.

The schedule of the USAC Indy car and stock car events continued unchanged until the 1978 season, when the American Speed Association Circuit of Champions stock cars was added. ASA and USAC stock cars ran their own events during the next few years, but the decline of the USAC division and declining attendance caused problems. Races were dropped from the schedule during the fair, and other events like midgets were added to the schedule, but problems continued.

Wisconsin Auto Racing lost its bid to get the promoting contract renewed after the 1983 season and the new promoter. GO Racing Limited, took over with the 1984 season.

Racing stock cars at the Wisconsin State Fair Park, in West Allis, Wisconsin.
Photo courtesy of Phil Hall.

NASCAR made its first appearance at the track with a sportsman race to start the 1984 season, but problems that would plague Fair Park and its new promoters surfaced early with a poor crowd.

The problem with the promoter, GO Racing, and the fair board continued and deepened until it was agreed after the 1991 season that their ten-year contract would be bought out by a new promoter.

After a search, Indy Car racing team owner, Carl A. Haas of Illinois was selected. A program of track improvement and improvement in relations with the fair board, fans, sponsors, and sanctioning bodies began. Goals were set to eventually bring about a NASCAR Winston Cup event.

Haas brought back NASCAR's junior Busch Grand National series after many years absence and tried other events to build the crowds back up.

The fair board has strongly stated that auto racing is in the future for the track, heading off rumors of a switch to horse racing that circulated during the dark days of the previous promoter.

It appears that the mile is well on its way towards celebrating its 100th anniversary as an auto-racing track in 2003.

History of Wisconsin License Plates

By Marly P. Hemp
Brookfield, Wisconsin

July 1, 1905, dawned the beginning of automobile license plate registration in the State of Wisconsin. Before the sun had set, 507 autos had been registered and single licenses issued.

As in numerous other states, two cities in Wisconsin were known to have earlier registration regulations on their books, those being Madison and Milwaukee. Although the Madison ordinance was approved on August 29, 1904, no evidence of actual vehicle registration has ever been found. The Milwaukee ordinance was passed on September 6, 1904; under the ordinance, for a $1.00 fee, a number was assigned and a certificate was issued.

The Milwaukee ordinance required the automobile owner to furnish his own single plate with four-inch-high metal numbers and an "M" letter suffix affixed to a dark background. The choice of plate material was left to the owner and ranged from metal to wood with one of the more popular choices being leather. Motorcycle plates were required to have two-inch-high numbers with no letter suffix. Examples of these very early automobile and motorcycle plates and registration certificates are still in existence, the earliest known being a motorcycle registration, #121, dated 9/19/04.

The first state-issued plate in Wisconsin was issued on July 1, 1905, to Dane County Judge A. E. Zimmerman of Madison, for his ten hp Ford touring car. This early date ranks Wisconsin as the fifth state to begin issuing plates. Massachusetts was the first state to issue plates in 1903; the last was Florida which began issuing plates in 1918.

Wisconsin law initially required a $1.00 fee for owners to obtain a single plate and certificate of registration. The original plates were manufactured by Schwaab Stamp & Seal Co. in Milwaukee. The plates consisted of three-inch-high metal numbers riveted to a black-painted zinc base. Although porcelain material plates were used extensively in other states, no porcelain material plates were ever manufactured or issued in Wisconsin.

Wisconsin plate numbers started with number 1, each with the suffix "W." The numbering system for dealer/manufacturers' plates employed a similar numbering system and in addition sported a large star, a designation which lasted until 1932. The first star plate was issued on July 1, 1905, to Rudolph Hokanson, a Madison dealer. For some unknown reason, a motorcycle registration system was not established until July 1, 1909.

Wisconsin law initially specified that plates be issued to the vehicle. As a result, as the years passed and vehicles were sold and resold, the registration system became very cumbersome. This factor, coupled with the state fathers' ever latent concern for the almighty dollar led to a revision in these procedures. In 1911 the state began issuing plates in dated pairs on an annual basis. The final issue under the old system established in 1905 was #21983; it was issued to G. W. Young of Algoma on July 31, 1911.

WISCONSIN AUTO LICENSE PLATE HISTORY 1905-1993

License plate display courtesy of the Wisconsin Department of Transportation, Division of Motor Vehicles, Bureau of Vehicle Services.

Figure 1

Year	Plate Number Issued	Number of Plates Issued
1905	1-1,492	1,492
1906	1,493-2,666	1,174
1907	2,667-4,147	1,481
1908	4,148-6,192	2,045
1909	6,193-9,832	3,640
1910	9,833-15,831	5,999
1911	15,832-21,983	6,152

Under the new system, established on August 1, 1911, plates were issued only to new registrations. Previously issued undated registrations would expire December 31, 1911. The new pairs of green plates had aluminum numbers and date tabs riveted onto a zinc base. A major change was in the more modern design of the numbers. Although not officially documented, experts believe 1,287 pairs were issued between August 1 and the end of 1911.

The plates issued in 1912 were identical in design to 1911 plates, but were painted red, 24,578 plates were issued in 1912.

The bases of the 1913 plates were painted blue, and there was one major change. The zinc base was discontinued and replaced with a rolled-edge steel base. A unique feature of the 1913 plates was a postage-stamp-size guarantee sticker affixed to the rear plate reading, "This plate is guaranteed — Defective or mis-matched plates will be replaced without charge — Schwaab Stamp & Seal Co."

In 1914 Wisconsin finally converted to the conventional steel-embossed design. In the same year, prison manufacturing began sharing the production load with Schwaab. It is believed that the prison made the first 40,000 of the 53,160 passenger plates issued in 1914 with Schwaab furnishing the remainder of the production. Today, the prison remains the sole producer.

From 1914 to 1932 there were no significant design changes. During this period, however, a system change lasting from 1924 to 1931 saw the addition of a letter which signified differentiated weight classifications.

The year 1932 saw a design change which introduced a taller plate issued in two sizes. In 1932 and 1933, three-digit plates were furnished in 6 x 8 3/4-inch size. This pattern was further applied to the four-digit plates from 1934-1939. All other plates were 6 x 13 1/2 inches. The smaller plates through these years are lovingly called "Wisconsin Shorties" by collectors.

1940 was an interesting year with the introduction of the "America's Dairyland" legend and smaller digits. Legend has it that law enforcement agencies complained about plate visibility during high-speed chases. The politicians relented at mid-season and effected yet another design change. The new design featured larger digits, and the horizontal "Wisconsin 1940" was replaced with "Wis 40" running vertically between the third and fourth digit. The changes were believed to have occurred at the 430,000 registrations of that year.

With the advent of World War II in 1942, Wisconsin issued plates on a semi-permanent basis. Rounded corners were added for steel conservation. For the year 1943, in lieu of new plates, windshield stickers were issued; motorists were instructed to remove their front plates and store them for future use. During this period, new registrants were issued single three-digit and four-digit motorcycle-sized plates. These small plates were characterized by strange combinations of letters and numbers. No real pattern has been established on the issuance of these plates, but it is known that, when number and letter combinations were exhausted, the remainder of the plates issued in 1945 were of the original 6 x 13 1/2-inch size plate. Collectors covet these small plates, referring to them as "Wisconsin War Plates." All sizes were yellow on black and updated with metal tags.

Following the war, new white-on-black plates were issued with a monthly staggered registration system. This series started with rounded plate corners with the final two years receiving square-cornered plates. All were validated with clip-on steel tabs. The new system lends much confusion to the plate collector. For example, a plate issued in January of a given year would be used during that full year, but would carry the expiration date of the following year.

The confusion is multiplied by the extended validations of older series plates which overlapped with newly-issued series plates.

Beginning in 1952 (dated 1953), plates were two-year plates with metal tag validations. The year 1956 is significant for the national standardization of all automobile license plates to the 6 x 12-inch size. The last metal validation tag for Wisconsin was issued in 1960. Validations in succeeding years were pressure-sensitive stickers.

The year 1967 saw the introduction of Wisconsin's first reflective plate (dated 1968). This yellow-on-black plate is often referred to as the "Yellow Butter Plate." This color scheme lasted through 1972 after which it was replaced by the red-on-white series which lasted through 1979. The butter yellow returned in 1979; at that time, the first Wisconsin vanity (personalized) plates became available to the public.

A new more decorative design was introduced in 1986. The blue-on-white plate sported a sailboat, sun, goose, cloud, barn, and fence logo. The scene was selected after many months of highly-publicized public competition; the selection process was not without significant political interjection. Rumor has it that local state officials lobbied the federal government for a variance for a larger plate so additional animals could be added to the design. Local wags refer to the logo as the "Sailing Farmer." Wisconsin was far from a trendsetter with its logo; the first logo presented on a plate was a steer head on the 1917 Arizona plate.

In the following year, with very little notice, the blue-on-white color scheme was replaced by a red-on-white scheme because it was noted, belatedly, that the blue-on-white scheme coincided with most of Wisconsin's neighbors. The red-on-white scheme has remained unchanged since that time.

Starting in 1997, motorists could choose Wisconsin's optional "1848/1998 Sesquicentennial Plate" commemorating Wisconsin's 150 years of statehood. This colorful plate which was an alternative to the standard red-on-white required an additional $15 fee. Standard registration fees for 1997 were $40, and personalized plates required an additional $15 fee.

As the 100th anniversary of license plate registration approaches, one must realize how far we have come from the early homemade leather license plate, and wonder what the future holds.

Appendix

This list is very long. It might not be inclined to hold the interest of the reader very long and is placed as an appendix at the end of the book for reference for those interested. You will note that the bulk of them are for a single year covering a very rudimentary and short-lived activity. Kane-Pennington is noted to list from 1894 to 1900. These were very early cars, some three-wheeled, and lends credence to the claim of Wisconsin cars, a 100-year history. Then a few list more than a five-year history, where little is known or has been written about the company, like Maibohm of Racine. Perhaps a reader might come up with a trove of information on one of these forgotten companies.

Here then is the Wisconsin Society of Automotive Historians listing, hopefully accurate.

WISCONSIN-BUILT VEHICLES

Vehicle	City	Years Built
Abel	Fond du Lac	1901
Abresch	Milwaukee	1899-1912
A.E.C.-Anger	Milwaukee	1913-14
Ajax	Racine	1925-26
Albrecht	Milwaukee	1900
American Motors	Kenosha & Milwaukee	1957-
American Steam	Milwaukee	1903-04
Ames	Owatonna	1895-98
Appleton Motor Trk.	Appleton	1922-34
Anheuser	Green Bay	1905
Auto Carriage	Milwaukee	1905
Auto Hoe	West DePere	1950
Badger	Clintonville	1909-12
Badger	Columbus	1910-12
Ballard	Oshkosh	1894-95
Banner Boy Buckboard	Milwaukee	1958
Battleship	Clintonville	1909
Billiken	Milwaukee	1914
B-O-E	Milwaukee	1914
Briggs & Stratton	Milwaukee	1919-24
Bril	Appleton	1909
Brodessor	Milwaukee	1909-11
Brodhead	Brodhead	1910
Burdick	Eau Claire	1909-10
Carhart Spark	Racine	1871
Case	Racine	1910-27
Champion	Milwaukee	1909-11
Chevrolet	Janesville	1922-
Clark Hatfield	Oshkosh	1908-09
Classic	Lake Geneva	1920-21
Cleaver	Fond du Lac	1903
Colt	Milwaukee	1958
Comet	Racine	1916-23
Commander	Milwaukee	1921-22
Continental	Superior	1912-18
Corliss	Corliss	1909-18
Crown	North Milwaukee	1911-16
Cruiser	Madison	1917-19
Doman	Oshkosh	1899-1900
Duesenberg II	Elroy	1978-
Earl	Milwaukee	1907-08
Earl	Kenosha	1908
Eclipse	Milwaukee	1905
Elite	Milwaukee	1909-10
Empress	Milwaukee	1908-10
Eugol	Kenosha	1921-22
Excalibur	Milwaukee	1952-53
Excalibur SS	Milwaukee	1964-
Falls	Sheboygan Falls	1924
Fawick Flyer	Milwaukee	1907
Field	Rice Lake	1924
Flagler	Sheboygan	1914-15
Four-Wheel Drive	Milwaukee	1902-07
FWD	Clintonville	1909-
F.S.	Milwaukee	1912
Francke	Milwaukee	1904
GMC	Janesville	1921 to present
Grass Premier	Sauk City	1923-33
Green Bay	Wequiock	1876-78
Green Bay	Green Bay	1887

Vehicle	City	Years Built
Greyhound	Eau Claire	1909
Haase	Milwaukee	1904
Hansen	Milwaukee	1906
Harley-Davidson	Milwaukee	1903-
Harris	Menasha	1923
Haushalter	Milwaukee	1910
Hay Berg	Milwaukee	1907-09
Hercules	Milwaukee	1902
Holbrook	Racine	1912
Howell	Racine	1900
Hudson	Kenosha & Milwaukee	1955-57
H.W.O.	Milwaukee	1922
Hyde	Milwaukee	1904
Ideal	Milwaukee	1914
Imhof	Racine	1900
Iverson	Milwaukee	1902-08
James	La Crosse	1904
Jeffery	Kenosha	1914-17
Johnson	Milwaukee	1905-12
Jonas	Milwaukee	1904
Juno	Juneau	1912-14
Kane-Pennington	Racine	1894-1900
Keen	Janesville	???
Keen Steam	Madison	1955-61
Kenosha-Winther	Kenosha	1918-28
Kissel	Hartford	1906-31
Klondike	Logansville	1914-17
Koehering	Milwaukee	1933
Krueger	Milwaukee	1904-09
Kunz	Milwaukee	1902-06
La Crosse	La Crosse	1914
LaFayette	Milwaukee	1920-24
Lang-Scharman	Marshfield	1909
Lewis	Racine	1913-16
Lipman	Beloit	1911
L.P.C.	Racine	1913
Madison	Madison	1878
Majestic	Milwaukee	1910-11
Maibohm	Racine	1916-22
Meiselbach	North Milwaukee	1904-09
Mitchell	Racine	1903-23
Motorbile	Beloit	1901
MPC	Milwaukee	1926-27
Mueller	Milwaukee	1909-10
Nash	Kenosha & Milwaukee	1917-57
National	Oshkosh	1901-03
National-Kissel	See Kissel	1927-30
Neville	Oshkosh	1910
New Monarch	Milwaukee	1903
Northwestern	Milwaukee	1904
Odenbrett	Milwaukee	1897
Ogren	Milwaukee	1919-23
Oride	Fond du Lac	1910
Oshkosh	Oshkosh	1918-
Oshkosh Steamer	Oshkosh	1876
Owen-Thomas	Janesville	1909
Parker	Milwaukee	1918-33
Pennington	Racine	1890-95
Petrel	Kenosha	1908-12
Pierce-Racine	Racine	1904-09
Piggins	Racine	1909
Pizazz	Milwaukee	1968
Progress	Milwaukee	1912-13
Pup	Spencer	1948
Racine	Racine	1895
Racine-Sattley	Racine	1910
Racine Wagon	Racine	1902
Radford	Oshkosh	1895
Rambler	Kenosha	1902-13
Rambler	Kenosha & Milwaukee	1950-70
Reinertsen	Milwaukee	1902
Reliance	Racine & Appleton	1917-27
Richards	Manitowoc	1910
Ritter	Madison	1912
Rocoit	Beloit	1909
Rogers	Beloit	1901-04
Rosenbauer	Milwaukee	1900-01
Russel-Deibler	Berlin	1908-10
Ruxton	Hartford	1929-30
Samson	Janesville	1922
Schaefer	Rion	1901
Schloemer	Milwaukee	1890

Vehicle	City	Years Built
Schuler	Slinger	1924
Scimitar	Milwaukee	1959
Seig	Milwaukee	1899
Shaver Steamer	Milwaukee	1895
Silent Smith	Milwaukee	1910-12
Silent Sioux	Milwaukee	1909-12
Smith	Milwaukee	1910-15
Special	Milwaukee	1909-10
Speedwell	Milwaukee	1903
Stegeman	Milwaukee	1910-17
Stephenson	Milwaukee	1910-13
Sterling	Milwaukee	1916-51
Sterling-Wite	Milwaukee	1951-52
Sternberg	Milwaukee	1908-15
Stoughton	Stoughton	1920-31
Superior	Superior	1901
Super-Traction	Fox Lake	1922-23
Termaat-Monahan	Oshkosh	1914
Terra-Tiger	Sheboygan Falls	1968-
Thayer-Isham	Marinette	1909
Time	Oostburg	1916
Titan	Milwaukee	1917-27
TMF	Oshkosh	1909
Toppins	Milwaukee	1916-29
True	Kenosha	1914
Utility	Milwaukee	1910
Vixen	Milwaukee	1914
Ward	Milwaukee	1914
Waukesha	Waukesha	1908
Weber	Milwaukee	1905
Weher	Whitewater	1910
Welc-Estberg	Milwaukee	1906
Whitcomb Wheel	Kenosha	1927-35
Winther-Marvin	Kenosha	1918-21
Winther	Kenosha	1920-23
Wisco	Janesville	1910
Wisconsin	Milwaukee	1899 & 1914
Wisconsin	Baraboo, Sheboygan & Loganville	1912-23
Z&B (Zachow & Basserdich)	Clintonville	1908
Zeibell	Oshkosh	1914-15

Index